RIVER GODS &
SPOTTED DEVILS

RIVER GODS & SPOTTED DEVILS

EDITED BY
JOHN CULLER AND CHUCK WECHSLER

ILLUSTRATIONS BY
JOSEPH BYRNE

LIVEOAK PRESS, INC.
CAMDEN, SOUTH CAROLINA

ISBN 0-929822-00-5

Dedicated to
SPORTING CLASSICS
*readers—and
the high ideals
to which they subscribe.*

FOREWORD

This book is a collection of stories from *Sporting Classics* magazine. Not just any stories, but some of the best outdoor pieces ever written.

In 1981, when the first issue of the magazine appeared, we announced we would feature outstanding sporting articles in our "classic" section, pieces our editors thought good enough to be called classic; articles with enough merit to interest sportsmen years after they were written. Not a single one of these great classics will ever get old.

I don't believe anyone can read the stories in this book and not be convinced they are fine literature; if emotion is any yardstick, it's no contest.

The editors of the magazine (readers all) found or knew about most of the articles here, but many were suggested by subscribers. In fact, a couple were nominated by senior readers who remembered them from the time they first appeared many years ago.

I'm sure there are other articles out there in long-forgotten volumes that deserve to be published again for a new generation of readers—after all, the game never changes, only the players.

Perhaps the greatest outdoor article ever written is in this book. We'll never know; I can't ever make up my mind which *I* like best. And it's a good bet your choice would be different from mine.

When I first read *The Shining Tides* by Win Brooks I was convinced it was the best I ever read. Strangely enough, this is part of a Brooks novel. The rest of the book is good, but the part about the striped bass is simply outstanding! I didn't want it to end.

"The Road to Tinkhamtown" by Corey Ford brought tears to my eyes, down my cheeks and into my not-so-macho beard. I had to take tough pills for a month to get over that one. Then came "The Ledge" by Lawrence Hall. I don't want to talk about it.

I'll tell you one thing: the best fishing story I ever read is in here—"The River God" by Roland Pertwee. A British playright who was hooked on fishing, Pertwee missed his calling.

Another book excerpt is "Ring of Spears" from Theodore Roosevelt's *African Game Trails*. Roosevelt was an excellent writer and a great role model.

As you read this book, you are going to learn some things: About yourself, about outdoor writing with feeling, and about the common brotherhood between sportsmen. Any of us could have been the subject of these stories; another time, another place—it's *us* all right. That's why they strike home.

I've taken up enough of your time—you've got more important reading to do.

JOHN CULLER
Camden, South Carolina

CONTENTS

xiii

RIVER GODS & SPOTTED DEVILS

THE
Shining
T I D E S

Winfield Brooks' powerful story about the life of
a striped bass takes you on an underwater journey
of violence and surprise.

by Winfield Brooks

Sun and a wafer edge of dissolving moon rose a few
minutes apart. From a late roost in a scrub oak on
Blake Point, Nycti the Quawk, the black-crowned
night heron, resented them hoarsely.

Roccus, a great striped bass, swinging a four-fathom curve
and following a tide press, passed south of Centerboard Shoal
and turned north. From deeper water she moved into nine feet
off Bird Island. Spiny and soft dorsal fins slashed a V-ream in
the stipple made by the breeze. Against a submerged granite
boulder cored with magnetite, lightning-split from the ledge five
hundred years before, she came to rest, tail and pectorals fanning
gently, at a meeting of tide and currents.

More than a quarter century had passed since Roccus first
rested beside this boulder during her original migration as a

1

three-year old in the company of a hungry thousand of her age and sex. To it she annually returned, sometimes with small pods of big fish, more recently as a solitary, in late May or June, when the spawning season of *Roccus saxatilis* was ended and the eggs were spilled in the milt-chalked Roanoke above Albemarle Sound or, on occasion, in the region of Chesapeake Bay.

This resting place off the southern coast of Massachusetts was her domain until October's northeasters sent her coursing southward. The boulder lie she had found good, and she returned to it as the experienced traveler returns time and again to tavern or hotel where he has found comfort, safety and food to his taste.

This year Roccus was making her earliest journey. For the sixth spring since she had attained a length of sixteen inches, no urge within her belly set her coursing up the Roanoke or Chesapeake feeders, past the thin tides to the gravel bars where, in other ecstatic Mays, she had reproduced. Instead, on the spangled night when the moon had waned, a counterurge had drawn her into the open Atlantic; and, passing migrating schoolfish too young to spawn, she had turned north and east along a thoroughfare as plainly marked for striped bass by current and tide and pressure, by food and temperature, by the instinct to avoid danger, as any broad, paved highway is posted for the guidance of man. The migrating shoals of small stripers, or rockfish, or rock, had remained in the Barnegat surf when Roccus passed between Sakonnet and Cuttyhunk into Buzzards Bay and into the tides of the Narrow Land where Muashop, giant of Cape Cod legend, still blew the smoke of his pipe down a southwest wind to make the fog.

Now the thirty-six foot beacon of Bird Island caught the first rays of sun and splinted the dazzling light of new day. The moon paled and Mars and Venus and Jupiter were snuffed out in the sky of azure. Gong buoy 9, better than a mile to the south, winked green at five-second intervals. East, against the sun, the old Wings Neck Light lost color. Roccus grooved her lie. She had come alone, too early, to a latitude of disquiet, troubled strangely, strangely drawn, and here in the merging, changing weights of waters familiar to the nerve ends along her laterals — in the surge of the sucking, thickening tide — she held her place while the light of the dying May moon transfused

2

the direct stream of brilliance of which it was only a reflection.

In an overhang of the same boulder, behind a curtain of rockweed and moss and bladder wrack, on a scour of sand ground from granite by the tides of thousands of years, Homarus the lobster lay partially embedded and concealed, expelling water through twenty pairs of gills, her stalked, compound eyes fixed on the fringe of weed shielding her cave. Her two pairs of antennae rippled with the flow of the weed in the sun's first strike.

Homarus weighed nineteen pounds and was nearly as old as Roccus. Since her final molt as a free-swimming surface lava she had shed shell, esophagus, stomach and intestine seventeen times as her body became too large for the armor encasing it. During her years she had carried more than a million eggs glued to the flexed pocket of her abdomen. She was almost uniformly black, with tinges of green at the edge of her back shell. She was a cannibal and a glutton, vicious and ugly. In her youth she had made an annual crawl to deep water. During recent years she had strayed little from Bird Island ledge. For her, as for Roccus, the boulder was a familiar lie, the lobster in the hole made by tide scour through the overhang, the bass above the overhang near the holdfast of the weed. Homarus was secure in her knowledge that anything small enough to enter the cavern was prey for her appetite. The aperture was too small for the green snout and jaws of the bass.

Each was aware of the other for hours.

Tide ebbed its extreme. In charging pressure, in degrees of salinity, in varying temperatures, there was conveyed to Roccus the memory of many feeding grounds. Around the boulder's westerly side in slow pouring came drained warmth from shallows over lutaceous bottoms, a peculiar freshness tasting of algae, alewives, larvae and shellfish. This current was the confluence of drainage from Sippican Harbor, the Weweantic and Wareham rivers, from Beaverdam Creek, Agawam River and Hammett Cove and a score of lesser waters into which anadromous fishes made their way. Around the boulder's easterly side swept an icy current from Cape Cod Bay, which plunged with the west-flowing current through Cape Cod Canal. This was underlay for a streak of warmer, less saline water which on the flood, covered Big Bay and Buttermilk Flats and the

Onset mudbanks and had been freshened slightly by Red Brook's discharge.

The separate currents ran and slowed, stirred and stilled, and there was a semblance of complete slack, a hushed suspension of motion.

Roccus turned outward from the boulder, and the broad fan of her tail made a roil of water and sand which parted the weed curtain of the overhang and caused Homarus to back deeper into her lodge, waving antennae in anger and spanning her crusher claw. Roccus resumed her lie.

The still of the sea was only an illusion; there was no dead calm. End of one tide was but the beginning of a new, and birth of the new tide aroused activity in the sea. Life about the ledge responded. Clams extended their siphons, clearing holes. Crabs settled carapaces deeper. Scallops thrust upward, dropped back like leaves falling through dead air. Sea robins changed lairs, crawling on the first three rays of their pectoral fins, and sculpins settled in the weeds on the rocks, awaiting questing green crabs. Soft-finned rock cod moved lazily through caverns; and from countless hiding places the sharp-toothed cunners emerged in schools, nibbling at barnacles and the sand tubes of annelids. The cunners were the bait-stealing curse of bottom fishermen.

New tide awakened hunger in the lobster. Before Roccus' arrival Homarus had dined on a two-pound male of her own kind. Later she had killed a flounder, which, by treading her legs, she had buried beneath her as a dog buries a bone for future reference.

Tide also awakened hunger in Roccus. She made a three-quarter leaping turn, a sprung bow of steel, and her tail drove into the overhang. Homarus, nearly dislodged, backed farther into her cave, gripping deeper. The disturbance of Roccus' thrust caused a surface commotion which excited seven herring gulls.

As the tide turned, Anguilla the eel swam to the ledge, surfaced, sucking larvae of a kind she had not tasted for seven years. Anguilla was a thirty-two-inch ripple of macrurous grace, blue-black but showing yellowish-white on her underside in a transformation which would make her a silver eel returned from fresh water to the sea for completion of her catadromous life. She carried within her ovaries, moving down from fresh water,

4

more than ten million eggs which would ripen swiftly when she reached the Sargasso deep. The urge to procreate swept her more relentlessly than any current.

As Anguilla approached Roccus' lie and Homarus' ledge, she deflated her air bladder and sank close to the bottom, moving with slow undulation like a weed torn from anchorage. At the base of the boulder she came to rest, arrowed head near the weed curtain, a third of her elongated body curled beneath her.

Homarus tasted oil from the eel. She withdrew her legs from the sand and buoyed her body and waved her antennae in excitement. She was fond of eels. Stealthily she extended her sharp cutter along the sand into the weed fringe.

Roccus saw the eel in the cone of vision of her gold-rimmed black left eye. She also tasted the eel's oil.

Anguilla moved an inch nearer the hole, though appearing not to move. Behind the weed Homarus moved an inch nearer Anguilla. Roccus saw the lobster's claw.

Though her superior nostrils sensed danger, Anguilla had no experience with lobsters or striped bass. She moved another inch, questing, tasting, testing. Her head, weaving, swung between the open jaws of Homarus' cutting claw, which snapped like a trap. The cutter slashed embedded linear scales, flesh and bone, its blades meeting between the severed head and body of the eel.

As Anguilla's body reacted in a hoop, Roccus made a violent tail smash against the weed curtain, and the compression dislodged the lobster, overturning her outside the hole. Before Homarus could right herself, Roccus overleaped and bit through her tail, crushing shell and flesh between double-toothed tongue and vomer plate.

In the strengthening tide, Roccus lay content. She had eaten the tail of Homarus and all of Anguilla. The claws and body of Homarus bumped along the bottom in the quickening pulse of the sea, all but concealed by a cloud of cunners, some already inside the body. Three days later her body shell, first crimsoned, then paled pink by the sun, was found on Indian Neck by a boy who showed it at home to the amazement of his parents. They had never seen one so large. The boy saved it a few days, but it grew rank and his mother made him bury it in their garden, where, in August it fed a clump of coral phlox envied by all their neighbors.

Out of the southern sky, against the afterglow of sun when flashes of the Wings Neck Light grew bolder, a wedge of birds come driving beneath the first sprinkling of stars. They flew in wavering formation, eighteen on the right flank, twenty on the left: Canada geese seeking rest. They were in flight from Texas to Crane Lake in Saskatchewan and since daybreak they had been on the wing. Cutting across Cape Cod, they flew at two thousand feet with a following breeze. As they passed over Bird Island the gander leader sighted the distant sheen of Big Bay and Little Bay, Buttermilk and Great Herring, and the mirrored, shadowed surfaces of Sandy and Long Pond and Gallows and Bloody and Boot, and a score of others. He honked and towered, circling, climbing, then all the flock began to honk and gabble, their voices like those of beagles chasing rabbits among the constellations.

Nine miles away, coursing a meadow where quail had roaded, a dog fox heard the geese and cocked mangy ears. Saliva drooled from his mouth because once he had tasted gosling in the yard of a farmer. Fear rose in his heart because he had met ganders, to his sorrow. He stood silent, listening, pretending not to listen.

The geese reached peak of tower and the old bird made his choice, which was Little Bay where the eelgrass was thick. Honking ceased, the wedge drove north in silence, losing altitude. The fox did not hear the geese again and was relieved that his appetite would not place a strain upon his fortitude. He wet where the quail had been and went off to hunt a mole.

Until the tide turned, Roccus occupied her boulder lie, at times suspended in the current, at times on the scour outside the empty lodge of Homarus.

Saturn was the evening star. The moon has crossed the meridian with the sun and was invisible from earth; it was dark o'the moon. When the blanket of stars lay close and heavy on the water, shimmering and opalescent, Roccus broke through it with a roll and tailslap and fell back on her side. The star scattered, danced, reformed in wavering pattern. The bass slashed the surface, sinuating on her right side, then on her left, leaped half clear. Three yellowish-brown sea lice fell from her shoulder and were promptly devoured by a cunner which an hour later was eaten by a crab which, before morning, was swallowed by a master sculpin.

Nycti the Quawk, belly yearning, flapped from the filth of his roost for a night of hunting in Planting Island Cove. His flight voice was harsh: *quuaawwk, quuaawwk!* Roccus leaped once more in the brief sustention of the tide.

From Dry Ledge, Roccus drove northwest again seeking warmth. Alewives were in abundance but their appetite was held in check by enervating cold. In the rivers a few bass which had wintered over began to lose sluggishness.

On a morning ebb there was a definite change of pressure and the wind backed into the northeast. Roccus swam to the sandy shoal between Warren Point and Long Beach Point, lay finning in three feet of water. Even the hermit crabs had moved off the shoal in advance of the storm. The wind made up and the surface ran angrily in lifts, sulkily in hollows, and Roccus gave herself to the conflicting movement of the water, warmed by water thinned by rain. Half buoyant, she was vibrant with storm, knowing it with all her body, comforted by its warmth; she was of the storm as well as of the sea. Wind pushed against the tide, tide pushed the surface; the surface waters ran counter to the movement of the tide. Roccus lent herself to the opposing actions and in the turbulence maintained her lie without effort, now feeling the scrape of sand against her belly and anal fins and tail, now delighting in the lash of raindrops along her dorsal.

By slack of ebb the wind was a halfgale and seas ran more regularly and higher over milky sands. Roccus dropped back into deeper water. The first northeaster of the reluctant spring gathered force from a thick, gray ceiling of clouds.

So the May was gone. The backward spring leaped to keep abreast of the sun's orbit. Anglers sandpapered rods, wound guides and tips, varnished with their fingers, cut sticks of glass, Burma, Calcutta cane; cleaned reels, tested old lines of nylon and linen and discarded them; applied emery to dulled metal squids; replaced rusted hooks in favorite plugs; built herring cars; wired squid rigs for bottom fishing; cast lead for surf weights; filed gaff hooks; counted eelskin rigs; stood hypnotized before tackle displays, mobbed tackle counters; made phone calls to charter boatmen.

7

The bass were in!

Gilligan wrote in the *New York Herald Tribune* that a few were being taken in the New Jersey surf. Ray Camp in the *New York Times* said they were off Shinnecock Inlet. Trullinger and Hurley and Brawley sent word to the *World-Telegram*, the *Mirror* and the *Journal* that they were knee-deep in them in the Sound. In *The Boston Herald* Henry Moore wrote that there were bright fish in Buzzards Bay. Earl Banner in *The Boston Globe* said he had reports they were in the Weweantic River but he wanted to be shown. Dirk Montreal in *The Boston Advertiser* outlined the Cape Cod Canal Derby, and Cliff Davis in the *Post* wrote of the Martha's Vineyards striped-bass tournament.

The bass were in and it was time for fishing!

There were at least four good months ahead. The sea, which gave earth life and might someday reclaim it, traced pattern and plot in the shining tides. The net was of greater strength and wider sweep than any Roccus had avoided. Roccus and the shining tides were one. She cleaved upriver.

Bobby Meade steered a twenty-five-degree course through the platinum haze, holding the bow of *Carey's Chicken* in line with the first left-hand buoy marking the Hog Island channel approach to Cape Cod Canal. Both engines were revved to twenty-one hundred and the slipstream was wet, pouring past the spray shield. He and Cal were taking her over from the Vineyard to the base on the river for the first of the fishing.

Cal Knight lay on his back, an ear close to the panel opening of the port engine housing; his eyes were closed under a frown of concentrated listening. If there was a fault in the engine the skipper'd find it, Bobby thought.

Hooking on as Cal's mate had taken a deal of doing. Not that Cal, who was his second cousin, didn't want him, knowing him able, but his ma, and Cal too, had needed convincing that three years of high school were enough for a boy not planning college, and that this particular boy could quit before the end of his third year as well off as ever he'd be.

"Your pa always said you can't learn navigation without you knowing your arithmetic," his ma warned, using the strongest argument she could muster.

But he had the need to earn some money. "Pa would figure

8

I should. I'll make more working for Cal than I can off the Vineyard on somebody else's boat."

"You'll spend, boarding places and suchlike."

"I'll sleep aboard and mostly eat aboard., And Cal will pay me ten dollars every day he has a charter."

"On days he doesn't you won't earn."

"He will most every day 'cept in foul weather. All the best fishermen want Cal. We'll go for tuna and make a lot of money."

"I don't care; you're too young."

"I'm seventeen!" He'd sounded as if seventeen were mighty close to man's expectancy. "Besides, I'm big enough."

He was, too — tall enough, at any rate, tall like his pa had been but skinny as the pole of a boathook. He had a knowledge of boats and fishing gained from his pa, who had always been a good earner, though with him it was easy come, easy go. It was Cal, in the conclusive argument, who'd won his ma over. "I'll look after him and Father O'Meara'll see that he gets to mass. Holds an early mass for the boatmen and anglers." It was Cal who'd . . .

"Mind your helm!" Cal said.

Bobby started from daydreaming and noticed he was three points off course. Cal still lay with eyes closed, listening. The boy turned the wheel gently.

"Hey Cal."

"Yuh?"

"How'd you know I was off course?"

"Wave slap changed on the bow."

"How can you hear the slap above the motor?"

"Pick a fiddle out of an orchestra, can't you?"

"You find the trouble?"

"Carburetor adjustment. Doesn't amount to anything." Cal slammed the panel back into the housing box and secured it and came standing without touching his hands to the deck. "I'll take her now. Bad water here for you to learn." He took the wheel.

"You sore, Cal?"

"Nope."

"I shouldn't have let her fall off like that."

"You shouldn't have."

"Nothing happened that time, but next time it could."

9

"That's right. Now you've said it all yourself without my having to say it. No next times. We set a course, we hold it. Right?"

"Right, Cal."

"Fetch one of the glass rods and rig a plug. Get that big hooper-dooper I made. Might's well wet a line."

Bobby fetched a rod from the cabin ceiling and snapped the big teak plug to the leader. Cal throttled down to four hundred, to two-fifty, and Bobby let the plug go astern, thumbing a free spool. "Boy, what action!" the boy said.

"Let out a couple hundred feet, get it deep. Any fish around here, they'll be deep. Tell you something."

"Yuh?"

"Throw your reel in gear and loosen the star drag. Strip your line off against the drag. Know why?"

"Guess so. Fish hits when I'm free spooling I maybe get a backlash or a burned thumb."

"And if you don't and you throw into gear with the drag set up, you break off. So you knew half it anyway." He grinned. "Guess I can't teach you much, mate."

Cal swung right rudder to a forty-degree course, leaving Abiel's close to port for the run along Stony Point Dike toward the canal proper. They bucked an outgoing tide with the rips strongly made. Revved down, they had barely steerage way. There was little traffic. A tanker was standing down past Mashnee, riding light, and a dragger, loaded to the gunwales, passed them with her diesels pounding, Bostonbound. There were a few small craft distant and one closing rapidly on their starboard bow.

Cal said "That's a fast job, Bobby. Coming up."

The approaching cruiser's bow was a brown dot in a ten-foot V-fountain of spray. She passed a hundred feet distant at not less than thirty knots, a low, three-quarter-decked mahogany hull built for speed and some weather. The big man at her wheel kept his eyes ahead, but the girl beside him, her hair streaming, waved. Cal waved back and Bobby pumped the rod and cranked the reel to give an imitation of handling a fish. The sucked-down stern of the boat showed the bronze letters, *Tiderunner*, and, beneath them, *Marblehead*.

Bobby stripped line, the action of the plug was in every fiber of the line and rod and in the nerves of his hands. Then he felt shock up his arms to his shoulders.

"Cal!"

When the tide ebbed with the west flow of colder water through the canal, Roccus in mid-channel dropped back with it under the railroad bridge, past State Pier, through the straits between Hog Neck and Hog Island into warmer waters of Buzzards Bay. She swam onto the shoal at Cedar Island Point and in three fathoms there hunted food, finding little except a few of the first of the humpbacked scup. These, in the adult growth, had dorsal fins too sharp to be relished. Some of the smaller ones she swallowed. She pursued and lost a small school of sand launce. She rooted for them but could not find where they had buried themselves.

With the wash of *Tiderunner's* wake over the shoal she swam into deeper water, not alarmed but wary, and within the cone of vision of her right eye detected an active, elongated shadow, something like a whiting, swimming in jerks as if wounded, and fluttering from one side to the other. She closed on its strangeness and followed leisurely until the object leaped away from her. She accelerated and swam beneath it and bunted it gently with her head. In her years Roccus had encountered many kinds of artificial lures, and a few, when they had proved sufficiently tantalizing in action and the conditions of light or approach were such to obscure leader and line, she had struck. Decision and action in this case were simultaneous. She swirled and took the hooper-dooper head on just as it jerked again. Two of the gang of head hooks embedded themselves in her upper lip.

"Cal!"

Cal heeded."You hung on the bottom, Bobby?"

"On fish!" Bobby grunted. The rod arched and the line hissed against the light drag, and hissed cutting the surface.

"Good boy!" He revved the port motor, turned right rudder to keep the line from the hull. "Take him easy. Bass?"

"Yuh. Big one, Cal."

"They all feel big first-out in the spring."

Bobby held the rod tip fairly high and kept the reel cranking,

11

but the line still payed out.

"You best tighten up a little on that drag."

"That's what I was going to tell you," Bobby grunted. "I'm buttoned down tight already."

"Oh." Could be a big fish at that, Cal thought, though it was awful early. He gunned the motors and began to follow the fish across the channel. Bobby picked up some line. The fish dogged deep and the rod butt, jumping alive, bruised his groin. "Get me a belt, Cal."

Cal reached into the cabin for a leather bib and buckled it on the boy and helped set the butt in the pocket, feeling as he did so the springy surge of power away out at the end of the line. The fish *was* big. Twenty minutes passed. The battle had taken them across the channel to the south end of Mashnee, a boulder-strewn bottom.

"That rod'll stand all you can give it and the line is new. Your fish is well hooked or you'd have lost him long ago. Better go to work son."

The young mate lowered the rod tip, reeling; pumped, lowered reeling; pumped again, repeated.

"Gets in those boulders, he'll cut off, Bobby."

"Know it. Moved him some. This can't be no bass."

"It's bass," Cal said. "Nothing else acts like that. Give it to him."

Bobby gained fifty feet, lost it, gained sixty, lost fifty. Ten minutes later after a series of short runs the fish had only a hundred feet of line.

"Coming up!" Bobby yelled in triumph.

Off the stern Roccus surfaced in a great shower of foam and Bobby called on the Mother of God to witness the sight. Cal kicked into slow reverse and said quietly, "Don't give him slack. Ease off a little on your drag and watch out. He just came up to look around; he's going to move sudden."

Roccus sinuated, swirled and sounded, and all the line so laboriously won was lost before the boat could be brought on a following coarse.

He ain't even winded," Cal said.

"Cal."

"Yuh."

12

"You take him."

"If you don't want him I'll cut him off."

"But you saw him."

"Yuh, and how!"

"How big, Cal?"

"Oh, maybe thirty, forty pounds." He knew it was wise not to say how big.

The fish lunged and the line sang.

"I saw him, too."

"Bigger than any bass I ever saw."

"That so? Well, watch your rod tip."

No kidding him, Cal thought. He saw as well as I. He knows he's hung to a record.

The rod was a glass half-circle.

"Not much line left."

"We'll run up on him again. Take in steadily, keep the pressure on him."

They'd worked back to the channel edge, and Cal noticed with apprehension that the mahogany speed cruiser which had passed them outbound was headed in again at high speed, bearing directly across their coarse. He sounded a sharp warning on his horn and saw the bow wave diminish sharply. They hadn't seen him before. He gave his attention to the fish.

With the help of the boat, Bobby had the fish within a hundred feet again, and surfacing. Cal kicked into neutral.

"You tired him some; don't let him rest now." He went below for the big gaff. When he came topside with it, he saw with consternation that *Tiderunner* was laying to, not a hundred feet beyond the surfaced, thrashing bass. He cupped his hands and shouted, "Ahoy, *Tiderunner!* Move off, please! This fish will run again!"

The man and the girl had taken seats on the cabin to watch the fight. The man gave no sign he heard; Cal saw the girl turn to speak to her companion, probably repeating the message. The man pointed at the fish and said something. Cal shouted a warning again but it was ignored.

"He's going to move again, Cal, I can tell. He's getting ready! There he goes!"

The surface leaped and boiled. The bass took line once more

13

and the tip of Bobby's rod was pointed directly at the other boat.

"I can't turn him, Cal," he called.

"He'll pass under that lardhead. I'll swing in an arc around him. Don't pressure him enough to keep him up."

He gunned both motors. He saw the man on *Tiderunner* leap for the wheel and shouted. "Don't start up! Lay where you are!"

The girl waved, but *Tiderunner's* motors came alive with a roar and the mahogany leaped, crossing *Carey's Chicken's* bow.

"He's going over my line!" Bobby shouted.

Cal kicked into neutral, slammed into reverse. *Tiderunner* jumped clear, the man at her wheel shaking a fist.

"He cut me off!" Bobby's cry was anguish. Life had gone from the rod, line drooped from its tip. The mahogany cruiser, her damage done, lay to, motors idling again, and the boy called to her skipper in Cal's own phrase, "You big lardhead!"

Cal said, "Easy. I can do better than that. Reel in your line." He ran over alongside *Tiderunner*, and the man emerged from her wheelhouse. He was younger than Cal had thought, and the girl was better looking. But even so...

He said, deliberately, easily, "You're a no-good son of a bitch. At first I wasn't going to say it in the presence of the lady, but then I figured anyone who'd be palling around with you wouldn't mind an understatement like that... You don't do you?" he asked, his eyes on the girl.

Her companion had a bull of a voice. "You wouldn't say that ashore, you clam mucker! You haven't got the guts!"

"I'd say it ashore, afloat, or flying. And with ditto marks. I base on the river at Farrell's Wharf and I'll be there in less than an hour. I'll be glad to say it then and there or any time later, anywhere."

He moved out and headed upchannel. *Tiderunner* passed him, heading in.

"Maybe he'll be waiting, Cal," Bobby said.

"Good. I need it."

"Looks pretty good. In good shape."

"I need a licking. Do me good. Shouldn't have said it — not in front of her."

"She didn't look the kind would be with him."

"Doesn't make any difference. Shouldn't have said it. Don't

14

you ever."

"I won't....Cal?"

"Yuh?"

"How big was that bass?"

"Really want to know? Make you feel bad."

"I want to know."

"Not less than one hundred pounds. Not less than five and a half feet long. Now you can cry in your pillow tonight."

"Maybe I'll get a bigger one."

Cal grinned. "I got me a good mate." He said. He put an arm around the boy's shoulder. "Listen, kid. No sense to tell a man not to feel bad when he loses a record fish. But if you'd caught it you wouldn't have had any fun bass fishing the rest of your life. Imagine that!"

They both laughed...

Tiderunner wasn't in sight when they tied up at Farrell's Wharf.

"Wash down and make up the bunks," Cal said. "I'm going up to see Tom Salter and tell him about that fish, and I'm going to call New Haven and tell Dan Merriman, who's doing striped-bass research at Yale. No sense telling anyone else; they'll just figure we're dreaming. If I'm not back in fifteen minutes get some chow cooking; anything suits me."

"Okay, Skipper." Bobby grinned.

Cal found Tom Salter at his boat station and told him of the fish. Tom told of the fish he and Father O'Meara had seen.

"Could be the same," Tom said. "Fish we saw wouldn't stay in the river long."

"How is the Father?"

"No younger. But well enough. And asking for you recently."

"I'll drop by the rectory and say hello. Someone I want him to keep an eye on."

"You won't find him this afternoon. Manuel Riba is giving him some worry and he went up to Manuel's place. That damnfool chief down at the Coast Guard Station, Maddox — you know him — he's got Father in a frame of mind to believe that all his works are in vain if he can't save Manuel from the devil."

"By the way, you know a sport cruiser, *Tiderunner?*"

"I've seen it lately. Seems to belong up the river. Saw it

moored off a new house up there where some professor and his daughter come to live. Why?"

"Quite a craft."

The soft, warm light was going. Cal paid his respects to Mrs. Salter and decided to go back to the boat without telephoning Merriman. He saw the riding and cabin lights were already turned on; Bobby would have something cooking. Maybe later they'd go uptown to the movies. Right now he was hungry.

He called when he walked out on the apron of the wharf, but Bobby didn't answer. The new tide hadn't raised *Carey's Chicken* much. He swung down four rungs of the ladder and jumped aboard. Bobby lay sprawled on the deck between the engine housings, his head in his hands, sobbing. Cal knelt swiftly.

"Hey, kid, what gives?"

The boy half turned his head. It was a bloody mess, mouth and cheeks cut, both eyes swollen, nose torn at one nostril.

"What happened?"

"That guy came looking for you. Said you'd run out on him. Called you a yellow bastard. I told him everything you'd said went for me, too. That's all. Except he's awful fast and awful good."

Cal got him sitting up and washed out the cuts. The nose wasn't broken. Nor the spirit.

"I wasn't crying because I took a licking."

"I know."

"It was because I'd lost the fish. Cal, you'd have had him if you'd been handling him. Would have meant a lot for the reputation of the boat."

So that was it.

"Listen, Bobby. I couldn't have done any better than you. Nobody could. You made no mistakes. That rod was too light to kill that fish in anything under an hour. Hadn't have been for that son of a bitch you'd have had him."

"Maybe."

"Come on, let's chow. You want to go to the movies later?"

"Sure, anything you say."

"I say the movies for you. I got an errand to do."

Roccus sank to the bouldered deeps off Mashnee. The hooks

of the plug were merely an annoyance, the weight of it a nuisance which did not greatly alarm her. She had rid herself of
similar lures before. Behind her, as she swam, trailed one
hundred and twenty feet of forty-five-pound-test nylon line and
three feet of nylon leader. Before dusk all except a foot of the
line had been cut off by the sharp edges of barnacles, mussels
and rocks. She expelled with an exertion that tired her and
somehow caused her to be tense. Awkwardly, she fed through
squid though she was not hungry. She sought the reassurance
of normality.

Roccus' jaw healed swiftly, causing her no pain. As June
waned she joined first one and then another of the many schools
of striped bass which remained in the area of Cape Cod Canal.
Some of these fish were from the Chesapeake region and more
were native to the Hudson and its tributaries. There were few
from the Roanoke; most of the migrating Roanoke fish had come
no farther north than the Jersey coast.

All these fish in the canal area moved back and forth with the
tides through the big ditch, driving whiting from the bottom to
the surface, where, in the rips, they skitted furiously, heads out
of water, terrorized. The bass rose beneath them in pursuit,
tail-smashing to stun them.

Day and night the anglers lined the canal riprap to cast for
the bass, using eelskins on weighted rigs during the darkness
and plugs in daylight hours. Favorite spots were crowded. These
were adjacent to the swiftest rips and had been given names
common among the angling fraternity. Some of the names were
Halfway Gate, Split Rock, the Mussel Bed, the Cradle, Lobster
Pound, Lumber Yard, Paddy's Rock, the Beacon, the Herring
Run, the High Tension, Portugee Hole and the Basin. There
were a score more. Some men fished all night and slept in the
daytime in cars parked in a wooded section under the Bourne
highway bridge. Some fished for market, some only for sport;
others fished for sport, yet marketed their catch so they could
meet expenses and continue to fish for fun. When the bass were
choosy, or chasing whiting far out in the middle of the canal,
hard to reach, many of the fishermen lived for days on nothing
more substantial than coffee and doughnuts. Restaurants stayed
open all night to cater to them, and these, on the slack tides,

17

were crowded with anglers who were waiting for rips to make up. They had only one subject of conversation — striped bass. There was none but dreamed of catching a record fish. None really expected to. They were a red-eyed, bewhiskered, somewhat odoriferous congregation of zealots.

Roccus scattered the stars and seized a compressed slab of moonlight, swallowing it.

The July moon beamed on waters slapped by the tails of late-arriving menhaden moving inshore along both sides of the Cape. There were many thousands in each school and there were countless thousands of schools. Into one dimpling over three fathoms Roccus drove again.

Other fish were feeding on the pogy — many other bass, squeteague, late pollock, the first of the bluefish, blue and hammerhead sharks, bonito, dolphin and, in deeper waters, broadbill swordfish and whales. Nearly all life of the ocean fed on the menhaden. Lobstermen seined them for bait. Fleets of white vessels seined them by the millions for oil and fertilizer. They swam fin to fin, tiers deep, the most abundant species in the Atlantic fishery. They were late arriving because the sea on the shoals had been late to warm. Now they would summer in the bays and harbors, the inlets and surf, waxing fatter and oilier on algae, sediment of organic decay and minute crustacean life, and their enemies from the land and of the sea would deplete their numbers by millions, yet fail appreciably to deplete their population. For each mature menhaden moving inshore had spawned more than one hundred thousand eggs. They were a countless streaming under the stars of the tide, showering as Roccus drove again.

When the July moon filled, Roccus returned to the lie by the Bird Island boulder, gorged with pogy, and at two o'clock of a morning, when the light on the water was one six-hundred-thousandth of the brilliance of the midday sun, she moved into the circle of a seine. She felt it against her tail before she saw it; she felt it against her side. Lesser bass, also trapped, began in excitement to mill around her. She surfaced and found no escape; she sounded and encountered wide-mesh twine. She swam the closing circle of the siene, brushing against it. Some of the smaller bass were gilled, thrashing, floundering. But she

18

was not greatly alarmed. In the Roanoke, in an arm of the Chesapeake, once in the Hudson, she had been in nets before. From traps, like most bass, she always found her way; these were the offshore weirs with openings never closed except on low water. This trap was different; its opening already had closed, its diameter was closing.

Roccus moved slowly in a half-circle, well inside the closing wall of mesh. Then, with a rush and thrust that scattered the smaller bass, she surged to the surface, flashed like a bright spearhead in the July moonlight, and re-entered the protecting water a fathom clear of the net floats. The thrust of the broad tail carried her to the channel past Bird Island and the safety of the flowing depths. She passed a pod of pogy, scattering them in a frenzy of flashing silver, then slowing to alert movement along the margin of the channel.

In the moon's last quarter Roccus reentered the canal, following schools of spike and tinker mackerel, feeding only at night, lying on the bottom with lesser fish during the hours of sun. Her appetite diminished and she was easily satisfied. She no longer pursued the darting whiting to the surface to whack them and gorge them. She moved lazily after eels, not eager for their taste. As the water warmed, her stripes darkened from brown to deep blue, and a reddish hue appeared on the edge of her gill covers. Sea lice left her for fish traveling to the surf. A benign lassitude of old age crept upon her.

Lovely and peaceful beat the sea of summer, cruel with death. Schools of small tuna were annihilating squid. Giant bluefins were decimating the mackerel shoals. Stalking the big tuna came the killers.

Through the canal with the tide eastflowing Roccus moved under Sagamore Highway Bridge, past Paddys Reef, past the dolphins in the mooring basin across from The Blinker, past breakwater and sandcatcher and into the surge of Cape Cod Bay, where the half-flood kicked a chop of seventy-one-degree surface water against the current disgorging between the riprap. A light easterly behind the fetch of sea added to surface commotion at the canal's east entrance. Roccus felt an uneasiness. She moved across the Sagamore bar where sand eels and sperling silvered the surf.

The school tuna harassing the summer squid were between twenty and forty pounds in weight, fish which in the larval stage three and four years before had measured only a quarter inch in length. Several hundred of these in two or three distinct schools had moved higher along the bay arm from the Barnstable traps where they had gorged on herring. Now they moved through and under acres of the small red squid, gorging again.

It was not coincidence that the adult members of their family were in the same area. Departing from the fathom curve of their migration highway between the tip of Cape Cod and Nova Scotia, they had moved in from Wood End to intercept the mackerel which swam with the east wind. They raced at great speed effortlessly. Between their bullet-shaped heads and their tails of tremendous power there was no line of water resistance; their giant fins fitted into grooves in their bodies. Sun rainbowed the spray above them when they surfaced, sporting; they made a slice caused by the slimy substance adhering to their tiny scales. The slick made a pattern of betrayal on the water.

Orcinus, the killer whale, was leader of a pack which had sped south with the Labrador Current, then followed a bent course inside the Gulf Stream to a point three miles off The Race. There they had been sighted, an even dozen of them, and reported by two draggers inbound from the Georges Bank. They had been seen in combat with a finback whale of sixty feet which they had mortally wounded but upon which they had not fed. They had come south to feed on the tuna.

Orcinus was twenty-nine feet long, with huge rounded flippers, great tail flukes and a dorsal fin, curved with age, more than five feet in length. About three quarters of his scaleless skin was black, but his chin and belly were white and there were white oval patches above each eye. In his pack were six males only slightly smaller. The five females were less than half as large, and their flippers, flukes and fins were disproportionately smaller, perhaps a quarter of the size of the males. These were the gangsters of the Atlantic and their molls, unmatched in ruthlessness, working with a mob instinct that struck terror into the hearts of the largest whales and sharks.

Off Barnstable the killers had intercepted the trail of the tuna and soon began to take toll of them in all sizes. A forty-pound schoolfish was a half-bite appetizer for Orcinus, a five-hundred-pound bluefin a two-bite hors d'oeuvre. Despite the speed of the tuna the killers overtook them at will. Yet they did not harry them ceaselessly. They withdrew as their appetites were satisfied, so that the bluefins were not completely stampeded.

Now, having swum outside the tuna for several miles during half a day while the bluefins, their alarm diminishing, resumed feeding, the killers drove toward the land again and the giant tuna fled before them among the schoolfish. The schoolfish turned over the shoals in terror.

Inside Roccus there was no hunger except a yearning which had no significance for her senses. She moved leisurely across the Sagamore bar and onto the shoals off Scorton Harbor Creek in Sandwich. There, encountering extreme shoaling, she finned farther off the land. And farther off the land, where the water deepened to eight fathoms, Orcinus hit her.

The bass had brief warning. A tuna of about twenty pounds arced into her vision, leaped and twisted and turned offshore again. Roccus followed from curiosity and met, nearly head on, a giant tuna in a glide of frenzy, in flight before the closely following killer.

Orcinus saw Roccus only as a blurred shadow suspended where no shadow should be. He chopped at her with one side of his jaw in the flash of his passing. His twenty-two conically pointed teeth on that side sliced into the caudal peduncle of the bass — nearly to the backbone — just failing to sever.

Tuna and killer whale vanished as quickly as they had appeared. Roccus, seeking shallower water, swam slowly and with great exertion. Her broad tail, the propeller of her normal action, was fouled and its driving force drastically reduced. She was severly injured.

On the second night after being wounded by Orcinus, Roccus swam awkwardly with the tide in the starry shallows past Sandwich Harbor Creek to the deep of the canal's east end; and as the west tide began to flow, she gave her hurt self to the pull of it and, dropping deep, moved through. The wound of both sides of the wrist of her tail attracted two lampreys, which she brushed off a mussell bed, but cunners followed her, as did dogfish, drawn by the flow of her life in the tide's life.

Her life was a life of great tides and currents but this life of the moon's tide was small; the moon was in quarter stage, and the rips were slow to make. This was a windless night when the eelrig bouncers got much distance in their casts but took few bass. Roccus saw a dozen slow-moving, blue-backed, white-bellied skins, inflated with water, move within her striking distance and withdraw with tantalizing tail action. Hungry, she might have struck. She did not hunger.

Before the new day crept under the span of the railroad bridge she had reversed her journey through the canal and was again in Buzzards Bay.

The wound confused her, rather than pained. The alarm building within her was the result of confusion.

Stena, the roseate tern, was fishing. From her lookout on the high bank of the point near where Roccus rested, the bird watched the schools of bait fish congregating near shore. The sun lay slightly behind her, past its zenith.

When there was a sufficient concentration of the small prey milling about, Sterna performed the Trick of the Menacing Shadow, launching herself and swooping to within a few feet of the water. Her shadow panicked the bait, which showered ahead of it, and the tern of greatest symmetry dipped to scoop baby herring and sand eels, some of which she took from the air.

Lying under four feet of water on the warm silt bottom, Roccus watched this performance for an hour, at the end of which Sterna had her fill. The bass moved slowly to feed on wounded fluttering bait.

Sun beat down on the surface of the river. No wind moved that surface, no fish, no bird. The tide had reached the peak of the salt mark on the marsh grass. Bait fish kept to the cooler depths over sand, worrying shell lately turned by the quahoggers. Plankton clouded the iris-blue water. A kingfisher swooped but held its dive over a cloud of minnows too deep to reach and returned with a cry of angry frustration to its lookout at the brittle tip of a dead cedar.

Blue crabs crawled the bottom and in the weed crept up on partially opened seed scallops, and on the bars snuggled with their hinges against small rocks, waiting for clam snouts to show. They could move fast and in any direction. A late-spawning horseshoe crab pushed sand like a bulldozer. Fiddlers, their homes flooded, crept along cautiously, hunting shrimps and sand fleas and the broker clams gulls had dropped for cracking when the tide was down.

In a hole fourteen feet deep, off an old windwheel once used to make electricity for a pump, Roccus rested with her chin in mud, expelling water at an accelerated count, turning on one side, then the other, to present the healing wound at the base of her caudal to the black ooze, the warm and salving ooze. So she had rested for days moving into weeks since Orcinus had struck her, feeding lightly and not more than twice a week. She wasted away. She was still a great fish, but her depth and thickness had diminished, the deep bulge of her belly had vanished; she was flabby in her underside, there was an unhealthy sheen on her gill covers and no sea lice sought her as host.

August waned. Days of intense heat were followed by brief tempests that failed to clear the air. The dawns were red beyond the eye of the sun. Chain lightning, distant, licked the evening sky. There was no thunder. A season was approaching its end and the approach communicated itself to all life.

Man witnessed the quick ripening of his tomatoes, the sudden, overnight toughening of his corn, the withering of his potato vines, the indefinable feeling that a chore so long delayed as tacking a new tin blade on his snow shovel had better be attended to. There were days and weeks and possibly months before a sterner season claimed the earth, yet the grasp of change was on it.

The terns, their young flown, were hungrier for themselves; the mackerel gulls were less lazy; the fierce-winged gannet dived from greater height. The curlew cried above the moor at night and the plovers called at daybreak. The young of the native black ducks tested their strengthening wings above the guzzles. Sandpipers and swallows flew in clouds, and in the march the redwinged blackbird tucked her song beneath her wing.

In the dunes the hares developed a scent the gray fox could follow, and in the marsh the muskrat made a tentative selection of winter quarters. The otter ranged far, and in the night his whistle was a distant locomotive.

The life of the sea also felt change. Tuna coursed east, the

23

killers in their wake. Cod and haddock began an inshore move-ment and the whiting went into the surf's first roller. Bluefish followed the whiting into the surf and the scup turned south. Off the beaches the young of the menhaden were nearly four inches long and the adult fish had disappeared; some said the pogy fleet had taken all of them, but they had merely moved into deeper water, a movement which was scarcely more than a drift accomplished on the ebb of a high-course tide.

Off Plum Island and Parver River, off the estuary of North and South rivers, off the Gurnet, outside Saquish and Clarks Island, off the Cape Cod Canal and Sandwich Harbor Creek, on shoals, the young striped bass began to school, school joining school, for southward migration, a movement of bait fish, which, in turn, depended completely upon the development of weather.

Roccus, mending slowly, felt a similar urge, though the schooling fish were mostly between five and fifteen pounds. Pods of the larger migrating fish usually formed later. She began to feed on the fugitive small bait, on a few late softshelled crabs. She mended slowly.

On the last night of the August moon, while a tempest cloud covered the crescent, Roccus dropped back through the narrows down, down the river and into the pulsing sea. Her wound had not healed completely and never would, she swam with half the strength of her usual tail thrust and only half her eager-ness of questing. Otherwise she had the fair health of old age and a sudden desire to be gone to the far waters of her birth. With the tide she dropped back, until she reached the Mashnee Shoals at the western approach of the canal.

To the submerged granite boulder on the Bird Island ledge, where she had paused in her migrations of many years, Roccus made her way, driven by the urge to begin her southward journey. For three days of early September she occupied this hold. She gained strength as the wound at the wrist of her caudal healed dispite its fouling, and her appetite returned. Here in May she had fed upon Anguilla, and here now the eels dropping back from the rivers to spawn swam in abundance and were tasty and nourishing.

These were bright days of mistrals at dawn, warming surface water the hours of sun, and cool nights when the pattern of the universe beyond earth was mirrored on the frosty tides.

No striped bass joined her on the Bird Island ledge and on the night of the third day of her lie there she returned to the Mashnee shore. The instinct of early migration remained strong within her, but she was possessed by a stronger urge to seek the company of her own kind.

Off Mashnee smaller bass were beginning to school. Some had passed through the canal from Cape Cod Bay, others were from the rivers and harbors adjacent to the canal's west end. These fish were restless, undetermined in their movements, uncertain, wavering with the tidal changes, held in the gathering place by the flow of feed on the canal edge, waiting on the weather.

Roccus joined a school of bass in the fifteen to twenty-pound class. She was neither welcomed nor made unwelcome. She swam in a flanking position like an outrider edging a herd of cattle.

Three pods of bull bass which had summered in Cape Cod Canal, one group of fish individually approaching half the size of Roccus, joined the school to which Roccus had attached herself. Two days later more than one hundred striped bass from six to twelve pounds each joined up. All acted in response to the same urging that moved the matriarch for company of her species in a journey of varying lengths, none short, to the warmer waters of early life.

In the rips and backwaters the young menhaden and herring and the silver eels were plentiful. The nights were noisy as the bass fed and strengthened yet did not grow in size. Despite her healing, her feeding, her strengthening, she continued to waste away.

Now the nights were cold, and the surface water, from the night air, was sometimes colder than the depths, and in the limitless element above the sea migrating birds were a-wing to lesser latitudes, quiet in the passage.

Roccus felt the change of pressure on the weight of waters at the Mashnee gathering place of the tides. Of the great and growing school of bass she alone felt it, being wiser in age and experience. It was a subtle change, not marked, telling her that heavy weather was definitely approaching, though not yet close. Only five barometers hinted this change; most did not. Yet next

25

day all the school felt it, the larger fish first.

It was a signal for application to appetite, for satiation beyond appetite, for gorging against the needs of a journey that would begin at the height of the storm and allow no interval for seeking food. With the storm the school might move along to Cuttyhunk or to Sakonnet area, or even as far as Montauk Point; it would positively move from Mashnee and during passage it would not feed. Roccus fed almost exclusively on the migrating eels, whose oily flavor, more pronounced now than that of young menhaden, she somehow needed. These she pursued at leisurely pace, approaching them from behind, accelerating to seize them broadside at the head. Some she bit in two, others she swallowed whole. Her best hunting was at night, when the eels were most active, emerging from their hiding places.

Because a high-pressure area from Canada slowed the storm's progress up the coast from Hatteras, the weather held fair beyond the time Roccus' instinct told her it would foul. The barometer even showed a slightly upward trend.

So came a cloudless night of thin moon, nearly dark o' the moon, a windless night, the sea flat, cold except for a distinguishable offshore ground swell. In the marshes, gathering black ducks were raucous. A flight of geese went over.

Hunger blinded caution or Roccus would not have struck at the false Anguilla that darted past a haze of phosphorescence. The very force of her strike, while it set the sharp hook, snapped the line with a vicious jerk that amazed the trolling, half-dozing angler.

Downtide, sounding, Roccus fought her doom with the utmost of her half-mended strength. Her savage strike had driven the head hook of the rigged eel through the roof of her mouth, and the barb of the middle hook had pierced her tongue and lower jaw. As pain stabbed her and she swirled, the tail hood of the false Anguilla slapped under her open gill cover and secured itself in her rakers.

A resistance which sought to turn her course, a sensation she had experienced in other misadventures, quickly ended. But one hook bled her gills, and the others, like a chain bolt on a door, secured her jaws, nearly locking them. Her breathing became labored. She was in a state of slow suffocation.

She surfaced in a flurry of panic, violently shaking her head, circling, creating a disturbance which in decent weather would have attracted the gulls from afar. This day the gulls were on the beaches or the pierheads or the rocks, or riding the updrafts of the wind above the faces of the dunes. None observed her.

She drove for the bottom again, but not to rest. Although the pain of the hooks, a sudden reflex of her nervous system, subsided, there grew within her a feeling of bursting and a terror of the unknown that gripped her jaws. Without sense of direction or purpose, regardless of changing pressures, she swam swiftly about, often striking the rocks.

This phase of her struggle lasted for hours, but her strength waned as the day waned and the storm gathered itself for night assault. Finally her terror vanished and her aimless movements ceased; and in the late afternoon, the ebb tide nearly spent, herself spent, she gave herself to the tide, unconscious, drifting with it, her fins moving only from the turbulence of the water, and an uncontrolled trembling in all her muscles. Her tail was completely paralyzed.

Through the quickfall of night, into the first of the tide's resurgence, life clung to Roccus rather than she to life.

Then it was full dark and, though the heavy clouds completely obscured the new moon and the constellations, there came a moment when it seemed as if Roccus had entered again the spangled shallows of her youth. The golden burst of Capella in Auriga fired the sea. Bright were Deneb and Altair and Algol, and bright was Jupiter below the Great Square of Pegasus. And suddenly all of the planets and their moons, every one of the myriad stars, were pouring down the tide, streaming down the tide that had turned for home.

RING
OF
Spears

Join Roosevelt as he hunts elephants and witnesses a daring spear hunt for lions in this excerpt from his classic, African Game Trails.

by Theodore Roosevelt

The next day we moved camp to the edge of a swamp about five miles from the river. Near the tents was one of the trees which, not knowing its real name, we called "sausage-tree;" the seeds or fruits are encased in a kind of hard gourd, the size of a giant sausage, which swings loosely at the end of a long tendril. The swamp was half or three-quarters of a mile across, with one or two ponds in the middle, from which we shot ducks. Francolins — delicious eating, as the ducks were also — uttered their grating calls nearby, while oribi and hartebeest were usually to be seen from the tents. The hartebeest, by the way, in its three forms, is much the commonest game animal of East Africa.

A few miles beyond this swamp we suddenly came on a small herd of elephants in the open. There were eight cows and two

28

calves, and they were moving slowly, feeding on the thorny tops of the scattered mimosas and on other bushes which were thornless. The eyesight of elephants is very bad; I doubt whether they see more than a rather near-sighted man; and we walked up to within seventy yards of these, slight though the cover was, so that Kermit could try to photograph them. We did not need to kill another cow for the National Museum, and so after we had looked at the huge, interesting creatures as long as we wished, we croaked and whistled, and they moved off with leisurely indifference. There is always a fascination about watching elephants; they are such giants, they are so intelligent — much more so than any other game, except perhaps the lion, whose intelligence has a very sinister bent — and they look so odd with their great ears flapping and their trunks lifting and curling. Elephants are rarely absolutely still for any length of time; now and then they flap an ear, or their bodies sway slightly, while at intervals they utter curious internal rumblings, or trumpet gently. These were feeding on saplings of the mimosas and other trees, apparently caring nothing for the thorns of the former; they would tear off branches, big or little, or snap off a trunk if the whim seized them. They swallowed the leaves and twigs of these trees; but I have known them to merely chew and spit out the stems of certain bushes.

After leaving the elephants we were on our way back to camp when we saw a white man in the trail ahead; and on coming nearer whom should it prove to be but Carl Akeley, who was out on a trip for the American Museum of Natural History in New York. We went with him to his camp, where we found Mrs. Akeley, Clark, who was assisting him, and Messrs. McCutcheon and Stevenson who were along on a hunting trip. They were old friends and I was very glad to see them. McCutcheon, the cartoonist, had been at a farewell lunch given me by Robert Collier just before I left New York, and at the lunch we had been talking much of George Ade, and the first question I put to him was "*Where is* George Ade?" for if one unexpectedly meets an American cartoonist on a hunting trip in mid-Africa there seems no reason why one should not also see his crony, an American playwright. A year previously Mr. and Mrs. Akeley had lunched with me at the White House, and we had talked

29

over our proposed African trips. Akeley, an old African wanderer, was going out with the especial purpose of getting a group of elephants for the American Museum, and was anxious that I should shoot one or two of them for him. I had told him that I certainly would if it were a possibility; and on learning that we had just seen a herd of cows he felt — as I did — that the chance had come for me to fulfill my promise. So we decided that he should camp with us that night, and that next morning we would start with a light outfit to see whether we could not overtake the herd.

An amusing incident occurred that evening. After dark some of the porters went through the reeds to get water from the pond in the middle of the swamp. I was sitting in my tent when a loud yelling and screaming rose from the swamp, and in rushed Kongoni to say that one of the men, while drawing water, had been seized by a lion. Snatching up a rifle I was off at a run for the swamp, calling for lanterns; Kermit and Tarlton joined me, the lanterns were brought, and we reached the meadow of short marsh grass which surrounded the high reeds in the middle. No sooner were we on this meadow than there were loud snortings in the darkness ahead of us, and then the sound of a heavy animal galloping across our front. It now developed that there was no lion in the case at all, but that the porters had been chased by a hippo. I should not have supposed that a hippo would live in such a small, isolated swamp; but there he was on the meadow in front of me, invisible, but snorting, and galloping to and fro. Evidently he was much interested in the lights, and we thought he might charge us; but he did not, retreating slowly as we advanced, until he plunged into the little pond. Hippos are sometimes dangerous at night, and so we waded through the swamp until we came to the pool at which the porters filled their buckets, and stood guard over them until they were through; while the hippo, unseen in the darkness, came closer to us, snorting and plunging — possibly from wrath and insolence, but more probably from mere curiosity.

Next morning Akeley, Tarlton, Kermit, and I started on our elephant hunt. We were travelling light. I took nothing but my bedding, wash kit, spare socks, and slippers, all in a roll of waterproof canvas. We went to where we had seen the herd and then took up the trail, Kongoni and two or three other gun-bearers walking ahead as trackers. They did their work well. The elephants had not been in the least alarmed. Where they had walked in single file it was easy to follow their trail; but the trackers had hard work puzzling it out where the animals had scattered out and loitered along feeding. The trail led up and down hills and through open thorn scrub, and it crossed and recrossed the wooded watercourses in the bottoms of the valleys. At last, after going some ten miles we came on sign where the elephants had fed that morning, and four or five miles farther on we overtook them. That we did not scare them into flight was due to Tarlton. The trail went nearly across wind; the trackers were leading us swiftly along it, when suddenly Tarlton heard a low trumpet ahead and to the right hand. We at once doubled back, left the horses, and advanced toward where the noise indicated that the herd was standing.

In a couple of minutes we sighted them. It was just noon. There were six cows, and two well-grown calves — these last being quite big enough to shift for themselves or to be awkward antagonists for any man of whom they could get hold. They stood in a clump, each occasionally shifting its position or lazily flapping an ear; and now and then one would break off a branch with its trunk, tuck it into its mouth, and withdraw it stripped of its leaves. The wind blew fair, we were careful to make no noise, and with ordinary caution we had nothing to fear from their eyesight. The ground was neither forest nor bare plain; it was covered with long grass and a scattered open growth of small, scantily leaved trees, chiefly mimosas, but including some trees covered with gorgeous orange-red flowers. After careful scrutiny we advanced behind an ant-hill to within sixty yards, and I stepped forward for the shot.

Akeley wished two cows and a calf. Of the two best cows one had rather thick, worn tusks; those of the other were smaller, but better shaped. The latter stood half facing me, and I put the bullet from the right barrel of the Holland through her lungs, and fired the left barrel for the heart of the other. Tarlton, and then Akeley and Kermit followed suit. At once the herd started diagonally past us, but half halted and faced toward us when

31

only twenty-five yards distant, an unwounded cow began to advance with her great ears cocked at right angles to her head; and Tarlton called "Look out; they are coming for us." At such a distance a charge from half a dozen elephant is a serious thing. I put a bullet into the forehead of the advancing cow, causing her to lurch heavily forward to her knees; and then we all fired. The heavy rifles were too much even for such big beasts, and round they spun and rushed off. As they turned I dropped the second cow I had wounded with a shot in the brain, and the cow that had started to charge also fell, though it needed two or three more shots to keep it down as it struggled to rise. The cow at which I had fired kept on with the rest of the herd, but fell dead before going a hundred yards. After we had turned the herd Kermit with his Winchester killed a bull calf, necessary to complete the museum group; we had been unable to kill it before because we were too busy stopping the charge of the cows. I was sorry to have to shoot the third cow, but with elephants starting to charge at twenty-five yards the risk is too great, and the need of instant action too imperative, to allow for any hesitation.

We pitched camp a hundred yards from the elephants, and Akeley, working like a demon, and assisted by Tarlton, had the skins off the two biggest cows and the calf by the time night fell; I walked out and shot an oribi for supper. Soon after dark the hyenas began to gather at the carcasses and to quarrel among themselves as they gorged. Toward morning, a lion came near and uttered a kind of booming, long-drawn moan, an ominous and menacing sound. The hyenas answered with an extraordinary chorus of yelling, howling, laughing, and chuckling, as weird a volume of noise as any to which I ever listened. At dawn we stole down to the carcasses in the faint hope of a shot at the lion. However, he was not there; but as we came toward one carcass a hyena raised its head seemingly from beside the elephant's belly, and I brained it with the little Springfield. On walking up it appeared that I need not have shot at all. The hyena, which was swollen with elephant meat, had gotten inside the huge body, and had then bitten a hole through the abdominal wall of tough muscle and thrust his head through. The wedge-shaped head had slipped through the hole all right, but the muscle had then contracted, and the hyena was fairly caught, with its body inside the elephant's belly, and its head thrust out through the hole. We took several photos of the beast in its queer trap.

After breakfast we rode back to our camp by the swamp. Akeley and Clark were working hard at the elephant skins; but Mrs. Akeley, Stevenson, and McCutcheon took lunch with us at our camp. They had been having a very successful hunt; Mrs. Akeley had to her credit a fine maned lion and a bull elephant with enormous tusks. This was the first safari we had met while we were out in the field; though in Nairobi, and once or twice at outlying bomas, we had met men about to start on, or returning from, expeditions; and as we marched into Meru we encountered the safari of an old friend, William Lord Smith — "Tiger" Smith — who, with Messrs. Brooks and Allen, were on a trip which was partly a hunting trip and partly a scientific trip undertaken on behalf of the Cambridge Museum.

From the 'Nzoi we made a couple days' march to Lake Sergoi, which we had passed on our way out; a reed-fringed pond, surrounded by rocky hills which marked about the limit to which the Boer and English settlers who were taking up the country had spread. All along our route we encountered herds of game; sometimes the herd would be of only one species; at other times we would come across a great mixed herd, the red hartebeest always predominating; while among them might be zebras, showing silvery white or dark gray in the distance, topis with beautifully colored coats, and even waterbuck. We shot what hartebeests, topis, and oribis were needed for food. All over the uplands we came on the remains of a race of which even the memory has long since vanished. These remains consist of large, nearly circular walls of stones, which are sometimes roughly squared. A few of these circular enclosures contain more than one chamber. Many of them, at least, are not cattle kraals, being too small, and built round hollows; the walls are so low that by themselves they could not serve for shelter or defense, and must probably have been used as supports for roofs of timber or skins. They were certainly built by people who were in some respects more advanced than the savage tribes who now dwell in the land; but the grass grows thick on

33

the earth mounds into which the ancient stone walls are slowly crumbling, and not a trace of the builders remains. Barbarians they doubtless were; but they have been engulfed in the black oblivion of a lower barbarism, and not the smallest tradition lingers to tell of their craft or their cruelty, their industry or prowess, or to give us the least hint as to the race from which they sprang.

We had with us an ox wagon with the regulation span of sixteen oxen, the driver being a young colonial Englishman from South Africa — for the Dutch and English Africanders are the best ox-wagon drivers in the world. On the way back to Sergoi he lost his oxen, which were probably run off by some savages from the mountains; so at Sergoi we had to hire another ox wagon, the South African who drove it being a Dutchman named Botha. Sergoi was as yet the limit of settlement; but it was evident that the whole Uasin Gishu country would soon be occupied. Already many Boers from South Africa, and a number of English Africanders, had come in; and no better pioneers exist today than these South Africans, both Dutch and English. Both are so good that I earnestly hope they will become indissolubly welded into one people; and the Dutch Boer has the supreme merit of preferring the country to the town and of bringing his wife and children — plenty of children — with him to settle on the land. The homemaker is the only type of settler of permanent value; and the cool, healthy fertile Uasin Gishu region is an ideal land for the right kind of pioneer homemaker, whether he hopes to make his living by raising stock or by growing crops.

At Sergoi Lake there is a store kept by Mr. Kirke, a South African of Scotch blood. With a kind courtesy which I cannot too highly appreciate he, with the equally cordial help of another settler, Mr. Skally — also a South African, but of Irish birth — and of the district commissioner, Mr. Corbett, had arranged for a party of Nandi warriors to come over and show me how they hunted the lion.

The Nandi are a warlike pastoral tribe, close kin to the Masai in blood and tongue, in weapons and in manner of life. They have long been accustomed to killing lions which become man-eaters or which molest their cattle overmuch; and the peace

which British rule has imposed upon them — a peace so welcome to the weaker, so irksome to the predatory tribes — has
left lion killing one of the few pursuits in which glory can be
won by a young warrior. When it was told them that if they
wished they could come to hunt lions at Sergoi, eight hundred
warriors volunteered, and much heart-burning was caused in
choosing the sixty or seventy who were allowed the privilege.
They stipulated, however, that they should not be used merely
as beaters, but should kill the lions themselves, and refused to
come unless with this understanding.

The day before we reached Sergoi they had gone out, and
had killed a lion and lioness; the beasts were put up from a
small covert and despatched with heavy throwing spears on
the instant, before they offered, or indeed had the chance to offer,
any resistance. The day after our arrival there was a cold rain and
we found no lions. Next day, November 20th, we were successful.

We started immediately after breakfast. Of course, we carried
our rifles, but our duty was merely to round up the lion and
hold him, if he went off so far in advance that even the Nandi
runners could not overtake him. We intended to beat the country
toward some shallow, swampy valleys twelve miles distant.

In an hour we overtook the Nandi warriors, who were
advancing across the rolling, grassy plains in a long line, with
intervals of six or eight yards between the men. They were
splendid savages, stark naked, lithe as panthers, the muscles
rippling under their smooth dark skins; all their lives they had
lived on nothing but animal food, milk, blood, and flesh, and
they were fit for any fatigue or danger. Their faces were proud,
cruel, fearless; as they ran they moved with long springy strides.
Their head-dresses were fantastic; they carried ox-hide shields
painted with strange devices; and each bore in his right hand
the formidable war spear, used both for stabbing and for
throwing at close quarters. The narrow spear heads of soft iron
were burnished till they shone like silver; they were four feet
long, and the point and edges were razor sharp. The wooden
haft appeared for but a few inches; the long butt was also of
iron, ending in a spike, so that the spear looked almost solid
metal. Yet each sinewy warrior carried his heavy weapon as if
it were a toy, twirling it till it glinted in the sun-rays. Herds of

game, red hartebeests and striped zebra and wild swine, fled right and left before the advance of the line.

It was noon before we reached a wide, shallow valley, with beds of rushes here and there in the middle, and on either side high grass and dwarfed and scattered thorntrees. Down this we beat for a couple of miles. Then, suddenly, a maned lion rose a quarter of a mile ahead of the line and galloped off through the high grass; and all of us on horseback tore after him.

He was a magnificent beast, with a black and tawny mane; in his prime, teeth and claws perfect, with mighty thews, and savage heart. He was lying near a hartebeest on which he had been feasting; his life had been one unbroken career of rapine and violence; and now the maned master of the wilderness, the terror that stalked by night, the grim lord of slaughter, was to meet his doom at the hands of the only foes who dared to molest him.

It was a mile before we brought him to bay. It was a sore temptation to shoot him; but of course we could not break faith with our Nandi friends. We were only some sixty yards from him, and we watched him with our rifles ready, lest he should charge either us, or the first two or three spearmen, before their companions arrived.

One by one the spearmen came up, at a run, and gradually began to form a ring round him. Each, when he came near enough, crouched behind his shield, his spear in his right hand, his fierce, eager face peering over the shield rim. As man followed man, the lion rose to his feet. His mane bristled, his tail lashed, he held his head low, the upper lip now drooping over the jaws, now drawn up so as to show the gleam of the long fangs. He faced first one way and then another, and never ceased to utter his murderous grunting roars. It was a wild sight; the ring of spearmen, intent, silent, bent on blood, and in the centre the great man-killing beast, his thunderous wrath growing ever more dangerous.

At last the tense ring was complete, and the spearmen rose and closed in. The lion looked quickly from side to side, saw where the line was thinnest, and charged at his topmost speed. The crowded moment began. With shields held steady, and quivering spears poised, the men in front braced themselves for the rush and the shock; and from either hand the warriors sprang forward to take their foe in the flank. Bounding ahead of his fellows, the leader reached throwing distance; the long spear flickered and plunged; as the lion felt the wound he half turned, and then flung himself on the man in front. The warrior threw his spear; drove deep into the life, for entering at one shoulder it came out of the opposite flank, near the thigh, a yard of steel through the great body. Rearing, the lion struck the man, bearing down the shield, his back arched; and for a moment he slaked his fury with fang and talon. But on the instant I saw another spear driven clear through his body from side to side; and as the lion turned again the bright spear blades darting toward him were flashes of white flame. The end had come. He seized another man, who stabbed him and wrenched loose. As he fell he gripped a spear-head in his jaws with such tremendous force that he bent it double. Then the warriors were round and over him, stabbing and shouting, wild with furious exultation.

From the moment when he charged until his death I doubt whether ten seconds had elapsed, perhaps less; but what a ten seconds! The first half-dozen spears had done the work. Three of the spear blades had gone clear through the body, the points projecting several inches; and these, and one or two others, including the one he had seized in his jaws, had been twisted out of shape in the terrible death struggle.

We at once attended to the two wounded men. Treating their wounds with antiseptic was painful, and so, while the operation was in progress, I told them, through Kirke, that I would give each a heifer. A Nandi prizes his cattle rather more than his wives; and each sufferer smiled broadly at the news, and forgot all about the pain of his wounds.

Then the warriors, raising their shields above their heads, and chanting the deep-toned victory song, marched with a slow, dancing step around the dead body of the lion; and this savage dance of triumph ended a scene of as fierce interest and excitement as I ever hope to see.

The Nandi marched back by themselves, carrying the two wounded men on their shields. We rode to camp by a roundabout way, on the chance that we might see another lion. The afternoon waned and we cast long shadows before us as we rode across the vast lonely plain. The game stared at us as we passed; a cold wind blew in our faces, and the tall grass waved ceaselessly; the sun set behind a sullen cloud bank; and then, just at nightfall, the tents glimmered white through the dusk.

From *African Game Trails,* copyright©1909 by Syndicate Publishing Co. and Charles Scribner's Sons.

PlayHouse

Guns fashioned from pine logs and piles of shot
made of mud balls. Suddenly, the flaming realism of
the old man's passion and adoration gripped me.

by Nash Buckingham

ousin Charlie and I had figured to turn the hunt
homeward. Quite a piece it was, too, across those
hardwood ridges, pine domes and sedged hollows
that made a skyline for Big Hatchie Basin. Leo and
Tom Cotton were off on cast. We trudged across the furrowed
aisles of a rustling corn patch and found them staunchly on
birds, just where a curlycue broom's end of weeds plaited in
among thinning stalks.

Leo was strictly in character, head and plume aloft, dog aris-
tocracy poised and posed. Brawny, lumbering pointer Tom,
having evidently swung offhill a trifle late, was bowed into an
upstanding study in pop-eyed liver and white. Since that day,
more than half a century agone, the memories of those two
valiant comrades and that particular happening have never left

39

me. Their like comes about once in a lifetime, and perhaps rightly so.

Leo belonged to the late Billy Joyner, and Tom Cotton to me. But in those brave days shooting interests were so unselfishly interlocked that dog sharing was an indissolubly companionate affair. Leo had handled prairie chickens from the Texas Panhandle to the wildrose hedges of Saskatchewan. Many a time he had stopped to stare at the dust trails of antelope. And fight? He and Tom Cotton met in many a sanguinary set-to at catchweight. But their issues, whatever they were, were never definitely settled. Sometimes Tom took the count and limped pitifully for a few days. Again, it was Leo who licked gaping gashes in his burr-curdled hide. From kennel to bird field, in a baggage can or buckboard, the air was electric with intoned mutters and snarled dares. Once thrown down on the job, however, and stretched out for a day's business, no more friendly, cooperative or loyal brace of comradely quail sleuths ever spoored an upland or fought tooth and toenail in common cause.

Many a mob of snipe-snouted shaggy mongrels have I seen surge forth and wolf down upon Leo and Tom. And just as often their frenzied yowls of impending mutilation would suddenly cresendo into notes of dismay as "our boys" met them more than halfway and filled the impromptu arena with whirling, top-sided casualties. They had a way, too, of traveling meekly past some rural danger zone, one in front as skirmishing decoy, the other lagging warily in support behind our horses. Out would bluster some chunky, coarse-pelted churlish bully; fat, meaty tail awhirl and ruff abristle, cocked and primed to swarm all over the apparently shrinking and submissive stranger. Camouflage and ambush! Apparently from thin air, a very devil incarnate in dog hair would suddenly fasten upon Shep's unprotected flanks, nosing for a rib-smashing roll-over and the deadly paw-hold. And sometimes it required apologies and peace offerings of cash after such flurries. But, their hunting done, Leo and Tom immediately resumed their private feud.

Well, that's how we came on them that particular afternoon. I was on the left, with left-handed Cousin Charley beside me. A segment of tumble-down rail fence t'wixt us and the birds. And a sign, "No Hunting," tacked to a nearby persimmon tree.

Funny how one remembers such things, but that was the setting. It had been an altogether gorgeous day. Lunchtime almost before we realized it. We found a sunny spot just off Fish Trap dam and lazed on the pine needles while we munched well-browned soda biscuits and lardy spareribs. The Big Hatchie is a rare study from the eminence of Fish Trap. It comes curving and slushing past an arrowhead island, above where the dark-some Sally Hole swamp juts its fist of cypress into the river bottoms among the hardwoods. Then it fans, as the light hits it, into a sheet of greenish-black enamel with a habit of switching to lumpy amber when heavy thunderstorms scour the scarred faces of the basin's red headlands.

But up and on our way again! It was ideal bird-finding time when we broke out atop the hogback and slanted down in search of our dogs. Our shooting coats were bulging toward completed quotas — much larger then than now. Another find or two meant finis. We paused in disturbed contemplation of that "No Hunting" sign. Cousin Charley grunted. "Got 'em sure as shootin', but that's jes' exactly what we kain't do — shoot."

"Why," I questioned, balancing gingerly on a rotting rail and peering past him at Tom and Leo, sculptured against the dun swale, "how come we can't shoot?"

"Ol' man Pomp Eddins' place — tha's how come — see that sign don't you? Well — he means it."

"Who th' — who is Pomp Eddins? Must be hard-boiled." Cousin Charley clucked tongue into cheek mournfully. The situation was ruinous. "Ol' man Pomp Eddins," he explained gravely, "is one o' them kind o'gent'mans it don't do no good t'fool with — that's all."

"Bad actor?"

"Well, naw, not exactly what we know as a bad actor, but if he gits in behin' you f' good cause, he'll jes' natcherly run you right on t' degredation — an' we're a long ways from home t' start running."

"Can't we ease around and drive those birds off his land?"

"Might, but I guess we better not — ou'h folks an' Master Pomp has always bin ve'y fren'ly — but I ain' presumin' nuthin' — they tell me folks that does don' hav' no luck."

To the infinite consternation of Leo and Tom, Cousin Charley

41

quietly flushed a luscious bevy that scattered enticingly on a hillside not far away. Cousin Charley as host-shooter was also using his wits and sense of propriety. "Now then," he grinned, "let's go to th' house an' as't permission to shoot a few birds on his property — I know him well enough t'do that — an' we ought to — anyhow — I hav't run poachers off my lan' ev'y now an' then."

We soon struck off up a winding road. "I know right where them birds lit," he remarked. I said I did, too. "I ain' see Mist' Pomp in quite a spell," he went on. "Him an' Papa was in th' Confederate Army t'gether-th' ol' gent'man is mighty queer an' his health ain't none to good." Leo and Tom, sensing, as dogs have a way of doing, that the hunt had suddenly taken an odd turn, were at heel. Charley told me more of Mister Eddins as the red road circled uphill. Retired now, he used to keep a store in town — president of the bank once upon a time. Knew some of my kinfolks in the city. "If he lets us shoot we can get cleaned up all-fired quick," concluded Charley.

The twists and turns of our way mounted higher among coniferous knobs. "Great folks, them Eddinses," puffed Charley, "th' Civil War 'bout cleaned them up — th' clan's seeded down t' ol' man Pomp; but he kep' things together — don't owe no man — an' had a sight o' cash money an' eight hunnerd acres — yep — daughter-in-law an' grandson — always bin' fine folks an' still are — them Eddinses." We walked out on top and into a clearing. Deeply set among holly and cedar squatted an antebellum, white-brick cottage. Its wide chimneys gave off squills of wood smoke into the keen sunshine.

It was young Mrs. Eddins who ushered us cordially into the cozy vastness of a low-ceilinged chamber filled with crowded bookshelves, hair sofas, armchairs and a grandfather clock that would have made a collector's acquisitive hair stand on end. She spoke gently to a tall, gray-haired, angular old gentleman who unwound from a deep rocker. "Daddy, here's some company come t' see you."

Cousin Charley stepped forward. "Mist' Eddins, this is Charley Johnson, good afternoon, suh."

"Yes," he acknowledged, bowing gravely, his direct, steely eyes measuring us both in rapid appraisal. "I know you well,

Charley, but it's been some time since we met howsomever. Yo' folks all coming' along all right, I hope?"

"Yes, suh, Mist' Pomp — uh — Mist' Pomp — this — uh — this is — uh — Mist' Buckin'ham — from down in th' city — comes out bird huntin' with me once in a while. Ou'h dogs got into a covey down yonder on th' brushy side o' yo' place, but we seen yo' posted sign an' come on up t'ast if you'd mind us shootin' a little if we run into another bunch on ou'h way home — we've 'bout got our limits an' we're headin thataway."

Mister Pomp's deeply recessed eyes, 'neath shaggy brows, swept me from head to foot. He slowly extended a leathery, toil-scarred hand. "Buckingham — is it?"

"Yes, suh."

"Gran'son o' ol' man Henry's?"

I nodded.

"He was from th' North — an' sided that way."

"Yes, suh."

"But his brother, yo' great-uncle Fred — he went out fust with Walker an' got set with th' Federals — crossed under a flag o' truce at midnight when his expired secon' day o' th' Battle o' Fredericksburg — an' reenlisted under Gin'l Lee — transferred later to th' Louisiana Wildcats — they blowed him up on th' Queen o' th' West." I listened in amazement. We had quickly gotten down to rock bottom on party platforms. A moment of hesitant recapitulation by Mister Pomp.

"Which one o' ol' man Henry's boys is yo' Daddy?"

"Miles!" And I said it proudly.

"Uummmm! in th' bank?"

"Yes, suh."

"Th' two younger boys — Gunn an' Hugh — in th' dry-foods business — they're yo' uncles, o' cose?"

"Yes, suh."

"Well, I didn' hav' no better friends than them boys — all o' them — back in th' hard-times panic o' ninety-three — they carried me — took care o' me an' mine an' a lot o' others in these parts."

His brilliant eyes turned from piercing scrutiny of me off through the window toward the basin's distant rim. A resurgent sun poured over it.

43

He quizzed rapidly. Another line of evidence must be established. He said: "Yo' wife's folks were th' ol' Cap'n Joneses, warn't they?"

"Yes, suh."

"Uuummmm — tho't I heard tell. Jones was my captain — fought all over his own land, too. Rich Yankees from up North own it all now — an' mighty fine folks they are, too, I'm told." He spat explosively into the fireplace.

"If I rec'lect rightly, yo' wife's a gran'niece o' ol man John Jarratt's, ain't she?"

"Yes, suh." No use to elaborate. Best to stand hitched and come clean.

"John an' me done some tall ridin' an shootin' t'gether. We rode with Forrest. Once in awhile we had som' all-fired hard runnin' t'do — too." An aquiline nose wrinkled into a grim snicker at the recollection. Half-reverie apparently swept us from his thoughts. Then — "You boys take chairs, git warm. You're welcome t'shoot on my land whenever you choose — I'll jes' go along a piece with you — I ain' shot at a bird in fifteen years. John Yancey — aw — John Yancey."

A rough-and-tumble specimen of shaver hardihood, with clear gray eyes and mop of tousled red hair, darted in from the hallway. The grandfather's eyes blazed with pride. "Say howdy' to th' gentlemen — say Howdy', John Yancey — then run an' fetch Granpa's gun."

With a whoop of joy the little fellow sprang away and soon returned lugging an old but beautiful muzzle-loading shotgun. It was in superb condition. Muzzles paper thin. Locks that sang like harp strings. Stock fit and balance that made shoulder-spot and eyes all one. With it was handed up belt, powder horn and shot pouch. I examined it avidly. A genuine Manton.

"Git yo' hat, John Yancey. You an' Granpa' goin' bird huntin'. I want you t' watch these good shots an' learn how t' hit 'em, boy — you'll be needin' some knowledge one o' these days."

There was a method in Charley's madness as we retraced that quarter of a mile to the vicinity of our scattered bevy. They had moved around an orchard's hem just outside some slash pine. Tom nailed them tightly. I believe to this good day he and Leo had an idea what was up.

44

How I wish more of today's "sports" with magazine guns could have watched that old gentlemen hustle his percussion Manton into action. In my own boyhood I had, of necessity, performed a like manual, but with nothing remotely comparable to his exhibition of rapid and orderly precision. Nipples capped, he stepped forward and to the left. Charley spun one victim from the rise. But old man Pomp Eddins laid down a bang-up right and left that served notice how he played the game. Congratulations over, we followed the singles across gully and into a patch of low broom sedge where we found both Leo and Tom on individual points.

"Do you boys mind," queried our host, "if I let this little chap try t' see kin he hit a quail on th' wing — he's shot a few rabbits an' some squirrels, settin' — but this'll be his first chance flyin' — an' over a dog?" He turned and smiled at the grandson. "Come on — boy." The Manton, recapped and hammers drawn, was thrust into the lad's eager hands. All must go well with Grandpa there to see it well done. Gun below the elbow, keen for contact with a long-awaited moment, John Yancey Eddins braced for his first rise. In every gunner's life, in every father's heart, there should be, at least, one such undying memory.

"Walk on in — walk right on pas' th' dog — when th' bird gits up — take yo' time." Step by step the child obeyed leadership that held his every faith. "Both eyes open, John Yancey, pick yo' bird if there's mo' n' one — an' keep both eyes jes' on it."

Singles began taking leave on every hand, I can still see that broth of a boy, stockinged legs and butternut knee pants spraddled into a resolute stance among the sedge clutter. Determined arms hefting the hurled stock — a long pause as the child leveled and swung. B-o-o-o-m — b-o-o-o-m! A boy on his knees peering beneath a smoke-screen; an old man's shrill cry, "you got 'im, son, you got 'im." A race through the stems as youth and old age broke for the retrieve. Oh! The radiance on their faces. Pomp's aglow with pride, the boy's alight with the greatest thrill any possessor of game heritage treasures as no other in life. For the next half hour neither Charley nor I fired a shot. Then, borrowing the Manton, we took turns at finishing our limits with the tool of a vanished gentility.

Gulch bottoms were beginning to darken. Shadows thrust

45

claws across the basin. The crest of a steep ridge split away cleanly, dropping almost a hundred feet sheer to the railway's gash. Behind Mister Pomp, we followed a sell-defined hump across the hump. It ended in a spacious alcove, swung like a dirtdauber's nest above the brink. I looked about me in wonder. Some grim business hereabouts. Pomp Eddins slackened pace and looked about him. "I thought maybe you'd like to see this place." He placed the Manton carefully aside and seated himself on a lichened boulder. "There was big doins' went on here — bloody doins' back in Shiloh times." Mister Pomp smiled reflectively. "I'll bet Charley ain't even been in this spot befo' in his life — y' see — from here this height commands th' railroad plum across the' basin — from whur th' ol' M. and C. come outa the' fur gap." Somehow, he seemed to kindle and take a fresh grip on himself. He lapsed into the speech of ancient action; words of almost broad patois leaped from him. "This he'ah wuz an' ol' fo'te — I hepp'd build it — look yonder at them timbered bastions still stickin' outa th' groun'."

He glanced ruminatively at worn, angled earthworks and crumbling casemate. Lethargic burrows in their aged blanket of peaceful silt and grasses. "We wuz dismounted an' ordered on detail t' mount two pieces — told t' hold this position at any an' all cost. H'it warn't no easy job, young man, gittin' them guns so high. But h'it wuz wuth th' sweat an' labor."

His eyes snapped fire. He was back at work again. "We come in from behin' yonderways-lak we com' awhile ago — with an infantry company in suppote fuh ambush." I visualized that scene. Gaunt, dog-tired gunners in ragged gray. Slobbery, lathered horses, sputtery whiplashes, straining traces, laborious heaving through steamy morass amd unwaxed swamp. What a beehive of slapdash, slaughterous activity and toxic hate. A steady voice continued. "I 'member how we stopped 'em th' fus' time — a supply train with guard — we wuz hid out an' ready when their locomotive come th'u th' gap an' pulled jes' onto th' trussle y'see down yonder." His eyes narrowed. "But we had it blocked with logs, they seen 'em jes' in time as they run outa th' curve. We let 'em get out an' start unloadin'. Then we cut that injin' t' ribbons — blowed h'it t' Hell-an'-Gone." He leaped to his feet and almost swarmed to a counterattack.

46

"Ou'h boys swung ov'ah th' hill an' flanked 'em — some tried t' make h'it away th'u yon valley." He chuckled. "But h'it warn't no use — we — we — had 'em — them hillsides yonder wuz strewn with dead." He was telling it to High Heaven. "We sho' raised Cain in these parts f' mo'n two months — but finally the Yanks com' in fo'ce with heavy guns an' shelled th' livin' hide offn' us — we — we — had t' abandon th' position an' fall back — damn it."

I looked about me carefully. Through worn embrasures grinned two dummy cannons, fashioned from peeled pine logs painted black and mounted upon hewn wooden gun carriages. About them, in orderly stacks, were piles of round shot — mud balls. As I half-grasped all their significance, the flaming realism of this old man's passion and adoration gripped me. I saw sweating, unshaven half-mad men lashing back on lanyards; blistering hands fumbling at red-hot gun muzzles; hell-and-damnation curses turning peaceful quail country into a sudden shambles of thudding smoothbores. Mister Pomp caught my look and smiled grimly. "This he'ah," he injected half-fancifully, "is what me an' John Yancey call ou'h 'Play House.'" He dropped a comradely arm about his grandchild's shoulder. The child cuddled lovingly against him.

"Y'see," he went on, a sort of proud wistfulness creeping into his tone, "y'see, I had t' raise this child — me an' his ma — that is — we come t' this ol' fo'te when he wuz jes'er toddler — almos' a babe in m'arms — h'it com't' me one day t'fix things up like you see 'em he'ah — I jes' built it all in mem'ry o' them times—an'—n'—as John Yancey growed up, we jes' kep' comin' an addin' t' things." His jaw suddenly tightened. He spoke proudly. "Anyhow, this he'ah ain' no bad play house t'bring a boy up in."

John Yancey spoke up softly. "Gran'pa, we hav' a lot o' fun he'ah don't we?"

The old man turned to me. "I fought — we all o'us — fought," he cried passionately, "f' ou'h conception o' homes an' rights jes' lik' th' side saw theirs. My father fought in Mexico — I fought with Forrest — an' — an' — this chile's daddy — th' only son God Himself could ever give me — was killed at San Juan Hill — he couldn' no mo' o' stayed at home when th' call come than John Jarratt coulda' hepped ridin' off with us boys."

We shook hands and exchanged "good-byes" and "come agains." He said simply, "Tell all yo' folks y' met ol' man Pomp Eddins — yo' Daddy'll remember me — an' — send me a bird-dog puppy sometime — I'll raise an' train him an' John Yancey t'gether — John's gittin' too big f' th' Play House anyhow." So, leaving them to turn back across their darkening trail through the hills, Charley and I slid down a precipitous path to the railroad ties and a starlit trek to home.

Fifteen or twenty years is a long, long time. Again, however, Cousin Charley and I munched cat-head biscuits and meaty hog ribs at Fish Trap dam. The bottomlands still challenged change, but it was there, however furtive. The drone of an airplane might impeach the years, or some distant, raucous motor change the face to things.

"Charley," I asked, "what ever became of the old gentleman way back over yonder across the Tubba — Mister Eddins — who knew my folds an' let us hunt on his land — and — showed us his Rebel Play House — I sent him a pointer puppy — afterward?"

"Daid," responded Charley, laconically. "He lived t' be past eighty but he passed on aroun' Christmas time — didn't last long after the' Worl' War."

"And the boy," I went on, "I suppose he turned out to be a bum bird hunter like us — and runs the old home place now?"

"Yep," replied Charley, and something in the way he spoke it made me look up. "There was sure one fine mighty fine, hones'-t'-God boy, too."

"He's — —?"

"Yep!" Cousin Charley was a direct narrator. "They hadn' no sooner started talkin' war with Mexico, back in 'sixteen, but that John Yancey an' his gran'pa showed up in town with John's gripsack all packed. That youngster signed up an' went on out with th' National Guard — an' I mean he lef' out right then." I might have guessed as much. Cousin Charley gnawed at a rib's end and caught up with his story. "Then, y'know, come sho'nuff war — with Germany. By that time John Yancey had turned out t' be a natural born soldier — his grandad damn near passed out, he was so proud when th' boy went to an

officers' trainin' school an' come out with a commission. I never
seen anyone quite so happy. Why — why — there wuz times
he'd talk about h'it an' tears com' to his eyes. Jon Yancey's wuz
a first unit overseas, too.

Charley paused. Tossed a welcome shred of fat meat to a
dog. The pair we were using were doing their best but they
weren't Tom Cotton and Leo by a hell of a sight. "Ol' man
Pomp Eddins come t' town a lot mo' in those days — wanted
news 'bout th' war — an' that boy —mebbe. He'd sit aroun' in
a big swivet till he got his mawning *Commercial Appeal* off th'
newsboy. Talked 'bout how he wish'd he coulda been along
with John Yancey. Whut's mo' — that ol' man meant ev'y word
he said. He'd say "This he'ah makes fo' wars f'us Eddinses —
fo' wars — an' th' Lord only knows how many mo'. John Yancey
— he'll be comin' home befo' long — an' — an' marryin' up."

A flock of ducks suddenly dipped through the chute and
whizzed across the spillway. Cousin Charley grabbed his gun
and sorrowfully watched them dwindle into specks. The old
codger loved to sneak mallards and jump them around bends.
He went back to his story.

"I happened t' be at th' sto' th' night th' telegraph operator
brought up th' message 'bout John Yancey. Somebody jus' had
t' ride out an' git the' news t' his folks. So I run out in m' Fode.
They'd done gone t'bed long ago. But ol' man Pomp he come
t' th' do'h with a lamp in one han' an' that ol' muzzle-loader
o' hisn' in t'other. He seen h'it wuz me an' say — 'why — com'
in, Charles,' he says. 'Glad t' see you — my daughter'll be right
down in a minute. Whut you got — a message fo'us 'bout John
Yancey winnin' another medal o'honor?' — says, 'How many
Germans is that boy done kilt this time.?' "

"Bout that time his ma — Miz Eddins — come into th' hallway
— I guess I musta looked — an'I sho'felt kinda queasy — maybe
h'it wuz whut they call mother's intuition — I don't know —
guess she jus' sorter suspicioned — you know? All I could do
wuz jes' hand her th' War Department's telegram — you
remember how they wuz' worded?" Charley looked at me, and
remembering, turned quickly away. He hadn't meant to put it
that way — good old scout.!

He clucked softly and sorrowfully. "Never s'long as I live,

Buck, will I ever fergit th' look that com' over his ma's face. She handed Mister Pomp th' wire — but he didn' hav' his specs, so she had t' read it to him — an' — man — her voice wuz as steady as — as — —" Charley clucked softly into his cheek. "Seemed at first lak Mist' Pomp couldn' understand. Then, all of a sudden lak' — it seemed t' com' t' him. I wuz lookin' t' see th' ol' gent'man bust out — but not a single tear com'hoppin' down his face. He warn't th' cryin' kind. Naw — he jes' sorta clutched out f' Miz Eddins — clasped her in his arms and sorta drawed himself up lak he wuz comin' t' attention — an' — an' half-listin' f' sump'n. They both jes' stood there an' shivered. I tried t' say sump'n comfortin' lak — but th' ol' man interrupted me. 'I'm obliged t' you, Charles,' he say, 'f' bringin' th' word — h'its sho' bad news,' he says. 'John Yancey Eddins has won th' highes' an' mos' distinguished honor that can befall a gallant soldier of *Our Country!*' When he drawed hisse'f up still straighter an' said 'Our Country' like he did — I cried." Charley wiped his greasy fingers on his stained and tattered hunting coat and turned to me again — reflectively. "Do you 'member whut an unreconstructed Confederate ol' man Pomp Eddins was? But in th' end he wuz sold jes' as strong on Uncle Sam." Charley had the threat of matters toward the knot. "'Bout that time," he concluded, "ol' man Pomp raised his face t'odes th' ceilin', an' his whole heart jes' seemed t' break out in one great cry. 'Aw — Gawd,' he says. You know,' he says, 'H'it ain't right!' Miz Eddins seen he wuz fixin' t' giv' down. She held him tighter in her arms an' says, soothing like, 'There — there — Daddy,' she says. 'Th' Lord giveth an' th' Lord taketh away, blessed be th' name o' th' Lord.' Buck, there warn't one single tear evah com' t' ol' man Pomp's eyes. 'I know,' he wailed, 'I take it all back — Gawd — but — oh!' He says, 'John Yancey — Oh! Christ!' he says. 'No mo' Eddinses fo' th' wars — no mo' Eddinses f' th' wars.' "

"Play House" is from *De Shootinest Gent'men* by Nash Buckingham. It originally appeared in the January 1929 issue of *Field & Stream*.

FROZEN
Terror

When Lewis Sweet suddenly found himself adrift
on the ice-floe, he had no idea of the chilling fate
that awaited him in the days to come.

by Ben East

Tramping across the rock-strewn, snowy beach of
Crane Island with two companions that bitter-cold
winter morning, on his way to the rough shore ice
and the lake-trout grounds beyond, Lewis Sweet had
no warning of what grim fate the next seven days had in store
for him, no intimation that before the week was up his name
would be on the lips of people and the front pages of newspapers
across the whole country. Nor did he guess that he was walking
that Lake Michigan beach for the last time on two good feet.

The date was Tuesday, January 22, 1929. There was nothing
to hint that the day would be any different from the many
others Sweet had spent fishing through the ice for lake trout,
there on the submerged reefs off Crane Island.

He'd walk out to his lightproof shanty, kindle a fire of dry cedar in the tiny stove, sit and dangle a wooden decoy in the clear green water beneath the ice, hoping to lure a prowling trout within reach of his heavy seven-tined spear. If he was lucky he'd take four or five good fish by midafternoon. Then he'd go back to shore and drive the thirty miles to his home in the village of Alanson, Michigan, in time for supper.

It would be just another day of winter fishing, pleasant but uneventful.

The Crane Island fishing grounds lay west of Waugoshance Point, at the extreme northwest tip of Michigan's mitten-shaped lower peninsula. The point is a long, narrow tongue of sand, sparsely wooded, roadless and wild, running out into the lake at the western end of the Straits of Mackinac, with Crane Island marking land's end. Both the island and the point are unpeopled. On the open ice of Lake Michigan, a mile offshore, Sweet and the other fishermen had their darkhouses.

Fishing was slow that morning. It was close to noon before a trout slid into sight under the ice hole where Sweet kept vigil. He maneuvered the wood minnow away and eased his spear noiselessly through the water. Stalking his decoy, the trout moved ahead a foot or two, deliberate and cautious. When it came to rest directly beneath him, eyeing the slow-moving lure with a mixture of hunger and wariness, he drove the spear down with a hard, sure thrust.

The steel handle was only eight or ten feet long, but it was attached to the roof of the shanty by fifty feet of stout line. When Sweet felt the barbed tines jab into the fish he let go the handle and the heavy spear carried the twisting trout swiftly down to the reef thirty feet below.

After the fish ceased struggling Sweet hauled it up on the line. When he opened the shanty door and backed out to disengage the trout, he noticed that the wind was rising and the air was full of snow. The day was turning blustery. Have to watch the ice on a day like that. Might break loose alongshore and go adrift. But the wind still blew from the west, onshore. So long as it stayed in that quarter there was no danger.

About an hour after he took the first trout the two men fishing near him quit their shanties and walked across the ice to his.

"We're going in, Lew," one of them hailed. "The wind is

hauling around nor'east. It doesn't look good. Better come along."

Sweet stuck his head out the door of his shanty and squinted skyward. "Be all right for a spell, I guess," he said finally. "The ice'll hold unless it blows harder than this. I want one more fish."

He shut the door and they went on, leaving him there alone.

Thirty minutes later Sweet heard the sudden crunch and rumble of breaking ice off to the east. The grinding, groaning noise ran across the field like rolling thunder, and the darkhouse shook as if a distant train had passed.

Sweet had done enough winter fishing there to know the terrible portent of that sound. He flung open the shanty door, grabbed up his ax and the trout he had speared, and raced across the ice for the snow-clouded timber of Crane Island.

Halfway to the beach he saw what he dreaded, an ominous, narrow vein of black, zigzagging across the white field of ice.

When he reached the band of open water it was only ten feet across, but it widened perceptibly while he watched it, wondering whether he dared risk plunging in. Even as he wondered, he knew the chance was too great to take. He was a good swimmer, but the water would be numbingly cold, and he had to reckon, too, with the sucking undertow set by 100,000 tons of ice driving lakeward with the wind. And even if he crossed the few yards of water successfully, he would have little hope of crawling up on the smooth shelf of ice on the far side.

He watched the black channel grow to twenty feet, to ninety. At last, when he could barely see across it through the swirling snowstorm, he turned and walked grimly back to his darkhouse.

He had a stove there, and enough firewood to last through the night. He wanted desperately to take shelter in the shanty but he knew better. His only chance lay in remaining out in the open, watching the ice floe for possible cracks and breaks.

He turned his back resolutely on the darkhouse, moved to the center of the drifting floe, and began building a low wall of snow to break the force of the wind. It was slow work with no tool but his ax, and he hadn't been at it long when he heard a pistol-sharp report rip across the ice. He looked up to see his shanty settling into a yawning black crack. While he watched, the broken-off sheet of ice crunched and ground back against the main floe and the frail darkhouse went to pieces like some-

53

thing built of cardboard.

Half an hour later the two shanties of his companions were swallowed up in the same fashion, one after the other. Whatever happened now, his last hope of shelter was gone. Live or die, he'd have to see it through right in the open on the ice, with nothing between him and the wind save his snow wall. He went on building it.

He knew pretty well what he faced, but there was no way to figure his chances. Unless the ice field grounded on either Hog or Garden Island, at a place where he could get to the beach, some sixty miles of open water lay ahead between him and the west shore of Lake Michigan. There was little chance the floe would hold together that long, with a winter gale churning the lake.

There was little chance, too, that the wind would stay steady in one quarter long enough to drive him straight across. It was blowing due west now but before morning it would likely go back to the northeast. By that time he'd be out in midlake if he were still alive, beyond Beaver and High and the other outlying island. And there, with a northeast storm behind him, he could drift more than one hundred miles without sighting land.

Sweet resigned himself to the fact that, when buffeted by wind and pounding seas, even a sheet of ice three miles across and two feet thick can stay intact only so long.

In midafternoon hope welled up in him for a little while. His drift carried him down on Waugoshance Light, a lighthouse abandoned and dismantled long before, and it looked for a time as if he would ground against its foot. But currents shifted the direction of the ice field a couple of degrees and he went past only one hundred yards or so away.

Waugoshance was without fuel or food; no more than a broken crib of rock and concrete and a gaunt, windowless shell of rusted steel. But it was a pinpoint of land there in the vast gray lake. It meant escape from the icy water all around; it spelled survival for a few hours at least, and Sweet watched it with hungry eyes as his floe drifted past, almost within reach, and the square red tower receded slowly in the storm.

By that time, although he had no way of knowing it, the search and rescue resources of an entire state were being marshaled in the hope of snatching him from the lake alive.

The two men who had fished with him that morning were still on Crane Island when the ice broke away. They had stayed on, concerned and uneasy, watching the weather, waiting for Sweet to come back to the beach. Through the snowstorm they had seen black water open offshore when the floe went adrift. They knew Sweet was still out there somewhere on the ice and they lost no more time. They piled into their car and raced for the hamlet of Cross Village, on the high bluffs of Sturgeon Bay ten miles to the south.

There was little the Cross Villagers or anybody else could do at the moment to help, but the word of Sweet's dramatic plight flashed south over the wires to downstate cities and on across the nation, and one of the most intense searches for a lost man in Michigan's history got under way.

The theme was an old one. Puny man pitted against the elements. A flyspeck of humanity out there alone, somewhere in an endless waste of ice and water, snow and gale, staving off death hour after hour — or waiting for it, numb and half frozen, with cold-begotten resignation. None heard the story unmoved. Millions sat at their own firesides that winter night, secure and warm and fed, and pitied and wondered about Lewis Sweet, drifting unsheltered in the bitter darkness.

The fast-falling snow prevented much action for the first twenty-four hours. But the storm blew itself out Wednesday forenoon, and the would-be rescuers went into action.

There was too much ice there in the north end of Lake Michigan for boats. The search had to be made from the air, and on foot along the shore of Waugoshance Point and around Crane Island, south into Sturgeon Bay and on the frozen beaches of the islands farther out.

Coast Guard crews and volunteers joined forces. Men walked the beaches for four days, clambering over rough hummocks of shore ice, watching for tracks, a thread of smoke, a dead fire, any sign at all that Sweet had made land. Other men scanned the ice fields and the outlying islands, Garden and Hog and Hat, from the air. Pilots plotted 2,000 square miles of lake and flew them systematically, one by one, searching for a black dot that would be a man huddled on a drifting floe.

Lewis Sweet, who on Monday of that week had hardly been known to anyone beyond the limits of his home town, was now an object of nation-wide concern. Men bought papers on the streets of cities 1,000 miles from Alanson to learn what news there might be of the lost fisherman.

Little by little, hour by hour, hope ebbed among the searchers. No man could survive so long on the open ice. The time spun out — a day, then two days, three — and still the planes and foot parties found no trace of Sweet. By Friday night hope was dead. Life could not endure through so many hours of cold and storm without shelter, fire, or food. On Saturday, the last day of the search, those who remained in it looked only for a dark spot on the beach, a frozen body scoured bare of snow by the wind. At dusk the search was reluctantly abandoned.

Folks no longer wondered whether Lewis Sweet would be rescued, or how. Instead they wondered whether his body would be found on some lonely beach when spring came, or whether the place and manner of his dying would never be known.

But Sweet had not died.

Twice more before dark on Tuesday he believed for a little time that he was about to escape the lake. The first time he saw Hat Island looming up through the storm ahead, a timbered dot on a gray sea that smoked with snow. His floe seemed to be bearing directly down on it and he felt confident it would go aground on the shingly beach.

No one lived on Hat. He would find no cabin there. But there was plenty of dry wood for a fire and he had his big trout for food. He'd make out all right until the storm was over and he had no doubt that some way would be found to rescue him when the weather cleared. But even while he tasted in anticipation the immense relief of trading his drifting ice floe for solid ground, he realized that his course would take him clear of the island and he resigned himself once more to a night of drifting.

The next time it was Hog Island, much bigger but also without a house of any kind, that seemed to lie in his path. But again the wind and lake played their tricks and he was carried past, little more than a stone's throw from the beach. As if to tantalize him deliberately, a solitary gull, a holdover from the big flock that bred there in summer, flew out from the ice hummocks

56

heaped along the shore, alighted for a few minutes on his floe, and then soared casually back to the island.

"That was the first time in my life I ever wished for wings!" Sweet told me afterward.

That night was pretty bad. The storm mounted to a raging blizzard. With the winter darkness coming down, the section of ice where Sweet had built his snow shelter broke away from the main field suddenly and without warning. He heard the splintering noise, saw the crack starting to widen in the dusk only a few yards away. He gathered up his fish and his precious ax and ran for a place where the pressure of the wind still held the two masses of ice together, grinding against each other. Even as he reached it the crevice opened ahead of him, but it was only a couple of feet wide and he jumped across to the temporary safety of the bigger floe.

Again he set to work to build a shelter with blocks of snow. When it was finished he lay down behind it to escape the bitter wind. But the cold was numbing, and after a few minutes he got to his feet and raced back and forth across the ice to get his blood going again, with the wind driven snow cutting his face like a whiplash.

He spent the rest of the night that way — lying briefly behind his snow wall for shelter, then forcing himself to his feet once more to fight off the fatigue and drowsiness that he knew would finish him if he gave in to it.

He was out in the open now, and the storm had a chance to vent its full force on the ice field. Before midnight the field broke in two near him, again, compelling him to abandon his snow shelter once more in order to stay with the main floe. Again he had the presence of mind to take his ax and the trout along. The same thing happened once more after that, sometime in the small hours of the morning.

Toward daybreak the cold grew even more intense. And now the storm played a cruel prank. The wind hauled around to the southwest, reversing the drift of the ice field and sending it back almost the way it had come, toward the distant north shore of Lake Michigan. In the darkness, however, Sweet was not immediately aware of the shift.

The huge floe — still some two miles across — went aground

an hour before daybreak, without warning. There was a sudden crunching thunder of sound, and directly ahead of Sweet the edge of the ice rose out of the water, curled back upon itself like the nose of a giant toboggan, and came crashing down in an avalanche of two-ton blocks! The entire field shuddered and shook and seemed about to splinter into fragments, and Sweet ran for his life, away from the spot where it was thundering aground.

It took the field five or ten minutes to lose its momentum and come to rest. When the splintering, grinding noise finally subsided, Sweet went cautiously back to learn what had happened. He had no idea where he was or what obstacle the floe had encountered.

To his astonishment, he discovered that he was at the foot of White Shoals Light, one of the loneliest lighthouses in Lake Michigan, rising from a concrete crib bedded on a submerged reef, more than a dozen miles from the nearest land. The floe, crashing against the heavy crib, had buckled and been sheared and piled up until it finally stopped moving.

Sweet was close to temporary safety at last. Just twenty-two feet away, up the vertical concrete face of the crib, lay shelter and fuel, food and survival. Only twenty-two feet, four times his own height. But it might as well have been twenty-two miles. For the entire crib above the waterline was encased in ice a foot thick, formed by freezing spray, and the steel ladder bedded in the concrete wall showed only as a bulge on the smooth, sheer face of the ice.

Sweet knew the ladder had to be there. He located it in the gray light of that stormy winter morning and went to work with his axe. He chopped away the ice as high as he could reach, standing on the floe, freeing the rungs one at a time. Then he stepped up on the first one, hung on with one hand, and went on chopping with the other, chipping and worrying at the flinty sheath that enclosed the rest of the ladder.

Three hours from the time he cut the first chip of ice away he was within three rungs of the top. Three steps, less than a yard — and he knew he wasn't going to make it.

His feet were wooden stumps on which he could no longer trust his weight. His hands had long since lost all feeling. They were so badly frozen that he had to look to make sure his fingers were hooked around a rung, and he could no longer keep a grip on the ax. He dropped it half a dozen times, clambering awkwardly down after it, mounting wearily up the rungs again. The first couple of times it wasn't so bad, but the climb got more and more difficult. The next time he dropped the ax he wouldn't be able to come back up the ladder. He took a few short, ineffectual strokes and the ax went clattering to the ice below. He climbed stiffly down and huddled on a block of ice to rest.

It's hard to give up and die of cold and hunger with food and warmth only twenty-odd feet overhead. Sweet didn't like the idea. In fact, he said afterward, he didn't even admit the possibility. There had to be some way to the top of that ice-coated crib, and he was bound he'd find it.

Hunched there on his block of ice, out of sight of land, with ice and water all around and the wind driving snow into his clothing at every buttonhole, the idea came to him. He could build a ramp of ice blocks up to the top of the crib!

The material lay waiting, piled up when the edge of the floe shattered against the base of the light. Some of the blocks were more than ten men could have moved but some were small enough for Sweet to lift. He went to work.

Three hours later he finished the job and dragged himself, more dead than alive, over the icy, treacherous lip of the crib.

Any man in normal surroundings and his right mind would have regarded Lewis Sweet's situation at that moment as pretty desperate. White Shoals Light had been closed weeks before, at the end of the navigation season. Sweet was on a deserted concrete island 100 feet square, in midlake, with frozen hands and feet, in the midst of a January blizzard — and ńo other living soul had the faintest inkling where he was or that he was alive. It wasn't exactly a rosy outlook, but in his fifty-odd years he had never known a more triumphant and happy minute!

The lighthouse crew had left the doors unlocked when they departed for the winter, save for a heavy screen that posed no barrier to a man with an ax. Inside the light, after his hours on the ice and his ordeal at the foot of the crib, the lost man found paradise.

Bacon, rice, dried fruit, flour, tea, and other supplies were there in abundance. There were three small kerosene stoves and plenty of fuel for them. There were matches. There was every-thing a man needed to live for days or weeks, maybe until spring!

At the moment Sweet was too worn out to eat. He wanted only to rest and sleep. He cut the shoes off his frozen feet, thawed his hands and feet as best he could over one of the oil stoves, and fell into the nearest bed.

He slept nearly twenty-four hours. When he awakened Thursday morning he cooked the first meal he'd had since eating breakfast at home forty-eight hours before. It put new life into him, and he sat down to take careful stock of his situation.

The weather had cleared and he could see the timbered shore of the lake both to the north and south, beckoning, taunting him, a dozen miles away. Off to the southeast, he could even see the low shape of Crane Island, where he had gone adrift. But between him and the land, in any direction, lay those miles of water all but covered over with fields of drifting ice.

From the tower of the light Lake Michigan was a curious patchwork of color. It looked like a vast white field veined and netted with gray-green. That network of darker color showed where constantly shifting channels separated the ice fields. Unless and until there came a still, cold night to close all that open water, Sweet must remain a prisoner here on his tiny concrete island.

At noon on Thursday, sitting beside his oil fire opening bloody blisters on his feet, Sweet heard the thrumming roar of a plane outside.

He knew it instinctively for a rescue craft sent out to search for him, and he bounded up on his crippled feet and rushed to a window.

But the windows were covered with heavy screen to protect them from wind and weather. No chance to wave or signal there. The door opening out on the crib, by which he had gained entrance, was two or three flights below the living quarters. No time to get down there. There was a nearer exit in the lens room at the top of the tower, one flight up. He made for the stairs.

The pilot of the plane had gone out of his way to have a look at White Shoals on what he realized was a very slim chance. He didn't really hope to find any trace of the lost man there and he saw no reason to linger. He tipped his plane in a steep bank and roared once around the light, a couple of hundred feet above the lake. Then seeking nothing but a jungle of ice and snow piled the length of the reef, he leveled off and headed for his home field for a fresh supply of gas to carry him out on another flight. He must have felt pretty bad about it when he heard the story afterward.

While the pilot made that one swift circle Lewis Sweet was hobbling up the flight of iron stairs as fast as his swollen painful feet would carry him. But he was too late. When he reached the lens room and stepped out through the door the plane was far out over the lake, disappearing swiftly in the south.

Most men would have lost heart then and there but Sweet had been through too much to give up at that point. Back in the living quarters he sat down and went stoically on the job of first aid to his feet.

"It doesn't hurt to freeze," he told me with a dry grin months later, "but it sure hurts to thaw out!"

Before the day was over another plane, or the same one on a return flight, roared over White Shoals. But the pilot didn't bother to circle that time and Sweet didn't even make the stairs. He watched helplessly from a screened window while the plane winged on, became a speck in the sky, and vanished.

Sweet was convinced then that if he got back to shore he'd have to do so on his own. It was plain that nobody guessed his whereabouts, or even considered the empty lighthouse a possibility.

After dark that night he tried to signal the distant mainland. There was no way for him to put the powerful beam of the light in operation, or he would almost certainly have attracted attention at that season. But he rigged a crude flare, a ball of oil-soaked waste on a length of wire, and went out on the balcony of the lens room and swung it back and forth, hoping its feeble red spark might be seen by someone on shore.

Twenty miles away, at the south end of Sturgeon Bay, he could see the friendly lights of Cross Village winking from their high bluff. How they must have mocked him!

On Friday morning he hung out signals on the chance that another plane might pass. But no one came near the light that day, and the hours went by uneventfully. Fresh blisters kept swelling up on his feet and he opened and drained them as fast as they appeared. He cooked and ate three good meals, and at nightfall he climbed back to the lens room, went outside in the bitter wind, and swung his oilrag beacon again for a long time. He did that twice more in the course of the night, but nothing came of it.

The lake still held him a prisoner Saturday. That night, however, the wind fell, the night was starlit and still and very cold. When he awoke on Sunday morning there was no open water in sight. The leads and channels were covered with new ice as far as he could see, and his knowledge of the lake told him it was ice that would bear a man's weight.

Whether he would encounter open water before he reached shore there was no way to guess. Nor did it matter greatly. Sweet knew his time was running out. His feet were in terrible shape and he was sure the search for him had been given up by this time. This was his only chance and he'd have to gamble on it. In another day or two he wouldn't be able to travel. If he didn't get away from White Shoals today he'd never leave it alive.

How he was to cross the miles of ice on his crippled feet he wasn't sure. He'd have to take that as it came, one mile at a time.

His feet were too swollen for shoes, but he found plenty of heavy woolen socks in the light. He pulled on three or four pairs, and contrived to get into the heavy rubbers he had worn over his shoes when he was blown out into the lake on Tuesday.

When he climbed painfully down from the crib that crisp Sunday morning and started his slow trek over the ice toward Crane Island he took two items along, his ax and the frozen trout he had speared five days before. If he succeeded in reaching shore they meant fire and food. They had become symbols of his fierce, steadfast determination to stay alive. So long as he kept them with him he was able to believe he would not freeze or starve.

Now an odd thing happened, one of those ironic quirks that seem to be Destiny's special delight at such times. At the very hour when Sweet was climbing down from the lighthouse and moving across the ice that morning, three of us were setting out from the headquarters of Wilderness State Park, on Big Stone Bay on the south shore of the Straits ten miles east of Crane Island, to have a final look for his body.

Floyd Brunson, superintendent of the park, George Laway, a fisherman living on Big Stone, and I had decided on one more last-hope search along the ice-fringed beach of Waugoshance Point.

We carried no binoculars that morning. We left them behind deliberately to eliminate useless weight, certain we would have no need for them. Had we had a pair along as we snowshoed to the shore and searched around the ice hummocks on the sand beach, and had we trained the glasses a single time toward White Shoals Light — a far-off gray sliver rising out of the frozen lake — we could not possibly have failed to pick up the tiny black figure of a man crawling at snail's pace over the ice.

Had we spotted him by nightfall, we could have had him in a hospital, where by that time he so urgently needed to be and where he was fated to spend the next ten weeks while surgeons amputated all his fingers and toes and his frozen hand and feet slowly healed.

But the hospital was still two days away. Toward noon Brunson and Laway and I trudged back from our fruitless errand, never suspecting how close we had come to a dramatic rescue of the man who had been sought for five days in the greatest mass search that lonely country had ever seen.

Lewis Sweet crept on over the ice all that day. His progress was slow. Inside the heavy socks he could feel fresh blisters swelling on his feet. They puffed up until he literally rolled on them as he walked. Again and again he went ahead a few steps, sat down and rested, got up and drove himself doggedly on. At times he crawled on all fours.

He detoured around places where the new ice looked unsafe. Late in the afternoon he passed the end of Crane Island, at about the spot where he had gone adrift. Land was within reach at last and night was coming on, but he did not go ashore. He had set his sights on Cross Village as the nearest place where he would find humans, and he knew he could make better time on the rocky beach of Sturgeon Bay.

Late that day, Sweet believed afterward, his mind faltered for the first time. He seemed to be getting delirious, and found

63

it hard to keep his course. At dark he stumbled into a deserted shanty on the shore of the bay, where fishermen sometimes spent a night. He was still seven miles short of his goal.

The shanty meant shelter for the night and in it he found firewood and a rusty stove, but no supplies except coffee and a can of frozen milk. He was still carrying his trout but he was too weak and ill now to thaw and cook it. With great effort he succeeded in making coffee. It braced him and he lay down on the bunk to sleep.

Before morning he was violently ill with cramps and nausea, perhaps from lack of food or from the frozen milk he had used with his coffee. At daybreak he tried to drive himself on toward Cross Village but he was too sick to stand. He lay helpless in the shanty all day Monday and through Monday night, eating nothing.

Tuesday morning he summoned the little strength remaining to him and started south once more, hobbling and crawling over the rough ice of Sturgeon Bay. It was quite a walk but he made it. Near noon of that day, almost a week to the hour from the time the wind had set him adrift on his ice floe, he stumbled up the steep bluff at Cross Village and called to a passing Indian for a hand.

Alone and unaided, Lewis Sweet had come home from the lake! When the Indian ran to him he put down two things he was carrying — a battered ax that had been dulled against the iron ladder of White Shoals Light, and a big lake trout frozen hard as granite.

"Frozen Terror" by Ben East first appeared in the January 1951 issue of Outdoor Life. Reprinted courtesy Mrs. Helen East.

THE
River God

Much of fishing lies in imagination, which makes it easy to see a river god, to seek his advice once more, and to benefit from his indomitable spirit.

by Roland Pertwee

When I was a little boy I had a friend who was a colonel. He was not the kind of colonel you meet nowadays, who manages a motor showroom in the West End of London and wears crocodile shoes and a small mustache and who calls you "old man" and slaps your back, independent of the fact that you may have been no more than a private in the war. My colonel was of the older order that takes a third of a century and a lot of Indian sun and Madras curry in the making. A veteran of the Mutiny he was, and wore side whiskers to prove it. Once he came upon a number of Sepoys conspiring mischief in a byre with a barrel of gunpowder. So he put the butt of his cheroot into the barrel and presently they all went to hell. That was the kind of man he was in the way of business.

65

In the way of pleasure he wore an old Norfolk coat that smelt of heather and brine, and which had no elbows to speak of. And he wore a Sherlock Holmesy kind of cap with a swarm of salmon flies upon it, that to my boyish fancy was more splendid than a crown. I cannot remember his legs, because they were nearly always under water, hidden in great canvas waders. But once he sent me a photograph of himself riding on a tricycle, so I expect he had some knickerbockers, too, which would have been that tight kind, with box cloth under the knees. Boys don't take much stock of clothes. His head occupied my imagination. A big, brave, white-haired head with cherry-red rugose cheeks and honest, laughing, puckered eyes, with gunpowder marks in their corners.

People at the little Welsh fishing inn where we met said he was a bore; but I knew him to be a god and shall prove it.

I was ten years old and his best friend.

He was seventy something and my hero.

Properly I should not have mentioned my hero so soon in this narrative. He belongs to a later epoch, but sometimes it is forgivable to start with a boast, and now that I have committed myself I lack the courage to call upon my colonel to fall back two paces to the rear, quick march, and wait until he is wanted.

The real beginning takes place, as I remember, somewhere in Hampshire on the Grayshott Road, among sandy banks, sentinel firs and plum-colored wastes of heather. Summer-holiday time it was, and I was among folks whose names have since vanished like lizards under the stones of forgetfulness. Perhaps it was a picnic walk; perhaps I carried a basket and was told not to swing it for fear of bursting its cargo of ginger beer. In those days ginger beer had big bulgy corks held down with a string. In a hot sun or under stress of too much agitation the string would break and the corks fly. Then there would be a merry foaming fountain and someone would get reproached.

One of our company had a fishing rod. He was a young man who, one day, was to be an uncle of mine. But that didn't concern me. What concerned me was the fishing rod and presently — perhaps because he felt he must keep in with the family — he let me carry it. To the fisherman born there is nothing so provoking of curiosity as a fishing rod in a case.

66

Surreptitiously I opened the flap, which contained a small grass spear in a wee pocket, and pulling down the case a little, I admired the beauties of the cork butt, with its gun-metal ferrule and reel rings and the exquisite frail slenderness of the two top joints.

"It's got two top joints — two!" I exclaimed ecstatically.

"Of course," said he. "All good trout rods have two."

I marveled in silence at what seemed to me then a combination of extravagance and excellent precaution.

There must have been something inherently understanding and noble about the young man who would one day be my uncle, for, taking me by the arm, he sat me down on a tuft of heather and took the pieces of rod from the case and fitted them together. The rest of the company moved on and left me in Paradise.

It is thirty-five years ago since that moment and not one detail of it is forgotten. There sounds in my ears today as clearly as then, the faint, clear pop made by the little cork stoppers with their boxwood tops as they were withdrawn. I remember how, before fitting the pieces together, he rubbed the ferrules against the side of his nose to prevent them sticking. I remember looking up the length of it through a tunnel of sneck rings to the eyelet at the end. Not until he had fixed a reel and passed a line through the rings did he put the lovely thing into my hand. So light it was, so firm, so persuasive; such a thing alive — a sceptor. I could do no more than say "Oo!" and again, "Oo!"

"A thrill, ain't it?" said he.

I had no need to answer that. In my new-found rapture was only one sorrow — the knowledge that such happiness would not endure and that, all too soon, a blank and rodless future awaited me.

"They must be awfully — awfully 'spensive," I said.

"Couple of guineas," he replied offhandedly.

A couple of guineas! And we were poor folk and the future was more rodless than ever.

"Then I shall save and save and save," I said.

And my imagination started to add up twopence a week into guineas. Two hundred and forty pennies to the pound, multiplied by two — four hundred and eighty — and then another twenty-four pennies — five hundred and four. Why, it would take a lifetime, and no sweets, no elastic for catapults, no penny novelty boxes or air-gun bullets or ices or anything. Tragedy must have been writ large upon my face, for he said suddenly, "When's your birthday?"

I was almost ashamed to tell him how soon it was. Perhaps he, too, was a little taken aback by its proximity, for that future uncle of mine was not so rich as uncles should be.

"We must see about it."

"But it wouldn't — it couldn't be one like that," I said.

I must have touched his pride, for he answered loftily, "Certainly it will."

In the fortnight that followed I walked on air and told everybody I had as good as got a couple-of-guineas rod.

No one can deceive a child, save the child himself, and when my birthday came and with it a long brown paper parcel, I knew, even before I had removed the wrappers, that this two-guinea rod was not worth the money. There was a brown linen case, it is true, but it was not a case with a neat compartment for each joint, nor was there a spear in the flap. There was only one top instead of two, and there were no popping little stoppers to protect the ferrules from dust and injury. The lower joint boasted no elegant cork hand piece, but was a tapered affair coarsely made and rudely varnished. When I fitted the pieces together, what I balanced in my hand was tough and stodgy, rather than limber. The reel, which had come in a different parcel, was of wood. It had neither check nor brake, the line overran and backwound itself with distressing frequency.

I had not read and reread Gramages' price list without knowing something of rods, and I did not need to look long at this rod before realizing that it was no match to the one I had handled on the Grayshott Road.

I believe at first a great sadness possessed me, but very presently imagination came to the rescue. For I told myself that I had only to think that this was the rod of all other rods that I desired most and it would be so. And it was so.

Furthermore, I told myself that, in this great wide ignorant world, but few people existed with such expert knowledge of rods as I possessed. That I had but say, "Here is the final word in good rods," and they would accept it as such.

Very confidently I tried the experiment on my mother, with inevitable success. From the depths of her affection and her ignorance on all such matters, she produced:

"It's a magnificent rod."

I went my way, knowing full well that she knew not what she said, but that she was kind.

With rather less confidence I approached my father, saying, "Look, father! It cost two guineas. It's absolutely the best sort you can get."

And he, after waggling it a few moments in silence, quoted cryptically:

"There is nothing either good or bad but thinking makes it so."

Young as I was, I had some curiosity about words, and on any other occasion I would have called on him to explain. But this I did not do, but left hurriedly, for fear that he should explain.

In the two years that followed I fished every day in the slip of a back garden of our tiny London house. And, having regard to the fact that this rod was never fashioned to throw a fly, I acquired a pretty knack in the fullness of time and performed some glib casting at the nasturtiums and marigolds that flourished by the back wall.

My parents' fortunes must have been in the ascendant, I suppose, for I call to mind an unforgettable breakfast when my mother told me that father had decided we should spend our summer holiday at a Welsh hotel on the river Lledr. The place was called Pont-y-pant, and she showed me a picture of the hotel with a great knock-me-down river creaming past the front of it

Although in my dreams I had heard fast water often enough, I had never seen it, and the knowledge that in a month's time I should wake with the music of a cataract in my ears was almost more than patience could endure.

In that exquisite, intolerable period of suspense I suffered as only childish longing and enthusiasm can suffer. Even the hank of gut that I bought and bent into innumerable casts failed to alleviate that suffering. I would walk for miles for a moment's delight captured in gluing my nose to the windows of tackleists' shops in the West End. I learned from my grandmother — a wise and calm old lady — how to make nets and, having mastered the art, I made myself a landing net. This I set up on a frame fashioned from a penny schoolmaster's cane bound to an old walking stick. It would be pleasant to record that this was a good and serviceable net, but it was not. It flopped over in a very distressing fashion when called upon to lift the lightest weight. I had to confess to myself that I had more enthusiasm than skill in the manufacture of such articles.

At school there was a boy who had a fishing creel, which he swapped with me for a Swedish knife, a copy of *Rogues of the Fiery Cross,* and an Easter egg which I had kept on account of its rare beauty. He had forced a hard bargain and was sure he had the best of it, but I knew otherwise.

At last the great day dawned, and after infinite travel by train we reached our destination as the glow of sunset was graying into dark. The river was in spate, and as we crossed a tall stone bridge on our way to the hotel I heard it below me, barking and grumbling among great rocks. I was pretty far gone in tiredness, for I remember little else that night but a rod rack in the hall — a dozen rods of different sorts and sizes, with gaudy salmon flies, some nets, a gaff and an oak coffer upon which lay a freshly caught salmon on a blue ashet. Then supper by candlelight, bed, a glitter of stars through the open window, and the ceaseless drumming of water.

By six o'clock next morning I was on the river bank, fitting my rod together and watching in awe the great brown ribbon of water go fleetly by.

Among my most treasured possessions were held a dozen flies, and two of these I attached to the cast with exquisite care. While so engaged, a shadow fell on the grass beside me and, an unhealthy face who, the night before, had helped with our luggage at the station.

"Water's too heavy for flies," said he, with an uptilting inflection. "This evening, yes; now, no — none whateffer. Better try with a worrum in the burrun."

He pointed at a busy little brook which tumbled down the steep hillside and joined the main stream at the garden end.

"C-couldn't I fish with a fly in the — the burrun?" I asked, for although I wanted to catch a fish very badly, for honor's sake I would fain take it on a fly.

70

"Indeed no," he replied, slanting the tone of his voice sky-ward. "You cootn't. Neffer. And that isn't a fly rod whatteffer."

"It is," I replied hotly. "Yes, it is."

But he only shook his head and repeated, "No," and took the rod from my hand and illustrated its awkwardness and handed it back with a wretched laugh.

If he had pitched me into the river I should have been happier.

"It is a fly rod and it cost two guineas," I said, and my lower lip trembled.

"Neffer," he repeated. "Five shilling would be too much."

Even a small boy is entitled to some dignity.

Picking up my basket, I turned without another word and made for the hotel. Perhaps my eyes were blinded with tears, for I was about to plunge into the dark hall when a great, rough, kindly voice arrested me with:

"Easy does it."

At the thick end of an immense salmon rod there strode out into the sunlight the noblest figure I had ever seen.

There is no real need to describe my colonel again — I have done so already — but the temptation is too great. Standing in the doorway, the sixteen-foot rod in hand, the deer-stalker hat, besprent with flies, crowning his shaggy head, the waders, like seven-league boots, braced up to his armpits, the creel across his shoulder, a gaff across his back, he looked what he was — a god. His eyes met mine with that kind of smile one good man keeps for another.

"An early start," he said. "Any luck, old fellar?"

I told him I hadn't started — not yet.

"Wise chap," said he. "Water's a bit heavy for trouting. It'll soon run down, though. Let's vet those flies of yours."

He took my rod and whipped it expertly.

"A nice piece — new, eh?"

N-not quite," I stammered; "but I haven't used it yet, sir, in water."

That god read men's minds.

"I know — garden practice; capital; nothing like it."

Releasing my cast, he frowned critically over the flies — a Blue Dun and a March Brown.

"Think so?" he queried. "You don't think it's a shade late in

71

the season for these fancies?" I said I thought perhaps it was. "Yes, I think you're right," said he. "I believe in this big water you'd do better with a livelier pattern. Teal and Red, Cock-y-bundy, Greenwell's Glory."

I said nothing, but nodded gravely at these brave names.

Once more he read my thoughts and saw through the wicker sides of my creel a great emptiness.

"I expect you've fished most in southern rivers. These Welsh trout have a fancy for a spot of color."

He rummaged in the pocket of his Norfolk jacket and produced a round tin which once had held saddle soap.

"Collar on to that," said he; "there's a proper pickle of flies and casts in that tin that, as a keen fisherman, you won't mind sorting out. Still, they may come in useful."

"But, I say, you don't mean *—" I began.

"Yes, go in; stick to it. All fishermen are members of the same club and I'm giving the trout a rest for a bit." His eyes ranged the hills and trees opposite. "I must be getting on with it before the sun's too high."

Waving his free hand, he strode away and presently was lost to view at a bend in the road.

I think my mother was a little piqued by my abstraction during breakfast. My eyes never, for an instant, deserted the round tin box which lay open beside my plate. Within it were a paradise and a hundred miracles all tangled together in the pleasantest disorder. My mother said something about a lovely walk over the hills, but I had other plans, which included a very glorious hour which should be spent untangling and wrapping up in neat squares of paper my new treasures.

"I suppose he knows best what he wants to do," she said.

So it came about that I was left alone and betook myself to a sheltered spot behind a rock where all the delicious disorder was remedied and I could take stock of what was mine.

I am sure there were at least six casts all set up with flies, and ever so many loose flies and one great stout, tapered cast, with a salmon fly upon it, that was so rich in splendor that I doubted if my benefactor could really have known that it was there.

I felt almost guilty at owning so much, and not until I had

done full justice to everything did I fasten a new cast on my line and go a-fishing.

There is a lot said and written about beginners' luck, but none of it came my way. Indeed, I spent most of the morning extricating my line from the most fearsome tangles. I had no skill in throwing a cast with two droppers upon it and I found it was an art not to be learned in a minute. Then, from over-eagerness, I was too snappy with my back cast, whereby, before many minutes had gone, I heard that warning crack behind me that betokens the loss of a tail fly. I must have spent half an hour searching the meadow for that lost fly and finding it not. Which is not strange, for I wonder has any fisherman ever found that lost fly. The reeds, the buttercups, and the little people with many legs who run in the wet grass conspire together to keep the secret of its hiding place. I gave up at last, and with a feeling of shame that was only proper, I invested a new fly on the point of my cast and set to work again, but more warily.

In that hard racing water a good strain was put upon my rod, and before the morning was out it was creaking at the joints in a way that kept my heart continually in my mouth. It is the duty of a rod to work with a single smooth action and by no means to divide its performance into three sections of activity. It is a hard task for any angler to persuade his line austerely if his rod behaves thus.

When, at last, my father strolled up the river bank, walking, to his shame, much nearer the water than a good fisherman should, my nerves were jumpy from apprehension.

"Come along. Food's ready. Done any good?" said he.

Again it was to his discredit that he put food before sport, but I told him I had had a wonderful morning, and he was glad.

"What do you want to do this afternoon, old man?" he asked.

"Fish," I said.

"But you can't always fish," he said.

I told him I could, and I was right and have proved it for thirty years and more.

"Well, well," he said, "please yourself, but isn't it dull not catching anything?"

And I said, as I've said a thousand times since, "As if it

could be."

So that afternoon I went downstream instead of up, and found myself in difficult country where the river boiled between the narrows of two hills. Stunted oaks overhung the water and great boulders opposed its flow. Presently I came to a sort of natural flight of steps — a pool and a cascade three times repeated — and there, watching the maniac fury of the waters in awe and wonderment, I saw a silver salmon leap superbly from the caldron below into the pool above. And I saw another and another salmon do likewise. And I wonder the eyes of me did not fall out of my head.

I cannot say how long I stayed watching that gallant pageant of leaping fish — in ecstasy there is no measurement of time — but at last it came upon me that all the salmon in the sea were careening past me and that if I were to realize my soul's desire I must hasten to the pool below before the last of them had gone by.

It was a mad adventure, for until I had discovered that stout cast, with the gaudy fly attached in the tin box, I had given no thought to such noble quarry. My recent possessions had put ideas into my head above my station and beyond my powers. Failure, however, means little to the young and, walking fast, yet gingerly, for fear of breaking my rod top against a tree, I followed the path downstream until I came to a great basin of water into which, through a narrow throat, the river thundered like a storm.

At the head of the pool was a plate of rock scored by the nails of fishermen's boots, and here I sat me down to wait while the salmon cast, removed from its wrapper, was allowed to soak and soften in a puddle left by the rain.

And while I waited a salmon rolled not ten yards from where I sat. Head and tail, up and down he went, a great monster of a fish, sporting and deriding me.

With that performance so near at hand, I have often wondered how I was able to control my fingers well enough to tie a figure-eight knot between the line and the cast. But I did, and I'm proud to be able to record it. Your true-born angler does not go blindly to work until he has first satisfied his conscience. There is a pride, in knots, of which the laity knows nothing,

74

and if through neglect to tie them rightly, failure and loss should result, pride may not be restored nor conscience salved by the plea of eagerness. With my trembling fingers I bent the knot and, with a pummeling heart, launched the line into the broken water at the throat of the pool.

At first the mere tug of the water against that large fly was so thrilling to me that it was hard to believe that I had not hooked a whale. The trembling line swung round in a wide arc into a calm eddy below where I stood. Before casting afresh I shot a glance over my shoulder to assure myself there was no limb of a tree behind me to foul the fly. And this was a gallant cast, true and straight, with a couple of yards more length than its predecesor, and with a wider radius. Instinctively I knew, as if the surface had been marked with an X where the salmon had risen, that my fly must pass right over the spot. As it swung by, my nerves were strained like piano wires. I think I knew something tremendous, impossible, terrifying, was going to happen. The sense, the certitude was so strong in me that I half opened my mouth to shout a warning to the monster, not to.

I must have felt very, very young in that moment. I, who that same day had been talked to as a man by a man among men. The years were stripped from me and I was what I was — ten years old and appalled. And then, with the suddenness of a rocket, it happened. The water was cut into a swath. I remember a silver loop bearing downward — a bright, shining, vanishing thing like the bobbin of my mother's sewing machine — and a tug. I shall never forget the viciousness of that tug. I had my fingers tight upon the line, so I got the full force of it. To counteract a tendency to go headfirst into the spinning water below, I threw myself backward and sat down on the hard rock with a jar that shut my teeth on my tongue — like the jaws of a trap.

Luckily I had let the rod go out straight with the line, else it must have snapped in the first frenzy of the downstream rush. Little ass that I was, I tried to check the speeding line with my forefinger, with the result that it cut and burnt me to the bone. There wasn't above twenty yards of line in the reel, and the wretched contrivance was trying to be rid of the line even faster than the fish was wretching it out. Heaven knows why it didn't

75

snarl, for great loops and whorls were whirling, like Catherine wheels, under my wrist. An instant's glance revealed the terrifying fact that there was not more than half a dozen yards left on the reel and the fish showed no sign of abating his rush. With the realization of impending and inevitable catastrophe upon me, I launched a yell for help, which, rising above the roar of the waters, went echoing down the gorge.

And then, to add to my terrors, the salmon leaped — a winging leap like a silver arch appearing and instantly disappearing upon the broken surface. So mighty, so all-powerful he seemed in that sublime moment that I lost all sense of reason and raised the rod, with a sudden jerk, above my head.

I have often wondered, had the rod actually been the two-guinea rod my imagination claimed for it, whether it could have withstood the strain thus violently and unreasonably imposed upon it. The wretched thing I held so grimly never even put up a fight. It snapped at the ferrule of the lower joint and plunged like a toboggan down the slanting line, to vanish into the black depths of the water.

My horror at this calamity was so profound that I was lost even to the consciousness that the last of my line had run out. A couple of vicious tugs advised me of this awful truth. Then, snap! The line parted at the reel, flickered out through the rings and was gone. I was left with nothing but the butt of a broken rod in my hand and an agony of mind that even now I cannot recall without emotion.

I am not ashamed to confess that I cried. I lay down on the rock, with my cheek in the puddle where I had soaked the cast, and plenished it with my tears. For what had the future left for me but a cut and burning finger, a badly bumped behind, the single joint of a broken rod and no faith in uncles? How long I lay there weeping I do not know. Ages, perhaps minutes, or seconds.

I was roused by a rough hand on my shoulder and a kindly voice demanding, "Hurt yourself, Ike Walton?"

Blinking away my tears, I pointed at my broken rod with a bleeding forefinger.

"Come! This is bad luck," said my colonel, his face grave as a stone. "How did it happen?"

76

"I c-caught a s-salmon."

"You what?" said he.

"I d-did," I said.

He looked at me long and earnestly; then, taking my injured hand, he looked at that and nodded.

"The poor groundlings who can find no better use for a river than something to put a bridge over think all fishermen are liars," said he. "But we know better, eh? By the bumps and breaks and cuts I'd say you made a plucky fight against heavy odds. Let's hear all about it."

So, with his arm around my shoulders and his great shaggy head near mine, I told him all about it.

At the end he gave me a mighty and comforting squeeze, and he said, "The loss of one's first big fish is the heaviest loss I know. One feels, whatever happens, one'll never —" He stopped and pointed dramatically. "There it goes — see! Down there at the tail of the pool!"

In the broken water where the pool emptied itself into the shallows beyond, I saw the top joints of my rod dancing on the surface.

"Come on!" he shouted, and gripping my hand, jerked me to my feet. "Scatter your legs! There's just a chance!"

Dragging me after him, we raced along by the river path to the end of the pool, where, on a narrow promontory of grass, his enormous salmon rod was lying.

"Now," he said, picking it up and making the line whistle to and fro in the air with sublime authority, "keep your eyes skinned on those shallows for another glimpse of it."

A second later I was shouting, "There! There!"

He must have seen the rod point at the same moment, for his line flowed out and the big fly hit the water with a plop not a couple of feet from the spot. He let it ride on the current, playing it with a sensitive touch like the brushwork of an artist.

"Half a jiffy!" he exclaimed at last. "Wait! Yes, I think so. Cut down to that rock and see if I haven't fished up the line."

I needed no second invitation, and presently was yelling, "Yes — yes you have!"

"Stretch yourself out then and collar hold of it."

With the most exquisite care he navigated the line to where

I lay stretched upon the rock. Then:

"Right you are! Good lad! I'm coming down."

Considering his age, he leaped the rocks like a chamois.

"Now," he said, and took the wet line delicately between his forefinger and thumb. One end trailed limply downstream, but the other end seemed anchored in the big pool where I had had my unequal and disastrous contest.

Looking into his face, I saw a sudden light of excitement dancing in his eyes.

"Odd," he muttered, "but not impossible."

"What isn't?" I asked breathlessly.

"Well, it looks to me as if the joints of that rod of yours have gone downstream."

Gingerly he pulled up the line, and presently an end with a broken knot appeared.

"The reel knot, eh? I nodded gloomily. "Then we lose the rod," said he. That wasn't very heartening news. "On the other hand, it's just possible the fish is still on — sulking."

"Oo!" I exclaimed.

"Now, steady does it," he warned, "and give me my rod."

Taking a pair of clippers from his pocket, he cut his own line just above the cast. "Can you tie a knot?" he asked.

"Yes," I nodded.

"Come on, then; bend your line onto mine. Quick as lightning."

Under his critical eye, I joined the two lines with a blood knot. "I guessed you were a fisherman," he said, nodded approvingly and clipped off the ends. "And now to know the best or the worst."

I shall never forget the music of that check reel or the suspense with which I watched as, with the butt of the rod bearing against the hollow of his thigh, he steadily wound up the wet slack line. Every instant I expected it to come drifting downstream, but it didn't. Presently it rose in a tight slant from the pool above.

"Snagged, I'm afraid," he said, and worked the rod with an easy straining motion to and fro. "Yes, I'm afraid — no, by Lord Bobs, he's on!"

I think it was only right and proper that I should have launched a yell of triumph as, with the spoken word, the point at which the line cut the water shifted magically from the left side of the pool to the right.

"And a fish too," said he.

In the fifteen minutes that followed, I must have experienced every known form of terror and delight.

"Youngster," said he, "you should be doing this, by rights, but I'm afraid the rod's a bit above your weight."

"Oh, go on and catch him," I pleaded.

"And so I will," he promised; "unship the gaff, young un, and stand by to use it, and if you break the cast we'll never speak to each other again, and that's a bet."

But I didn't break the cast. The noble, courageous, indomitable example of my river god had lent me skill and precision beyond my years. When at long last a weary, beaten silver monster rolled within reach of my arm into a shallow eddy, the steel gaff shot out fair and true, and sank home.

And then I was lying on the grass, with my arms round a salmon that weighed twenty-two pounds on the scale and contained every sort of happiness known to a boy.

And best of all, my river god shook hands with me and called me "partner."

That evening the salmon was placed upon the blue ashet in the hall, bearing a little card with its weight and my name upon it.

And I am afraid I sat on a chair facing it, for ever so long, so that I could hear what the other anglers had to say as they passed by. I was sitting there when my colonel put his head out of his private sitting room and beckoned me to come in.

"A true fisherman lives in the future, not the past, old man," said he; "Though for this once, it'd be a shame to reproach you."

I suppose I colored guiltily — at any rate, I hope so.

"We got the fish," said he, "but we lost the rod, and a future without a rod doesn't bear thinking of. Now" — and he pointed at a long wooden box on the floor, that overflowed with rods of different sorts and sizes — "rummage among those. Take your time and see if you can find anything to suit you."

"But do you mean — can I —"

"We're partners, aren't we? And p'r'aps as such you'd rather we went through our stock together."

"Oo, sir," I said.

"Here, quit that," he ordered gruffly. "By Lord Bobs, if a

show like this afternoon's doesn't deserve a medal, what does? Now, here's a handy piece by Hardy — a light and useful tool — or if you fancy greenheart in preference to split bamboo—"

I have the rod to this day, and I count it among my dearest treasures. And to this day I have a flick of the wrist that was his legacy. I have, too, some small skill in dressing flies, the elements of which were learned in his company by candlelight after the day's work was over. And I have countless memories of that month-long, month-short friendship — the closest and most perfect friendship, perhaps, of all my life.

He came to the station and saw me off. How I vividly remember his shaggy head at the window, with the whiskered cheeks and the gunpowder marks at the corners of his eyes! I didn't cry, although I wanted to awfully. We were partners and shook hands. I never saw him again, although on my birthdays I would have colored cards from him, with Irish, Scotch, Norwegian postmarks. Very brief they were: "Water very low." "Took a good fish last Thursday." "Been prawning, but don't like it."

Sometimes at Christmas I had gifts — a reel, a tapered line, a fly book. But I never saw him again.

Came at last no more cards or gifts, but in the *Fishing Gazette*, of which I was a religious reader, was an obituary telling how one of the last of the Mutiny veterans had joined the great majority. It seems he had been fishing half an hour before he died. He had taken his rod down and passed out. They had buried him at Totnes, overlooking the River Dart.

So he was no more — my river god — and what was left of him they had put into a box and buried it in the earth.

But that isn't true; nor is it true that I never saw him again. For I seldom go a-fishing but that I meet him on the river banks.

The banks of a river are frequented by a strange company and are full of mysterious and murmurous sounds — the cluck and laughter of water, the piping of birds, the hum of insects, and the whispering of wind in the willows. What should prevent a man in such a place having a word and speech with another who is not there? So much of fishing lies in imagination, and mine needs little stretching to give my river god a living form.

"With this ripple," says he, "you should do well."

"And what's it to be," say I — "Blue Upright, Red Spinner?

What's your fancy, sir?"

Spirits never grow old. He had begun to take an interest in dry-fly methods — that river god of mine, with his seven-league boots, his shaggy head, and the gaff across his back.

Dodie's Duck

All he wanted was a mallard duck for his beloved
Dodie. But then life — and even hunting
regulations — ain't always fair.

by Walter Clare Martin

This morning I received a copy of *S. R. A. — B. S. 83*,
issued by the Bureau of Biological Survey, a promul-
gation of the national duck law.

In this important booklet I find innumerable rules,
regulations, statistics, etc., etc., but I note one deplorable omis-
sion. Nothing is said about the duck-hunting activities of Coyne
McCreagh of Coon Ridge, whose experience, I think throws
more light on the federal conservation program than all the
leaflets you could set a match to.

It was not jealousy, I am sure, which inspired the Bureau of
Biological Survey to ignore Mr. McCreagh so effectively. More
likely they considered him outside their scope, because, that
hazy dawning of November, he did not set out to hunt ducks.

The truth is, he set out to hunt rabbits.

He set out with three rocks, having no civilized arms except an erratic muzzle-fed musket. And for the musket he had no munitions.

He talked some of borrowing a Twenty-two from the Flints; but they lived a right smart down the holler. The Flints' shotgun had been reduced to historic scrap-iron when Bud fired it with snow in the snout.

So Coyne equipped himself with three rocks, round and cold, about the size of baseballs.

It is a matter of record that such missiles, addressing a rabbit broadside, may detail him with catastrophic effects.

So Coyne McCreagh, crunching the frosted leaves, stalked from one brush-pile to another. Into each pile he peered, and each pile he kicked hard with the heel of his home-soled boots.

Coyne was no Houdini, however, and the rabbits failed to appear. Two rocks chunked heavily into his skunk-perfumed coat, and the third chilled his throwing hand until it stiffened.

Coyne shifted this rock to his right perfumed pocket and rubbed his hands between his legs with much vigor. He then put his hand inside his pants pocket to warm it against his thigh.

A rabbit some thirty-odd feet away, blurring into a background of buck brush, sat watching these human maneuvers. With the infernal perversity which animates all cottontails he waited until Coyne's throwing hand was tightly tucked into his pants, then he jumped like a guilty conscience.

Coyne caught the insulting white flick of his tail as he scooted between the rough legs of the forest.

With a startled "gawd blast!" Coyne wrenched free his hand and fumbled a rock from his coat. He hurled it with desperate violence.

The beast was too far, and the total effect of the throw was to increase his ambition to travel.

Coyne McCreagh's body sagged as he watched the meat disappear.

"I'm sure sorry, Dodie," he said.

This Dodie, as the Biological Survey should know, was Coyne's young faithful wife, very expectant. She expected a baby, in three or four months, and today she expected a rabbit.

Budgetty matrons whose caloric adventures begin with

the telephone, who year-round visit smiling vendors of T-bones and sidewalks piled high with fresh spinach, can but weakly conceive what that rabbit meant in the life of young Mrs. McCreagh.

Six weeks she had rationed on salt sowbelly and corn-pone, with slippery-elm bark to chew, when too hungry. Dodie needed no Johns Hopkins guide-book to tell her she was not doing right by Coyne's baby. Her stomach, without publicity, turned upside down and the mountain bloom began to fade from her cheek.

It had reached such a crisis, Dodie had said to her man:

"If you don't get some fresh meat, I'll take fits."

That was why Coyne said he was sorry. He did not want his young mate to take fits. He did not want his heir to be born chicken-breasted or too crooked to swing a man's ax.

He was sorry, but he tightened his rawhide belt and trudged farther on, down the hollow. He probed and kicked every brush-pile. He thrust twistin' poles into old secret logs. He circled patches of briarbrush and peeped under bunch-grass, and the one thing he did not find was a rabbit.

"Taint no use," he muttered. "They clubbed 'em too close."

Just to keep the Biological records straight, this "clubbed 'em too close" referred to the winter before, when a fifteen-inch snow smothered the Ozarks. A vaste horde of pat-hunters, with clubs and with dogs, waded out and enjoyed a snow massacre.

From Coyne's county alone, 50,000 dead bunnies were piled upon trucks going east.

A great week! Kettles simmered. Coins clinked in surprised pockets. But it so happened that not one of those 50,000 dead bunnies laid an egg to be hatched the next Easter.

Great sport for the pot-hunters; but now Coyne tramped the hard hills without sighting a living creature. He began to doubt the one flicker of fur he had seen was anything more than a ghost. A rabbit ghost haunting the scene of the massacre.

Hungry, chilled, disillusioned, he paused on a bald knob to take bearings. He could see his home smoke, miles across bristling gulches, and told himself he should be there, chopping firewood.

But Dodie was expecting a rabbit.

Off south lay the river, smeared with fog like whipped cream. Some ten or twelve miles, by the tumbling road half a mile to a crow, or an airplane.

An automobile horn sounded along the ridge road, across the still vale from Coyne's knob. Sportsmen, probably, bound for the duck blinds. Lordy, lord, couldn't Coyne eat a duck! Dodie could eat a duck, too, he reckoned. How her anxious brown eyes would light and dance if he came swinging a fat duck by the neck.

It burst over Coyne, then, that despite war, flood, and damnation he was going to get Dodie a duck.

Furiously he plunged into the hollow. Through bramble and briar, through sassafras and blackjack he made for the nearest arm of the river. If he could get to the blind before the sportsmen arrived, he could offer to work — for a duck.

The car beat him, by a couple of minutes. The hunters were dragging out guns. Automatics, pump-actions, double-barrels, all sizes and chokes — Coyne never had beheld such an arsenal of shotguns.

Three men in the party and three guns to each man: short range, middle range and long distance.

The financier of the party was Lawrence Bogart, husky-voiced, impatient, red-shaven, meat-fed; a man who had inherited much and made more. He operated an overall factory.

The other two were physicians — Doc Pyne and Doc Smith. One lean and sardonic as a wolf at the door; his fellow thick, swarthy, coarse, friendly.

They were transferring luggage from the car to the blind. Coyne McCreagh hurried up, half winded.

"I reckon I could help you unload," he said.

Bogart sized him up.

"How much?"

"I'd do it for one mallard duck," said Coyne.

The thick friendly Doc laughed:

"You like 'em better than I do."

Bogart said:

"Can you keep your mouth shut?"

"A feller can't talk with his mouth full o' duck," said Coyne.

"Very shrewd, indeed," said the wolf.

"You're hired," said Bogart. "Just do what we want, and you'll eat duck till you quack for a week. There's a bonus, also,

85

at the end of the day, if everything goes off smoothly. All right, pitch in. We'll unpack the car and run it into the willows. Then lug all the stuff to the blind."

Coyne McCreagh pitched in, his heart singing. He was quite willing to quack for a week.

The junk was unloaded; the big car concealed; and the four men laddered into the blind. It was half sunk in lush slumps at the shore of the stream, warm and roomy, finer far than Coyne's cabin.

There were shelves for tall bottles; built-in boxes, bug-proof; fold-up couches; wall lights, operated by electric dry cells.

Coyne asked several questions about these smart lights, resolving to buy one for Dodie's Christmas.

As the program progressed, the men talked and drank. Coyne inferred that Doc Pyne was a novice. He was an expert skeet shooter, and office partner to Smith, who was striving to outdoorize him.

"When do you put out the decoys?" Pyne said to Bogart.

"Not legal this year," said Bogart.

"What about your phonograph records?"

"They're legal if made from mechanical quacks; but not legal if made from live fowl."

"Which are these?" inquired Pyne.

Bogart spun a phonograph disk with his thumb.

"I didn't ask when I bought them," he said.

They tried out the records. Quack, quack, quack, quack — a lively medley of friendly duck voices. Coyne would have sworn, had he not been standing there staring at it, that the river was swarming with mallards.

"Guess I'll plug my guns now," said Bogart.

"Plug?" said Doc Pyne, puzzled.

"Sure thing, that's the law. Repeating shotguns must have their magazines plugged to three shells. A damned silly thing, if you ask me. We have a bag limit of ten. Since we can take only ten what the hell does it matter if the gun shoots five loads or three?"

"Five loads would be better, I reckon," said Coyne.

"Why?" all the hunters looked at him.

"'Cause the more shots in a gun the less the number of flocks would be banged at to fetch down the limit of ten. That means fewer bunches is disturbed from their feed. It's breakin' rest and feed that hurts most."

"The man is right, Bogart," said Smith.

"Maybe so," said Bogart, "but it's no hair off my neck. I know how to beat the law — legal. Three loads in three guns are nine loads, as I figure. Here, McCreagh, you take charge of these two extra guns, and when I reach, hand 'em to me — like this."

He practiced Coyne in the art of gun-passing.

Smith was boring the sky with a hand telescope.

"Mallards!" he cried. "Drop the roof."

Bogart pulled a lever which let down the grassed roof. The men snapped to their shooting positions. Through the sloping glass panes, camouflaged with tall reeds, they could scan the smoking face of the river.

Smith set the phonograph calling. Coyne held the gun ready to pass.

A triangle of mallards dipped down through the haze to discover the source of the quacking.

Disappointed, they rose and circled the woods, their hollow wing-bones whistling, "Follow."

"They're gone," complained Pyne. The others signalled him "Hush." Soon the birds reappeared, dipping lower.

"They're tired," whispered Bogart. "Next time they'll drop."

The air in the room seemed to stiffen.

Around came the ducks, stretching, eager, convinced that no foe lingered near. They supposed the friendly ducks, whose voices they heard, were concealed somewhere in the weeds.

The shrill whistling ceased as by signal. Nervous wings relaxed in midair.

Tail rudders snapped down to check landing speed. One instant they hung in suspended power as if a still camera had caught them. The instant hunters rave about in their sleep.

Up sprang the camouflaged roof of the blind. Fire and thunder shattered the picture. Scatter loads, choked loads, and long range charges of shot ripped to pieces the gallant formation.

Surprised by the furious cannonade, the ducks climbed away from the death trap. Courageously they re-formed their torn ranks. Leaving wounded and dead whom they were unable to help, they cut a swift path through the ghostly haze and steered for less sinister waters.

The dead mallards and wounded, of all degrees, floated on the white water like lilies. The boat lay concealed at the weedy shore of the stream; but the men made no attempt to retrieve.

One by one the fine dinners for which Coyne would have given his cornfield headed into the strong flow and shot down. He stared at the ducks and the boat and men. When he could endure it no longer, he blurted:

"Ain't you aimin' to fetch in them ducks?"

"Hell no," said Bogart.

Coyne hesitated a moment. To him the idea was incredible. Enough dinners to support him and Dodie for two weeks were drifting away, for the turtles.

It must be a mistake. He persisted.

"Don't none of you fellers enjoy to eat duck?"

The men were annoyed, and showed it.

"Sure we like duck" said Bogart, "but we like shooting a damned sight better. If we picked up all the ducks, we would about have our bag limits and be heading home before we got started. We won't have our bag limits until sundown."

Coyne's hungry jaw stiffened, indignant. "It don't rest my mind none," he retorted. "That's the way it went with the rabbits. Last year they was growin' on every bush and nobody showed 'em no mercy. This year you can tramp till your tongue hangs out and not get enough hair for your eyebrow."

Bogart growled irritably:

"There's plenty of ducks."

"They ain't," said Coyne, "and if they was, this kind of business would soon blot 'em out."

"Take a drink and forget it," suggested Smith. Pyne added:

"It's strictly our business; and strictly within the law."

"Lawful or not," said Coyne, "It' ain't right. Wild game to you fellers is just something to bust; but it's serious meat to us here in the hills. It ain't right to waste meat and it ain't right to let cripples float off and die slow."

"We can't get 'em," said Bogart, "they are too far out."

"Loan me your boat," said Coyne, "I'll fetch em."

"Like hell! and get us all in a jam. This river is patrolled by state and federal men. One might chance along any moment."

"Let 'em come," said Coyne, "I ain't breakin' no law."

"Then for your information," said Bogart, "it is unlawful to use any kind of boat more than one hundred feet from the shore."

Coyne gaped: "Is that the law?"

"Yes, that's the law," they all nodded.

"It's a damned funny law, I reckon," said Coyne, "if a man can't pick up shot birds."

"There's a lot of damned funny laws," said Bogart, "but we manage to have our fun. And this particular law suits us just fine; it's an excuse for not picking up birds."

"I don't·like it," said Coyne, "it ain't right."

"And I don't like lectures," said Bogart. "We won't need you any more today. Here" — he held out a one dollar bill.

Deliberately Coyne turned and climbed from the blind; ignoring the proffered pay.

Again Coyne found himself on a ridge; alone, cold, rabbit-less, duckless.

Instinct urged him to go back home; eat cornbread; chop wood; get warm. Pride told him to keep on trudging.

His eyes toured the hills for suggestions. The nearest smoke flew from the roof of the Flints, two or three hours across hollows; tough going.

The Flints, he recalled, had a rifle. They might have a car-tridge or two. Coyne knew a place, down the river, where frog-weeds grew on mud flats. There often fed ducks; which a man could approach, if he used enough patience and cunning.

Resolutely he scraped down the hillside and worked across the oak deeps towards the Flints. It was mid-afternoon when he sat astride their worn fence and shouted at the clay-clinked log cabin.

It was bad manners to approach without shouting.

At his voice, mongrel dogs set up a fierce brawl. In the doorway a sockless woman appeared. She turned and spoke to Squirrel Flint — patching boots by his fire — and Squirrel Flint shuffled out to meet Coyne.

Squirrel Flint, tall, fibrous, bald, weather-warped, hard, made Coyne think of his old hickory ax-handle.

Coyne skipped the weather and all the usual small chat, and

told Flint why he had come. He wanted a gun to hunt ducks.

"I'm plumb sorry," said Squirrel, "but my shotgun is broke. Buddy stodged some snow in the muzzle."

"I reckon you don't have no ca'tridges for your twenty-two target," said Coyne.

"I mought," said Flint, "but you would be wasting your time. You can't fetch no ducks with a rifle."

"I mought fetch down one," said Coyne.

"With a heap o'luck maybe," said Flint. "We shore wouldn't need no bag limit for ducks if everybody used a single-shot rifle. I won't say a feller can't do it; but you shore need to take plenty of pains."

"I aim to take pains," said Coyne.

Flint got the rifle and six twenty-two shots; of which Coyne borrowed three. He declined an invitation to cider. Flint's cider was ripe and went to a man's eye. Dodie's duck required him to shoot straight.

Coyne warmed his raw hands at Flint's fireplace; and looked briefly at Flint's 'possum pelts. He then struck with gaunt strides through Flint's turnip patch, on the last leg of his march to the river.

Almost to the river, keeping close under shade, he saw a flock circling the fog.

He listened: the mud flats were quacking. He crouched until the flying birds settled from sight beyond the tangle of high weeds and willows.

His heart bounced. Dodie's dinner was waiting. Indian-like he moved forward, half crawl, half run, towards the thick dank vegetation below.

He made it without being seen. In the willows and poison white sumacs he paused and held open his ears.

No ducks jabbered now. His hopes trembled. A dog, a loose rock, a fishing boat on the stream would fill the fog with a wild hurry of feathers.

He had borrowed a cord from Flint's rafters. He tied a loose loop and slung the gun on his back, to avoid jabbing mud into the muzzle.

Belly-flat in the herbage he wriggled along like a crocodile with a man's head. Inch by inch his muddy track lengthened. The closer he wormed to the edge of his cover, the more pains he took to be noiseless.

Light broke, at last, his screen thinning. He could see the frog-flats just ahead. Half a hundred gay waterfowl disported themselves — mallards, blue-wings, mergansers, and sprig-tails.

Wet and shivering, Coyne huddled behind a drift-log and studied the situation. A single-shot rifle — one chance. The nearest duck was a teal, a bright blue-wing cock, wrestling with a live fish in the puddle.

About fifty yards to the teal, Coyne figured. If the gun was any good, he could hit it. But a teal was a small profit; just one tempting bite, and beyond that teal, ten yards, sat a mallard.

Desperate, like any gambler who stakes his world on one throw, Coyne decided to try for the mallard.

"Now gawd damn you, little rifle, shoot straight!" He nosed the sly weapon across the drift-log and laid his right eye in the sights. The front bead appeared to blur slightly. Slowly, cautiously, holding his breath, he withdrew the gun from the log. With his bandanna, he wiped off the fine web.

Again the determined muzzle crept over the concealed log. Again Coyne rose into the sights. He pinned the head on the sheen of the lusty drake's wing, on the whistling bone that carries mallards to safety.

Tenderly he tightened his finger. The rifle let go its canned death. Powder smoke stung his eyes as the flat roared into air and the sycamore tops sprouted feathers.

Coyne jerked his breech bolt, forced in the fresh load, and fired his farewell at the mallards. His slug punched a harmless hole in the zenith. He shoved in his third cartridge and turned his mind to the flat.

There lumped his duck, dead as a doorknob.

A fine human pride caroused in his chest as he hurried to take up his bird. The muddy sop was adhesive.

He squished. Ankle deep in frog-pudding he retrieved the big drake and imagined what Dodie would say.

A motor-boat came rippin up-river. Two men in warm clothes scanned the shores. When they glimpsed Coyne, they swerved, swung the boat up a slough, and split the weeds within a stone's throw of the hunter.

They stepped from the boat with a business-like air, their legs sheathed in high boots. They came over.

"Did you kill that duck with that gun?" said one.

"Sure did," said Coyne, "plumb center."

The spokesman showed his credentials.

"You're under arrest," he said.

"Get into the boat," said the other.

"Hey! Hold on!" said Coyne, "you fellers got the wrong hunch. I bought my license last June. I got it here, in my shirt pocket."

"License or no license," the first officer said, "you killed a duck with a rifle. That's a violation of the federal law."

Coyne gawked.

"Crazy or not, that's the law." The man reached into a pocket. He brought forth a soiled copy of *S.R.A. — B.S. 83* and read pointedly:

" ... *migratory game birds may be taken during the open season with a shot gun only.*"

"Get into the boat," the other man said.

Coyne stood, staring queerly at the duck he had shot. Then he blurted:

"I tell you what, warden. Let me take this duck home to Dodie, my wife, then I'll cheerful go with you to jail."

"Can't be done," said the spokesman. "That bird is evidence now. It is proof you have violated Regulation Three which provides for the protection of wildfowl."

"Get into the boat," said the other one.

Coyne walked to the boat, his face tightening. The mud pulled with a loud sucking sob. The men took his duck and his rifle and seated him in the bow end of the boat.

They pulled from the flat, towards the current.

Up the river a sudden noisy bombardment gave Coyne his farewell salute.

THE ROAD TO

Tinkhamtown

Most remember Corey Ford for his "Lower Forty" column, but this short story, perhaps his best ever, wasn't discovered until after his death.

by Corey Ford

It was a long way, but he knew where he was going. He would follow the road through the woods and over the crest of a hill and down the hill to the stream, and cross the sagging timbers of the bridge, and on the other side would be the place called Tinkhamtown. He was going back to Tinkhamtown.

He walked slowly at first, his legs dragging with each step. He had not walked for almost a year, and his flanks had shriveled and wasted away from lying in bed so long; he could fit his fingers around his thigh. Doc Towle had said he would never walk again, but that was Doc for you, always on the pessimistic side. Why, now he was walking quite easily, once he had started. The strength was coming back into his legs, and he did not have to stop for breath so often. He tried jogging a few steps, just to

93

show he could, but he slowed again because he had a long way to go.

It was hard to make out the old road, choked with alders and covered by matted leaves, and he shut his eyes so he could see it better. He could always see it when he shut his eyes. Yes, here was the beaver dam on the right, just as he remembered it, and the flooded stretch where he had picked his way from hummock while the dog splashed unconcernedly in front of him. The water had been over his boot tops in one place, and sure enough, as he waded it now his left boot filled with water again, the same warm squishy feeling. Everything was the way it had been that afternoon, nothing had changed in ten years. Here was the blowdown across the road that he had clambered over, and here on a knoll was the clump of thorn-apples where a grouse had flushed as they passed. Shad had wanted to look for it, but he had whistled him back. They were looking for Tinkhamtown.

He had come across the name on a map in the town library. He used to study the old maps and survey charts of the state; sometimes they showed where a farming community had flourished, a century ago, and around the abandoned pastures and in the orchards grown up to pine the birds would be feeding undisturbed. Some of his best grouse covers had been located that way. The map had been rolled up in a cardboard cylinder; it crackled with age as he spread it out. The date was 1857. It was the sector between Cardigan and Kearsarge mountains, a wasteland of slash and second-growth timber without habitation today, but evidently it had supported a number of families before the Civil War. A road was marked on the map, dotted with Xs for homesteads, and the names of the owners were lettered beside them: Nason, J. Tinkham, Allard, R. Tinkham. Half the names were Tinkham. In the center of the map — the paper was so yellow that he could barely make it out — was the word "Tinkhamtown."

He had drawn a rough sketch on the back of an envelope, noting where the road left the highway and ran north to a fork and then turned east and crossed a stream that was not even named; and the next morning he and Shad had set out together to find the place. They could not drive very far in the jeep, because washouts had gutted the roadbed and laid bare the ledges and boulders. He had stuffed the sketch in his hunting-coat pocket, and hung his shotgun over his forearm and started walking, the setter trotting ahead with the bell on his collar tinkling. It was an old-fashioned sleighbell, and it had a thin silvery note that echoed through the woods like peepers in the spring. He could follow the sound in the thickest cover, and when it stopped he would go to where he heard it last and Shad would be on point. After Shad's death, he had put the bell away. He'd never had another dog.

It was silent in the woods without the bell, and the way was longer than he remembered. He should have come to the big hill by now. Maybe he'd taken the wrong turn back at the fork. He thrust a hand into his hunting coat; the envelope with the sketch was still in the pocket. He sat down on a flat rock to get his bearings, and then he realized, with a surge of excitement, that he had stopped on this very rock for lunch ten years ago. Here was the waxed paper from his sandwich, tucked in a crevice, and here was the hollow in the leaves where Shad had stretched out beside him, the dog's soft muzzle flattened on his thigh. He looked up, and through the trees he could see the hill.

He rose and started walking again, carrying his shotgun. He had left the gun standing in its rack in the kitchen when he had been taken to the state hospital, but now it was hooked over his arm by the trigger guard; he could feel the solid heft of it. The woods grew more dense as he climbed, but here and there a shaft of sunlight slanted through the trees. "And there were forests ancient as the hills," he thought, " enfolding sunny spots of greenery." Funny that should come back to him now; he hadn't read it since he was a boy. Other things were coming back to him, the smell of dank leaves and sweetfern and frosted apples, the sharp contrast of sun and cool shade, the November stillness before snow. He walked faster, feeling the excitement swell within him.

He paused on the crest of the hill, straining his ears for the faint mutter of the stream below him, but he could not hear it because of the voices. He wished they would stop talking, so he could hear the stream. Someone was saying his name over and over. "Frank, Frank," and he opened his eyes reluctantly

95

and looked up at his sister. Her face was worried, and there was nothing to worry about. He tried to tell her where he was going, but when he moved his lips the words would not form. "What did you say, Frank?" she asked, bending her head lower. "I don't understand." He couldn't make the words any clearer, and she straightened and said to Doc Towle: "It sounded like Tinkhamtown."

"Tinkhamtown?" Dock shook his head. "Never heard him mention any place by that name."

He smiled to himself. Of course he'd never mentioned it to Doc. Things like a secret grouse cover you didn't mention to anyone, not even to as close a friend as Doc was. No, he and Shad were the only ones who knew. They had found it together, that long ago afternoon, and it was their secret.

They had come to the stream — he shut his eyes so he could see it again — and Shad had trotted across the bridge. He had followed more cautiously, avoiding the loose planks and walking along a beam with his shotgun held out to balance himself. On the other side of the stream the road mounted steeply to a clearing in the woods, and he halted before the split-stone foundations of a house, the first of the series of farms shown on the map. It must have been a long time since the building had fallen in; the cottonwoods growing in the cellar hole were twenty, maybe thirty years old. His boot overturned a rusted ax blade and the handle of a china cup in the grass, that was all. Beside the doorstep was a lilac bush, almost as tall as the cottonwoods. He thought of the wife who had set it out, a little shrub then, and the husband who had chided her for wasting time on such frivolous things with all the farm work to be done. But the work had come to nothing, and still the lilac bloomed each spring, the one thing that had survived.

Shad's bell was moving along the stone wall at the edge of the clearing, and he strolled after him, not hunting, wondering about the people who had gone away and left their walls to crumble and their buildings to collapse under the winter snows. Had they ever come back to Tinkhamtown? Were they here now, watching him unseen? His toe stubbed against a block of hewn granite hidden by briars, part of the sill of the old barn. Once it had been a tight barn, warm with cattle steaming in

96

their stalls, rich with the blend of hay and manure and harness leather. He liked to think of it the way it was; it was more real than this bare rectangle of blocks and the emptiness inside. He'd always felt that way about the past. Doc used to argue that what's over is over, but he would insist Doc was wrong. Everything is the way it was, he'd tell Doc. The past never changes. You leave it and go on to the present, but it is still there, waiting for you to come back to it.

He had been so wrapped in his thoughts that he had not realized Shad's bell had stopped. He hurried across the clearing, holding his gun ready. In a corner of the stone wall an ancient apple tree had littered the ground with fallen fruit, and beneath it Shad was standing motionless. The white fan of his tail was lifted a little and his backline was level, the neck craned forward, one foreleg cocked. His flanks were trembling with the nearness of grouse, and a thin skein of drool hung from his jowls. The dog did not move as he approached, but the brown eyes rolled back until their whites showed, looking for him. "Steady, boy," he called. His throat was tight, the way it always got when Shad was on point, and he had to swallow hard. "Steady, I'm coming."

"I think his lips moved just now," his sister's voice said. He did not open his eyes, because he was waiting for the grouse to get up in front of Shad, but he knew Doc Towle was looking at him. "He's sleeping," Doc said after a moment.

"Maybe you better get some sleep yourself, Mrs. Duncombe."

He heard Doc's heavy footsteps cross the room. "Call me if there's any change," Doc said, and closed the door, and in the silence he could hear his sister's chair creaking beside him, her silk dress rustling regularly as she breathed.

What was she doing here, he wondered. Why had she come all the way from California to see him? It was the first time they had seen each other since she had married and moved out West. She was his only relative, but they had never been very close; they had nothing in common, really. He heard from her now and then, but it was always the same letter: why didn't he sell the old home place, it was too big for him now that the folks had passed on, why didn't he take a small apartment in town where he wouldn't be alone? But he liked the big house, and

97

he wasn't alone, not with Shad. He had closed off the other rooms and moved into the kitchen so everything would be handy. His sister didn't approve of his bachelor ways, but it was very comfortable with his cot by the stove and Shad curled on the floor near him at night, whinnying and scratching the linoleum with his claws as he chased a bird in a dream. He wasn't alone when he heard that.

He had never married. He had looked after the folks as long as they lived; maybe that was why. Shad was his family. They were always together — Shad was short for Shadow — and there was a closeness between them that he did not feel for anyone else, not his sister or Doc even. He and Shad used to talk without words, each knowing what the other was thinking, and they could always find one another in the woods. He still remembered the little things about him: the possessive thrust of his paw, the way he false-yawned when he was vexed, the setter stubbornness sometimes, the clownish grin when they were going hunting, the kind eyes. That was it; Shad was the kindest person he had ever known.

They had not hunted again after Tinkhamtown. The old dog had stumbled several times walking back to the jeep, and he had to carry him in his arms the last hundred yards. It was hard to realize he was gone. He liked to think of him the way he was; it was like the barn, it was more real than the emptiness. Sometimes at night, lying awake with the pain in his legs, he would hear the scratching again, and he would be content and drop off to sleep, or what passed for sleep in these days and nights that ran together without dusk or dawn.

Once he asked Doc point blank if he would ever get well. Doc was giving him something for the pain, and he hesitated a moment and finished what he was doing and cleaned the needle and then looked at him and said: "I'm afraid not, Frank." They had grown up in town together, and Doc knew him too well to lie. "I'm afraid there's nothing to do." Nothing to do but lie here and wait till it was over. "Tell me, Doc," he whispered, for his voice wasn't very strong, "what happens when it's over?" And Doc fumbled with the catch of his black bag and closed it and said well he supposed you went on to someplace else called the Hereafter. But he shook his head; he always

98

argued with Doc. "No, it isn't someplace else," he told him, "it's someplace you've been where you want to be again." Doc didn't understand, and he couldn't explain it any better. He knew what he meant, but the shot was taking effect and he was tired.

He was tired now, and his legs ached a little as he started down the hill, trying to find the stream. It was too dark under the trees to see the sketch he had drawn, and he could not tell direction by the moss on the north side of the trunks. The moss grew all around them, swelling them out of size, and huge blowdowns blocked his way. Their upended roots were black and misshapen, and now instead of excitement he felt a surge of panic. He floundered through a pile of slash, his legs throbbing with pain as the sharp points stabbed him, but he did not have the strength to get to the other side and he had to back out again and circle. He did not know where he was going. It was getting late, and he had lost the way. There was no sound in the woods, nothing to guide him, nothing but his sister's chair creaking and her breath catching now and then in a dry sob. She wanted him to turn back, and Doc wanted him to, they all wanted him to turn back. He thought of the big house; if he left it alone it would fall in with the winter snows and cottonwoods would grow in the cellar hole. And there were all the other doubts, but most of all there was the fear. He was afraid of the darkness, and being alone, and not knowing where he was going. It would be better to turn around and go back. He knew the way back.

And then he heard it, echoing through the woods like peepers in the spring, the thin silvery tinkle of a sleighbell. He started running toward it, following the sound down the hill. His legs were strong again, and he hurdled the blowdowns, he leapt over fallen logs, he put one fingertip on a pile of slash and sailed over it like a grouse skimmering. He was getting nearer and the sound filled his ears, louder than a thousand churchbells ringing, louder than all the choirs in the sky, as loud as the pounding of his heart. The fear was gone; he was not lost. He had the bell to guide him now.

He came to the stream, and paused for a moment at the bridge. He wanted to tell them he was happy, if they only knew how happy he was, but when he opened his eyes he could not see them anymore. Everything else was bright, but the room was dark.

The bell had stopped, and he looked across the stream. The other side was bathed in sunshine, and he could see the road mounting steeply, and the clearing in the woods, and the apple tree in a corner of the stone wall. Shad was standing motionless beneath it, the white fan of his tail lifted, his neck craned forward and one foreleg cocked. The whites of his eyes showed as he looked back, waiting for him.

"Steady," he called, "steady, boy." He started across the bridge. "I'm coming."

The Road to Tinkhamtown by Corey Ford, copyright© 1970 by Holt, Rinehart & Winston, Inc., is reprinted by permission of Harold Ober Associates Incorporated.

The Bear

It was Old Ben who taught him courage and honor and pity and pride ... and that whatever the heart holds to, becomes truth.

by William Faulkner

He was ten. But it had already begun, long before that day when at last he wrote his age in two figures and he saw for the first time the camp where his father and Major de Spain and old General Compson and the other spent two weeks each November and two weeks again each June. He had already inherited then, without even having seen it, the tremendous bear with one trap-ruined foot which, in an area almost a hundred miles deep, had earned for itself a name, a definite designation like a living man.

He had listened to it for years; the long legend of corn-cribs rifled, of shotes and grown pigs and even calves carried bodily into the woods and devoured, of traps and deadfalls overthrown and dogs mangled and slain, and shotgun and even rifle charges delivered at point-blank range and with no more effect than so many peas blown through a tube by a boy — a corridor of wreck-age and destruction beginning back before he was born, through which sped, not fast but rather with the ruthless and irresistible deliberation of a locomotive, the shaggy tremendous shape.

It ran in his knowledge before ever he saw it. It looked and towered in his dreams before he even saw the unaxed woods where it left its crooked print, shaggy, huge, red-eyed, not malevolent but just big — too big for the dogs which tried to bay it, for the horses which tried to ride it down, for the men and the bullets they fired into it, too big for the very country which was its constricting scope. (He seemed to see it entire with a child's complete divination before he ever laid eyes on either — the doomed wilderness whose edges were being con-stantly and punily gnawed at by men with axes and plows who feared it because it was wilderness, men myriad and nameless even to one another in the land where the old bear had earned a name, through which ran not even a mortal animal but an anachronism, indomitable and invincible, out of an old dead time, a phantom, epitome and apotheosis of the old wild life at which the puny humans swarmed and hacked in a fury of abhorrence and fear, like pygmies about the ankles of a drowsing elephant; the old bear solitary, indomitable and alone, wido-wered, childless and absolved of mortality — old Priam reft of his old wife and having outlived all his sons.

Until he was ten, each November he would watch the wagon containing the dogs and the bedding and food and guns and his father and Tennie's Jim, the Negro, and Sam Fathers, the Indian, son of a slave woman and a Chickasaw chief, depart on the road to town, to Jefferson, where Major de Spain and the others would join them. To the boy, at seven and eight and nine, they were not going into the Big Bottom to hunt bear and deer, but to keep yearly rendezvous with the bear which they did not even intend to kill. Two weeks later they would return, with no trophy, no head and skin. He had not expected it. He had not even been afraid it would be in the wagon. He believed that even after he was ten and his father would let him go too, for those two November weeks, he would merely make another one, along with his father and Major de Spain and General Compson and the others, the dogs which feared to bay it and

102

the rifles and shotguns which failed even to bleed it, in the yearly pageant of the old bear's furious immortality.

Then he heard the dogs. It was in the second week of his first time in the camp. He stood with Sam Fathers against a big oak beside the faint crossing where they had stood each dawn for nine days now hearing the dogs. He had heard them once before, one morning last week — a murmur, sourceless, echoing through the wet woods, swelling presently into separate voices which he could recognize and call by name. He had raised and cocked the gun as Sam told him and stood motionless again while the uproar, the invisible course, swept up and past and faded; it seemed to him that he could actually see the deer, the buck, blond, smoke colored, elongated with speed, fleeing, vanishing, the woods, the gray solitude, still ringing even when the cries of the dogs had died away.

"Now let the hammers down," Sam said.

"You knew they were not coming here too," he said.

"Yes," Sam said. "I want you to learn how to do when you didn't shoot. It's after the chance for the bear or the deer has done already come and gone that men and dogs get killed.!

"Anyway," he said, "it was just a deer."

Then on the tenth morning he heard the dogs again. And he readied the too-long, too-heavy gun as Sam had taught him, before Sam even spoke. But this time it was no deer, no ringing chorus of dogs running strong on a free scent, but a moiling yapping an octave too high, with something more than indesicion and even abjectness in it; not even moving very fast, taking a long time to pass completely out of hearing, leaving even then somewhere in the air that echo thin, slightly hysterical, abject, almost grieving, with no sense of a fleeing, unseen, smoke-colored, grass-eating shape ahead of it, and Sam who had taught him first of all to cock the gun and take position where he could see everywhere, and then never move again, had himself moved up beside him; he could hear Sam breathing at his shoulder and he could see the arched curve of the old man's inhaling nostrils.

"Hah," Sam said, 'Not even running. Walking.'

"Old Ben!" the boy said, "But up here!" he cried. "Way up here!"

"He do it every year, Sam said, "Once. Maybe to see who

103

in camp this time, if he can shoot or not. Whether we got the dog yet that can bay and hold him. He'll take them to the river, then he'll send them back home. We may as well go back, too; see how they look when they come back to camp."

When they reached the camp the hounds were already there, ten of them crouching back under the kitchen, the boy and Sam squatting to peer back into the obscurity where they huddled, quiet, the eyes luminous, glowing at them and vanishing, and no sound, only that effluvium of something more than dog, stronger than dog and not just animal, just beast, because still there had been nothing in front of that abject and almost painful yapping save the solitude, the wilderness, so that when the eleventh hound came in at noon and with all the others watching — even old Uncle Ash, who called himself first a cook — Sam daubed the tattered ear and the raked shoulder with turpentine and axle grease, to the boy it was still no living creature, but the wilderness which leaning for the moment down, had patted lightly once the hound's temerity.

"Just like a man," Sam said. "Just like folks. Put off as long as she could having to be brave, knowing all the time that sooner or later she would have to be brave once to keep on living with herself, and knowing all the time beforehand what was going to happen to her when she done it."

That afternoon, himself on the one-eyed wagon mule which did not mind the smell of blood nor, as they told him, of bear, and with Sam on the other one, they rode for more than three hours through the rapid, shortening winter day. They followed no path, no trail even that he could see; almost at once they were in a country which he had never seen before. Then he knew why Sam had made him ride the mule which would not spook. The sound one stopped short and tried to whirl and bolt even as Sam got down, blowing its breath, jerking and wrenching at the rein while Sam held it, coaxing it forward with his voice, since he could not risk tying it, drawing it forward while the boy got down from the marred one.

Then, standing beside Sam in the gloom of the dying afternoon, he looked down at the rotted overturned log, gutted and scored with claw marks and, in the wet earth beside it, the print of the enormous warped two-toed foot. He knew now what he

104

had smelled when he peered under the kitchen where the dogs huddled. He realized for the first time that the bear which had run in his listening and loomed in his dreams since before he could remember to the contrary, and which, therefore, must have existed in the listening and dreams of his father and Major de Spain and even old General Compson, too, before they began to remember in their turn, was a mortal animal, and that if they had departed for the camp each November without any actual hope of bringing its trophy back, it was not because it could not be slain, but because so far they had had no actual hope to.

"Tomorrow," he said.

"We'll try tomorrow," Sam said. "We ain't got the dog yet."

"We've got eleven. They ran him this morning."

"It won't need but one," Sam said. "He ain't here. Maybe he ain't nowhere. The only other way will be for him to run by accident over somebody that has a gun."

"That wouldn't be me," the boy said. "It will be Walter or Major or — —"

"It might," Sam said. "You watch close in the morning. Because he's smart. That's how come he has lived this long. If he gets hemmed up and has to pick out somebody to run over, he will pick out you."

"How?" the boy said. "How will he know —" He ceased, "You mean he already knows me, that I ain't had time to find out yet whether I —" He ceased again, looking at Sam, the old man whose face revealed nothing until it smiled. He said humbly, not even amazed, "It was me he was watching. I don't reckon he did need to come but once."

The next morning they left the camp three hours before daylight. They rode this time because it was too far to walk, even the dogs in the wagon; again the first gray light found him in a place which he had never seen before, where Sam had placed him and told him to stay and then departed. With the gun which was too big for him, which did not even belong to him, but to Major de Spain, and which he had fired only once — at a stump on the first day, to learn the recoil and how to reload it — he stood against a gum tree beside a little bayou whose black still water crept without movement out of a canebrake and crossed a small clearing and into cane again, where, invisible, a bird — the big woodpecker called Lord-to-God by Negroes — clattered at a dead limb.

It was a stand like any other, dissimilar only in incidentals to the one where he had stood each morning for ten days; a territory new to him, yet no less familiar than that other one which, after almost two weeks, he had come to believe he knew a little — the same solitude, the same loneliness through which human beings had merely passed without altering it, leaving no mark, no scar, which looked exactly as it must have looked when the first ancestor of Sam Fathers' Chickasaw predecessors crept into it and looked about, club or axe or bone arrow drawn and poised; different only because, squatting at the edge of the kitchen, he smelled the hounds huddled and cringing beneath it and saw the raked ear and shoulder of the one who, Sam said, had had to be brave once in order to live with herself, and saw yesterday in the earth beside the gutted log the print of the living foot.

He heard no dogs at all. He never did hear them. He only heard the drumming of the woodpecker stop short off and knew that the bear was looking at him. He never saw it. He did not know whether it was in front of him or behind him. He did not move, holding the useless gun, which he had not even had warning to cock and which even now he did not cock, tasting in his saliva that taint as of brass which he knew now because he had smelled it when he peered under the kitchen at the huddled dogs.

Then it was gone. As abruptly as it had ceased, the woodpecker's dry, monotonous clatter set up again, and after a while he even believed he could hear the dogs — a murmur, scarce a sound even, which he had probably been hearing for some time before he even remarked it, drifting into hearing and then out again, dying away. They came nowhere near him. If it was a bear they ran, it was another bear. It was Sam himself who came out of the cane and crossed the bayou, followed by the injured bitch of yesterday. She was almost at heel, like a dog, making no sound. She came and crouched against his leg, trembling, staring off into the cane.

I didn't see him,' he said, 'I didn't, Sam!'

"I know it," Sam said. "He done the looking. You didn't hear

106

him neither, did you?"

"No," the boy said. "I — —"

"He's smart, Sam said, "Too smart." He looked down at the hound, trembling faintly and steadily against the boy's knee. From the raked shoulder a few drops of fresh blood oozed and clung. "Too big. We ain't got the dog yet. But maybe someday. Maybe not next time. But someday."

So I must see him, he thought. *I must look at him.* Otherwise, it seemed to him that it would go on like this forever, as it had gone on with his father and Major de Spain, who was older than his father, and even with old General Compson, who had been old enough to be a brigade commander in 1865. Otherwise, it would go on so forever, next time and next time, after and after and after. It seemed to him that he could see the two of them, himself and the bear, shadowy in the limbo from which time emerged, becoming time; the old bear absolved of mortality and himself partaking, sharing a little of it, enough of it. And he knew now what he had smelled in the huddled dogs and tasted in his saliva. He recognized fear. *So I will have to see him*, he thought, *without dread or even hope, I will have to look at him.*

It was in June of the next year. He was eleven. They were in camp again, celebrating Major de Spain's and General Compson's birthdays. Although the one had been born in September and the other in the depth of winter and in another decade, they had met for two weeks to fish and shoot squirrels and turkey and run coons and wildcats with the dogs at night. That is, he and Boon Hoggenbeck and the Negroes fished and shot squirrels and ran the coons and cats, because the proved hunters, not only Major de Spain and old General Compson, who spent those two weeks sitting in a rocking chair before a tremendous iron pot of Brunswick stew, stirring and tasting, with old Ash to quarrel with about how he was making it and Tennie's Jim to pour whiskey from the demijohn into the tin dipper from which he drank it, but even the boy's father and Walter Ewell, who were still young enough, scorned such, other than shooting the wild gobblers with pistols for wagers on their marksmanship.

Or, that is, his father and the others believed he was hunting squirrels. Until the third day he thought that Sam Fathers

107

believed that too. Each morning he would leave the camp right after breakfast. He had his own gun now, a Christmas present. He went back to the tree beside the little bayou where he had stood that morning. Using the compass which old General Compson had given him, he ranged from that point; he was teaching himself to be a better-than-fair woodsman without knowing he was doing it. On the second day he even found the gutted log where he had first seen the crooked print. It was almost completely crumbled now, healing with unbelievable relinquishment, back into the earth from which the tree had grown.

He ranged the summer woods now, green with gloom; if anything, actually dimmer than in November's gray dissolution, where, even at noon, the sun fell only in intermittent dappling upon the earth, which never completely dried out and which crawled with snakes — moccasins and water snakes and rattlers, themselves the color of the dappled gloom, so that he would not always see them until they moved, returning later and later, first day, second day, passing in the twilight of the third evening the little log pen enclosing the log stable where Sam was putting up the horses for the night.

"You ain't looked right yet," Sam said.

He stopped. For a moment he didn't answer. Then he said peacefully, in a peaceful rushing burst as when a boy's miniature dam in a little brook gives way, "All right. But how? I went to the bayou. I even found that log again. I — —"

"I reckon that was all right. Likely he's been watching you. You never saw his foot?"

"I," the boy said — "I didn't — I never thought —"

"It's the gun," Sam said. He stood beside the fence, motionless — the old man, the Indian, in the battered faded overalls and the frayed five-cent straw hat which in the Negro's race had been the badge of his enslavement and was now the regalia of his freedom. The camp — the clearing, the house, the barn and its tiny lot with which Major de Spain in his turn had scratched punily and evanescently at the wilderness faded in the dusk, back into the immemorial darkness of the woods. *The gun*, the boy thought. *The gun.*

"Be scared," Sam said. "You can't help that. But don't be afraid. Ain't nothing in the woods going to hurt you unless you corner it,

108

or it smells that you are afraid. A bear or a deer, too, has got to be scared of a coward the same as a brave man has got to be.

The gun, the boy thought.

"You will have to choose," Sam said.

He left the camp before daylight, long before Uncle Ash would wake in his quilts on the kitchen floor and start the fire for breakfast. He had only the compass and a stick for snakes. He could go almost a mile before he would begin to need the compass. He sat on a log, the invisible compass in his invisible hand, while the secret night sounds, fallen still at his movements, scurried again and then ceased for good, and the owls ceased and gave over to the waking of day birds and he could see the compass. Then he went fast yet still quietly; he was becoming better and better as a woodsman, still without having yet realized it.

He jumped a doe and a fawn at sunrise, walked them out of the bed, close enough to see them — the crash of undergrowth, the white scut, the fawn scudding behind her faster than he had believed it could run. He was hunting right, upwind, as Sam had taught him; not that it mattered now. He had left the gun; of his own will and relinquishment he had accepted not a gambit, not a choice, but a condition in which not only the bear's heretofore inviolable anonymity but all the old rules and balances of hunter and hunted had been abrogated. He would not even be afraid, not even in the moment when the fear would take him completely — blood, skin, bowels, bones, memory from the long time before it became his memory — all save, that thin, clear, quenchless, immortal lucidity which alone differed him from this bear and from all the other bear and deer he would ever kill in the humility and pride of his skill and endurance, to which Sam had spoken when he leaned in the twilight on the lot fence yesterday.

By noon he was far beyond the little bayou, farther into the new and alien country than he had ever been. He was traveling now not only by the compass but by the old, heavy, biscuit-thick silver watch which had belonged to his grandfather. When he stopped at last, it was for the first time since he had risen from the log at dawn when he could see the compass. It was far enough. He had left the camp nine hours ago; nine hours from now, dark would have already been an hour old. But he didn't think that. He thought, *All right. Yes. But what?* and stood for a moment, alien and small in the green and topless solitude, answering his own question before it had formed and ceased. It was the watch, the compass, the stick — the three lifeless mechanicals with which for nine hours he had fended the wilderness off; he hung the watch and compass carefully on a bush and leaned the stick beside them and relinquished completely to it.

He had not been going very fast for the last two or three hours. He went no faster now, since distance would not matter even if he could have gone fast. And he was trying to keep a bearing on the tree where he had left the compass, trying to complete a circle which would bring him back to it or at least intersect itself, since direction would not matter now either. But the tree was not there, and he did as Sam had schooled him — made the next circle in the opposite direction, so that the two patterns would bisect somewhere, but crossing no print of his own feet, finding the tree at last, but in the wrong place — no bush, no compass, no watch — and the tree not even the tree, because there was a down log beside it and he did what Sam Fathers had told him was the next thing and the last.

As he sat down on the log he saw the crooked print — the warped, tremendous, two-toed indentation which, even as he watched it, filled with water. As he looked up, the wilderness coalesced, solidified — the glade, the tree he sought, the bush, the watch and the compass glinting where a ray of sunlight touched them. Then he saw the bear. It did not emerge, appear; it was just there, immobile, solid, fixed in the hot dappling of the green and windless noon, not as big as he had dreamed it, but as big as he had expected it, bigger dimensionless against the dappled obscurity, looking at him where he sat quietly on the log and looked back at it.

Then it moved. It made no sound. It did not hurry. It crossed the glade, walking for an instant into the full glare of the sun; when it reached the other side it stopped again and looked back at him across one shoulder while his quiet breathing inhaled and exhaled three times.

Then it was gone. It didn't walk into the woods, the under-

110

growth. It faded, sank back into the wilderness as he had watched a fish, a huge old bass, sink and vanish back into the dark depths of its pool without even any movement of its fins.

He thought, *It will be next fall.* But it was not next fall nor the next nor the next. He was fourteen then. He had killed his buck, and Sam Fathers had marked his face with the hot blood, and in the next year he killed a bear. But even before that accolade he had become as competent in the woods as many grown men with the same experience; by his fourteenth year he was a better woodsman than most grown men with more. There was no territory within thirty miles of the camp that he did not know — bayou, ridge, brake, landmark tree and path. He could have led anyone to any point in it without deviation, and brought them out again. He knew game trails that even Sam Fathers did not know; in his thirteenth year he found a buck's bedding place, and unbeknown to his father he borrowed Walter Ewell's rifle and lay in wait at dawn and killed the buck when it walked back to the bed, as Sam had told him how the old Chickasaw fathers did.

But not the old bear, although by now he knew its footprint better than he did his own, and not only the crooked one. He could see any one of the three sound ones and distinguish it from any other, and not only by its size. There were other bears within those thirty miles which left tracks almost as large, but this was more than that. If Sam Fathers had been his mentor and the back-yard rabbits and squirrels at home his kindergarten, then the wilderness the old bear ran was his college, the old male bear itself, so long unwifed and childless as to have become its own ungendered progenitor, was his alma mater. But he never saw it.

He could find the crooked print now almost whenever he liked, fifteen or ten or five miles, or sometimes nearer the camp than that. Twice while on stand during the three years he heard the dogs strike its trail by accident; on the second time they jumped it seemingly, the voices high, abject, almost human in hysteria, as on that first morning two years ago. But not the bear itself. He would remember that noon three years ago, the glade, himself and the bear fixed during that moment in the windless and dappled blaze, and it would seem to him that it

111

had never happened, that he had dreamed that too. But it had happened. They had looked at each other, they had emerged from the wilderness old as earth, synchronized to that instant by something more than the blood that moved the flesh and bones which bore them and touched, pledged something, affirmed something more lasting than the frail web of bones and flesh which any accident could obliterate.

Then he saw it again. Because of the very fact that he thought of nothing else, he had forgotten to look for it. He was still-hunting with Walter Ewell's rifle. He saw it cross the end of a long blowdown, a corridor where a tornado had swept, rushing through rather than over the tangle of trunks and branches as a locomotive would have, faster than he had ever believed it could move, almost as fast as a deer even, because a deer would have spent most of that time in the air, faster than he could bring the rifle sights up to it, so that he believed the reason he never let off the shot was that he was still behind it, had never caught up with it. And now he knew what had been wrong during all the three years. He sat on a log, shaking, trembling as if he had never seen the woods before nor anything that ran them, wondering with incredulous amazement how he could have forgotten the very thing which Sam Fathers had told him and which the bear itself had proved the next day and had now returned after three years to reaffirm.

And he now knew what Sam Fathers had meant about the right dog, a dog in which size would mean less than nothing. So when he returned alone in April — school was out then, so that the sons of farmers could help with the land's planting, and at last his father had granted him permission, on his promise to be back in four days — he had the dog. It was his own, a mongrel of the sort called by Negroes a fyce, a ratter, itself not much bigger than a rat and possessing that bravery which had long since stopped being courage and had become foolhardiness.

It did not take four days. Alone again, he found the trail on the first morning. It was not a stalk; it was an ambush. He timed the meeting almost as if it were an appointment with a human being. Himself holding the fyce muffled in a feed sack and Sam Fathers with two of the hounds on a piece of plowline rope, they lay down wind of the trail at dawn of the second morning. They were so close that the bear turned without even running, as if in surprised amazement at the shrill and frantic uproar of the released fyce, turning at bay against the trunk of a tree, on its hind feet; it seemed to the boy that it would never stop rising, taller and taller, and even the two hounds seemed to take a sort of desperate and despairing courage from the fyce, following it as it went in.

The he realized that the fyce was actually not going to stop. He flung, threw the gun away, and ran; when he overtook and grasped the frantically pin-wheeling little dog, it seemed to him that he was directly under the bear.

He could smell it, strong and hot and rank. Sprawling, he looked up to where it loomed and towered over him like a cloudburst and colored like a thunderclap, quite familiar peacefully and even lucidly familiar, until he remembered. This was the way he had used to dream about it. Then, it was gone. He didn't see it go. He knelt, holding the frantic fyce with both hands, hearing the abased wailing of the hounds drawing farther and farther away, until Sam came up. He carried the gun. He laid it down beside the boy and stood looking down at him.

"You've done seed him twice now with a gun in your hands, he said. "This time you couldn't have missed him."

The boy rose. He still held the fyce. Even in his arms and clear of the ground, it yapped frantically, straining and surging after the fading uproar of the two hounds like a tangle of wire springs. He was panting a little, but he was neither shaking nor trembling now.

"Neither could you!" he said. "You had the gun! Neither did you!"

"And you didn't shoot," his father said. "How close were you?"

"I don't know, sir," he said. "There was a big wood tick inside his right hind leg. I saw that. But I didn't have the gun then."

"But you didn't shoot when you had the gun," his father said. "Why?"

But he didn't answer, and his father didn't wait for him to, rising and crossing the room, across the pelt of the bear which the boy had killed two years ago and the larger one which his father had killed before he was born, to the bookcase beneath

113

the mounted head of the boy's first buck. It was the room which his father called the office, from which all the plantation business was transacted; in it for the fourteen years of his life he had heard the best of all talking. Major de Spain would be there and sometimes old General Compson, and Walter Ewell and Boon Hoggenbeck and Sam Fathers and Tennie's Jim, too, because they, too, were hunters, knew the woods and what ran them.

He would hear it, not talking himself but listening — the wilderness, the big woods, bigger and older than any recorded document of white man fatuous enough to believe he had bought any fragment of it or Indian ruthless enough to pretend that any fragment of it had been his to convey. It was of the men, not white nor black nor red, but men, hunters with the will and hardihood to endure and the humility and skill to survive, and the dogs and the bear and deer juxtaposed and reliefed against it, ordered and compelled by and within the wilderness in the ancient and immitigable rules which voided all regrets and brooked no quarter, the voices quiet and weighty and deliberate for retrospection and recollection and exact remembering, while he squatted in the blazing firelight as Tennie's Jim squatted, who stirred only to put more wood on the fire and to pass the bottle from one glass to another. Because the bottle was always present, so that after a while it seemed to him that those fierce instants of heart and brain and courage and wiliness and speed were concentrated and distilled into that brown liquor which not women, not boys and children, but only hunters drank, drinking not of the blood they had spilled but some condensation of the wild immortal spirit, drinking it moderately, humbly even, not with the pagan's base hope of acquiring thereby the virtues of cunning and strength and speed, but in salute to them.

His father returned with the book and sat down again and opened it. "Listen," he said. He read the five stanzas aloud, his voice quiet and deliberate in the room where there was no fire now because it was already spring. Then he looked up. The boy watched him. "All right," his father said. "Listen." He read again, but only the second stanza this time, to the end of it, the last two lines, and closed the book and put it on the table beside him. "She cannot fade, though thou hast not thy bliss, for ever

114

wilt thou love, and she be fair," he said.

'He's talking about a girl,' the boy said.

'He had to talk about something,' his father said. Then he said, 'He was talking about truth. Truth doesn't change. Truth is one thing. It covers all things which touch the heart — honor and pride and pity and justice and courage and love. Do you see now?''

He didn't know. Somehow it was simpler than that. There was an old bear, fierce and ruthless, not merely just to stay alive, but with the fierce pride of that liberty and freedom, proud enough of that liberty and freedom to see it threatened without fear or even alarm; nay, who at times even seemed deliberately to put that freedom and liberty in jeopardy in order to savor them, to remind his old strong bones and flesh to keep supple and quick to defend and preserve them. There was an old man, son of a Negro slave and an Indian king, inheritor on the one side of the long chronicle of a people who had learned humility through suffering, and pride through the endurance which survived the suffering and injustice, and on the other side, the chronicle of a people even longer in the land than the first, yet who no longer existed in the land at all save in the solitary brotherhood of an old Negro's alien blood and the wild and invincible spirit of an old bear. There was a boy who wished to learn humility and pride in order to become skillful and worthy in the woods, who suddenly found himself becoming so skillful so rapidly that he feared he would never become worthy because he had not learned humility and pride, although he had tried to, until one day and as suddenly he discovered that an old man who could not have defined either had led him, as though by the hand, to that point where an old bear and a little mongrel dog showed him that, by possessing one thing other, he would possess them both.

And a little dog, nameless and mongrel and many-fathered, grown, yet weighing less than six pounds, saying as if to itself, "I can't be dangerous, because there's nothing much smaller than I am; I can't be fierce, because they would call it just noise; I can't be humble, because I'm already too close to the ground to genuflect; I can't be proud, because I wouldn't be near enough to it for anyone to know who was casting that shadow, and I

115

don't even know that I'm not going to heaven, because they have already decided that I don't possess an immortal soul. So all I can be is brave. But it's all right. I can be that, even if they still call it just noise."

That was all. It was simple, much simpler than somebody talking in a book about a youth and a little girl he would never need to grieve over, because he could never approach any nearer her and would never have to get any farther away. He had heard about a bear, and finally got big enough to trail it, and he trailed it four years and at last met it with a gun in his hands and he didn't shoot. Because the little dog —— But he could have shot long before the little dog covered the twenty yards to where the bear waited, and Sam Fathers could have shot at any time during that interminable minute while Old Ben stood on his hind feet over them. He stopped. His father was watching him gravely across the spring-rife twilight of the room; when he spoke, his words were as quiet as the twilight, too, not loud, because they did not need to be because they would last. Courage and honor, and pride, his father said, "and pity, and love of justice and of liberty. They all touch the heart, and what the heart holds to becomes truth, as far as we know truth. Do you see now?"

Sam, and Old Ben, and Nip he thought. And himself too. He had been all right too. His father had said so. "Yes sir," he said.

Tenth Legion

Tenth Legion, Tom Kelly's self-published classic on the wild turkey, has undergone five printings. You'll see why in this condensation of "Spring."

by Tom Kelly

From the middle of May until the first of the following March a turkey gobbler is straight-forward. He is reliable, he is sober and sedate and reasonable. There may from time to time pass through his head erotic flashes of pleasant passages last spring, but these constitute no more than twinkles in his eyes.

Upon occasion, possibly in an excess of fond recollection, he may gobble once or twice. Perhaps this is simply to clear his throat, or perhaps it is just for old times sake. But principally throughout this period he conducts himself and his business with the disciplined dignity of retired colonels in their seventies.

Retired Colonels of Artillery, with white moustaches.

Upon your first meeting with him you would unhesitantly cash his check, solicit his advice on municipal bonds, or approach him hat in hand for a donation to build the county orphanage. He looks and acts as if he were about to be elected Chairman of the Board of Censors.

And then spring comes, and on or about the first of March his behavior patterns change, and the transition of Dr. Jekyll into Mr. Hyde is by comparison a minor aberration.

Dignity not only drops from his shoulders, he uses it to wipe his feet.

The wattles at the base of his neck swell and grow red. Instead of standing still he shifts his weight from one foot to the other all the time, as if the ground were hot. The set of his head upon his neck is different — it leans forward, looking for something. If he had eyebrows, one eyebrow would be raised all the time.

His feathers brighten and take on an iridescence they have not shown previously. He approaches the world and everything in it with the thought processes of a twenty year old who had been at sea for eighteen months.

There is in the air around him an electricity, a magnetism, an aura of bright danger.

He is single minded, dedicated and sole purposed. There is nothing on his mind but girls.

Girls for breakfast, girls for lunch, girls in the middle of the afternoon. Girls for tea and girls for dinner and girls before he goes to bed. And when he does go to bed he flies up and cranes his neck in all directions to pick out the roosting places of nearby girls in order that he will not take a single step in the wrong direction when getting an early start on tomorrow's girls.

None of this interferes with his native caution or with his ingrained suspicion, rather one set of emotions is overlain upon the other; or one instinct upon the other, if you prefer.

The two emotions experienced concurrently make him almost vibrate. I suspect that close to, he hums, like high voltage lines.

His sole purpose in life is lovemaking — as often as possible, as rapidly as possible, and with as many partners as possible. He begrudges the night when he must sleep and thereby interrupt the pressing business of his days.

He is cocked — all the time.

So single functioned and so dedicated is he in his purpose now, that he frequently neglects to eat. A gobbler who means

118

it and is tending to his business (and during this time of the year it is difficult to find a gobbler who is not so occupied) will quite often lose two or three pounds during the spring — an amount that approaches twenty percent of his body weight.

He will strut and drum for as much as half an hour at a time. Strutting is technically supposed to be done to attract the female, and to do it he drops his wings until their ends drag upon the ground. I have seen turkeys who had worn off the outer four or five primaries, strutting, as cleanly as if they had been cut off with scissors. When he struts he stands the tail feathers upright and spreads them out in a fan. His head is drawn back in between what would be his shoulders, if he had shoulders, and he walks in a measured and stately manner.

I am not a hen turkey, and therefore presumably cannot adequately judge what is attractive to a hen turkey, but my private opinion is that he looks ridiculous.

A creature who is normally the epitome of slim, sleek alertness, whose feathers lie close to the body, smooth and luminous to the point of being burnished, who normally moves as if all his joints were oiled, turns all of a sudden into a clumsy ball. Every feather looks as if had been plucked out and then glued back on, wrong side to. The neck, which had a sinuous, flowing, and nearly serpentine grace is cramped back into his shoulders in the posture of a retired 80-year-old bookkeeper with arthritis.

He drums often. This sound, which Audubon calls the pulmonic puff, defies description. It is not, to me at any rate, audible at distances beyond seventy or eighty yards. A poor approximation of its sound is to say "shut" as quickly and as explosively as you can with the tongue against the front teeth, and then say "varoom" in two syllables, with the "oom" coming up out of the diaphragm and drawn out and resonated against the roof of the mouth as much as possible. When I hear it in the woods I do not so much hear the sound as I feel it under my breast bone. It is ventriloquistic, pervading and is a sensation partway between sound and vibration.

This sound is far from ridiculous. It personifies wilderness and solitude and lonely places. Nothing in my experience approaches it in this respect except the wild, far-off calling of geese at night, drifting down out of an early autumn sky.

119

A turkey even during this season does naturally have to eat a little. He is after all a bird, and the metabolic processes of a bird are far more active than those of any mammal, saving some of the shrews. There are birds for instance with body temperatures of 105° when normal, and with extremely fast heartbeats. And while a turkey is not keyed to the same pitch as a warbler, he is tuned pretty high. But during this period he eats seldom and what he does eat he eats quickly, and acts as if everything he took was tasteless. He is edgy and fidgety and nervous and appears to have his nerve not only exposed, but sticking out an inch or two, like antennae.

He has become not so much a bird as a psychological force. He reminds you of a good general. When you are in the company of the right kind of general officer you are not so much in contact with a man as you are with a presence. A turkey, tuned to the pitch at which he stays throughout the spring, is such a presence.

He will now stake out his own territory, his *lek,* and restrict his movements largely to that location. He may move away some from time to time, go off to visit maybe, but it is not at all uncommon to find the same turkey gobbling on the same five acres every morning and roosting there at night, too.

He will gobble a little in the afternoon. He often gobbles once after he flies up to roost at night, but he gobbles primarily first thing in the morning. And he will begin to gobble sometimes as much as fifteen or twenty mintues before daylight, especially if he is a river swamp turkey.

River swamp turkeys for some reason begin to gobble noticeably earlier on any given morning than do hill turkeys. And from the standpoint of the hunter it is fortunate that they do so. As clean and open as a big river swamp can be, you would never be able to get close enough to call him if he waited till daylight to begin. He would see you coming and hush, a long time before you got there, if you couldn't go to him in the dark.

On any morning that you go to hunt you will be in the woods at daylight or preferably fifteen minutes before. You will have left your car and will have walked to the place from which you intend to listen. And then you are going to prop your gun up against a tree and wait.

If you have gotten there as early as you should, the first thing

120

you are going to hear is nothing. Nothing but you is up yet. The only birds awake are a few owls and an occasional tardy whip-poor-will that hasn't knocked off and gone home to bed. Deer are still abroad, and you will hear them shuffling off ahead of you or boiling in herds out of thickets with all the ill bred snorting and blowing of which they are capable. Possums and coons will still be prowling and you will hear some of these. But all of these things are night creatures that are supposed to be up. The only day creature there is you.

Just as the sky in the east begins to change from black into a steely blue-white, the owls will begin to sound off, and then the cardinals, and late in the spring, the yellow billed cuckoos. These three birds make by far most of the noise, though there are dozens and dozens of lesser bird noises in the background.

I have no idea how far you can hear an owl — one who is really leaning into his hoot and means it. I sometimes think it is like the folk song, the one that says "you can hear the whistle blow a hundred miles," but it is a hell of a long way, and early in the morning like this, most of them sound as if they were calling from across the River Styx.

It is a lovely time of the year. There is as yet not much color to the woods but there are some early hints and stirrings, mostly muted pastels or pale chalks with only two or three brights for contrast. The shrub form of Buckeye is in full leaf and flower, and the Red pale is in fruit. Both the buckeye flower and the maple seed are a bright red — a gaudy, primitive, barbaric red. Blackberry, sweetgum, and huckleberry will be in the beginning of early leaf in the understory, and witch hazel, tag alder and river birch in the middle story with both stories in pale, pale greens. All the oaks are in catkins, the long fuzzy strings that come before the leaf, and make a background of pale buff and brown. Dogwood shows occasional streaks of white, and in the swamps the yellow top makes splashes of chromium yellow.

Only rarely, and then only early in the year is there a hint of frost. Mostly the forest floor is a flat brown. Other than the floor, none of the colors are in masses but the catkins of the oaks. The sharper colors occur as isolated highlights scattered here and there at random.

When the owls come into full voice, just at daylight, turkeys

121

will often gobble back at them. I don't know why turkeys gobble at owls but they do, and most men who kill a lot of turkeys have learned to do at least a presentable imitation of an owl, and do it.

Turkeys gobble primarily for girls, either to attract them or to let other turkey gobblers know they are on the job; that the situation is comfortably in hand, and that they need no help in handling anything that comes up. They can handle all the girls in hearing, thank you. But they do have a proclivity for gobbling at sudden sounds. Sometimes I think they may do it for the same reason that a man shouts in the woods. For high spirits, just for the hell of it, to hear it ring down through the trees and hear the echo come back.

Turkeys will, for I have heard them, gobble at saw mill whistles, at train and tugboat horns, at thunder, at owls as we said, at the slamming of a car door, at crows, and at each other. Once, on an artillery range, I heard two turkeys gobble at the sound of the first round arriving at the registration point.

The purpose in hooting like an owl (I do not really recommend slamming car doors or firing off artillery pieces) is to get a turkey to gobble who didn't really mean to do it — finesse him into it as it were.

There are mornings when every turkey in the county will begin to gobble at daylight, and will do it so much it sounds as if he were in danger of choking himself. The very next morning you can go and stand in yesterday's footprints, as far as you can tell under identical conditions of wind, temperature, and barometric pressure, and you will stand in the midst of silence.

These are the days when you must trick him into gobbling, or surprise him into it, because until he gobbles you do not know where he is and so you cannot get to him. You want to get within two hundred yards of the tree he is sitting in, gobbling, before he flies down, in order to try to call him to you from there. You want, very badly, to get there before he flies down if you can, and you have absolutely no idea of how long that is going to be. Sometimes he will stay on the limb fifteen minutes, sometimes an hour and a half, and since you never know ahead of time which one it will be you need to get there quickly. Since it is possible for you to hear him at half a mile or better, it makes for an awfully interesting athletic contest conducted at daylight in the woods on calm spring mornings. The fat businessman's quarter-mile dash, with shotgun.

The reason you want to get to him so quickly is that unlike with men, courting with turkeys goes both ways, girls seeking out boys if anything even more avidly than the reserve, and your chances are immensely improved if you can get to his tree before the ladies do.

They can come in from the opposite direction, of course, and shut you off, but if you are quick you will be right half the time at least. Furthermore, so long as he stays in the tree and gobbles, you know exactly where he is. After he flies down he is apt to move. You can tell if he is still up, or if he has flown down by the sound of his gobble, it sounds considerably muffled and has less clarity after he is on the ground.

The point is though, that until he gobbles the first time, either on his own or until you have tricked him into it, you could be within a hundred yards of a turkey in the dark, or be beyond three quarters of a mile from one and not know the difference.

A turkey can gobble only one time and give you direction. But direction is only half of what you need. The other necessary element you need is distance, and unless he is very close when he first gobbles, you cannot tell exactly how far away he is. Experience will help you here to a degree, but a turkey can gobble at different levels of volume. If he is still on the roost when he gobbles he could be looking in the other direction, which changes the level of sound and helps to build confusion.

It is generally-considered safest to start toward him the minute you hear him, and if he will gobble three or four more times at reasonably spaced intervals, you can get his location fixed and get to the proper place to try to kill him.

All kinds of things can happen during this procedure, which in military circles is called a movement to contact.

Assuming he did not sound so far away when he first gobbled that you considered it impossible, you can, because you know the country, know that there is impassable water between you and him and so you cannot go. Or you can start and find some obstacle in your way that you were not aware of. Later in the spring, with many of the trees in leaf and the wood thickening,

123

sound carries much more poorly. A turkey that sounds as loud the last of April as he sounded the last of March may be three hundred yards nearer than he sounds. It adds one more little uncertainty to what is often already a cloudy affair.

You can start toward a gobbling turkey who is so far away that he does not gobble regularly enough for you to get there. This can be the most frustrating of all. You go as far as you dare, and then stand there shifting from one foot to the other. You don't know whether to sit where you are and yelp at imagination, or to keep going in what you think is the proper direction at the very real risk of running him off or hushing him up.

The point to be taken here, though, is that whether he gobbled on his own, or whether you have tricked him into doing it, he almost has to do it more than once unless he is very close, and throughout the whole approach the contact having been established by him must be maintained by him. During this period you are absolutely under his control and are utterly at his whim.

There are some very old and very wise turkeys who gobble only a little bit. They cannot be tricked into gobbling very much and they are often silent for two or three days consecutively. If you can find the area one of them is using, you can then go back day after day because even if he is silent, the contact has been partially established — but only partially. Four or five acres is a big place, even if he roosts on the same four or five acres nightly, and he can just as easily be on one side of it as he can be on the other. In such a situation he can perhaps be best located the night before. On still afternoons the sound he will make flying up to roost is so loud as to be shocking after sitting in the quiet for so long. But you must then sit there until darkness comes and lets you slip out, if he is close, and then come back at daylight in the morning.

These kind are tough. These are the kind that people spend the season with. These are the kind that if you do finally kill, you stand and look down upon with real regret because you have established such a close rapport over the days or weeks it took you to kill him.

I have never picked up one like this after killing him without a real sense of loss, a little bit sorry that I had done it, but not sorry enough to quit.

124

Again, while I have no log book to refer to, nor any documents to consult, in thinking back over the years I feel that in dealing with gobbling turkeys you will kill one for every three or four that you work.

Some turkeys are just not going to come. No skill, no expertise in yelping, no combination of moves and countermoves is going to make the least particle of difference. There is no egotism in this either. I do not intend to imply that if I cannot kill a certain turkey then nobody else can kill him either, or that what is impossible for me, is impossible for anyone. I have been humbled and humiliated far too many times to have any shred of an illusion left. I have given turkeys away to experts. To men I knew were experts, who tried three or four or five times and then offered them back. But I had already abandoned hope, and left it abandoned.

There just happen to be turkeys that will gobble on the roost a hundred times. Turkeys you can get to quickly, and hide from easily, and do everything perfectly, and be at the right place at the right time. Turkeys who will then fly down and gobble three hundred times on the ground over a period of two hours. Turkeys who will then come to within 80 yards of where you sit and not one step farther. Turkeys who will parade and strut and drum there, and who wild horses could not drag that last 20 steps.

And there are a thousand stories about what you ought to do to kill them.

I have listened to men seriously discuss scratching in the leaves behind them with their hands, to imitate turkeys feeding. I have heard men say with a perfectly straight face that they took off their hat and slapped it repeatedly on their leg to imitate the wing flapping of a gobbler fight. You can get sacks full of advice about gobbling back at turkeys, or drumming back at them. I have heard all my life nearly, that if a turkey ever answers you he will come there eventually even if you have to sit until noon to wait for him. Maybe he will, but if it takes him that long the hell with it. I am not about to sit in the woods till noon listening to squirrels and bluejays while waiting for turkeys that may be a mile and a half off.

I have never tried scratching in the leaves either, or hitting my leg with my hat. I have never done so because I am convinced that it is going to sound exactly like a man scratching in the leaves

125

with his hand or hitting his leg with his hat.

Gobbling back, I am willing to admit, may work, may be even rarely worth trying. Drumming is just barely within the realm of possibility. But I regard the large body of this kind of advice as being in the same category as saying, "Kitty, kitty, kitty," or standing up and whistling and calling ,"Here, Rattler, here."

I am a big believer in moving. I think that unless a gobbler comes in very quickly, one of the most difficult things in the world is to firmly plant your ass under a tree and stubbornly refuse to move an inch until you have called the turkey up and killed him.

A great many turkeys will come to your calling from the roost and will then take up a regular pattern of movement, first toward you and then away, never coming close enough to shoot and never getting out of hearing, and all the time gobbling every thirty seconds or so. You know where they are every minute of the time but a fat lot of good it does you. I have upon occasion waited them out to the other end of their track, yelped once to turn them back, and then gotten up and ran a fast forty yards toward them and hidden quickly and shut up. Occasionally they will come back gobbling, and when they do stop they are forty yards closer than they think they are, and you can point out this error to them with a Battery, one round.

On just as many occasions I have jumped up to perform this ingenious maneuver and when I got forward and hid I did not ever hear another sound. This led me to believe that the turkey was not as far away as I thought he was when I moved, and when he saw me move he ran off. I have gotten up to move, either forward, or to get around turkeys, have heard them go off on the ground gobbling until they faded out of hearing.

One final word on the whole subject. As much as I believe in it personally and feel comfortable doing it, and recommend it every chance I get, there are places and instances where moving is impossible.

A big river swamp is one of those places.

In the first place it is absolutely flat in there. There may be six-inch ridges from time to time and there are eight-inch depressions, where overcup oak grows. There are some striking falls of a foot and a half down into tupelo or cypress ponds, but there is no other relief — none. In the fall when the sloughs dry up you can get down into the bottom of the slough bed, some six or eight feet below the normal floor, but only for this particular period of the year. Taking advantage of the terrain to move about in river swamps must be left out of your bag of tricks. In almost every case there, you can sit down and see a man walking a quarter of a mile away.

Except in exceptional instances, attempting to move on turkeys in this area is stupid. There will be all kinds of situations that arise with turkeys 200 hundred yards off and in absolutely plain sight and no matter how badly you want to do it, you cannot move.

If there is a rule for river swamps it may be stated simply that where you sit is where you stay.

In plain fact the mere selection of a place to hide and call from in there is extremely difficult. There are some blowdowns of course, and some places where tangles of vines wrap around the base of trees. After the timber has been cut, if single tree selection or patch clear cutting were used, there will be clumps of briars and some low seedlings. Yellow top in the spring will make thick clumps of foliage, often too thick, and there are some patches of palmetto. By and large, though, if you hunt in river swamps, whatever you intend to hide behind you must bring into the swamp with you. Whether you use a roll of camouflage netting or intend to cut bushes, you had better have them with you when you go. In there, as in Macbeth, Birnam Wood must come to Dunsinane.

And you have to hide. Hill or swamp, in the spring you have got to do it. There is all sorts of evidence to suggest that a turkey is color blind. Maybe he is. But he can damn well tell dark colors from light ones, and he is the world's best at picking out motion. Picking it out at a long distance too.

Perhaps in the early fall, if a man could sit with the utter stillness of a professional naturalist, he could depend upon calling up young gobblers, remaining immobile against a dark background, and raising the gun to shoot in one motion at the last. I say maybe only because I am willing to listen to another man's point of view, not because I really believe in it.

To go through life in the spring, dealing with old gobblers, attempting to sit out in the open and depending upon immobility to get the job done, is folly.

127

Nobody, nowhere, no time, is going to get away with it on anything like a regular basis.

From *Tenth Legion,* copyright© 1973 by Tom Kelly, Wingfeather Press.

The Ledge

Every sportsman can relate to this tale ... a grim
reminder of our own vulnerability to the
awesome, unrelenting powers in nature.

by Lawrence Sargent Hall

On Christmas morning before sunup the fisherman
embraced his warm wife and left his close bed. She
did not want him to go. It was Christmas morning.
He was a big, raw man, with too much strength,
whose delight in winter was to hunt the sea ducks that flew in
to feed by the outer ledges, bare at low tide.

As his bare feet touched the cold floor and the frosty air struck
his nude flesh, he might have changed his mind in the dark of
this special day. It was a home day, which made it seem natural
to think of the outer ledges merely as some place he had shot
ducks in the past. But he had promised his son, thirteen, and
his nephew, fifteen, who came from inland. That was why he
had given them his present of an automatic shotgun each the
night before, on Christmas Eve. Rough man though he was

129

known to be, and no spoiler of boys, he kept his promises when he understood what they meant. And to the boys, as to him, home meant where you came for rest after you had your Christmas fill of excitement.

His legs astride, his arms raised, the fisherman stretched as high as he could in the dim privacy of his bedroom. Above the snug murmur of his wife's protest he heard the wind in the pines and knew it was easterly as the boys had hoped and he had surmised the night before. Conditions would be ideal, and when they were, anybody ought to take advantage of them. The birds would be flying. The boys would get a man's sport their first time outside on the ledges.

His son, at thirteen, small but steady and experienced, was fierce to grow up in hunting, to graduate from sheltered waters and the blinds along the shores of the inner bay. His nephew, at fifteen, an overgrown farm boy, had a farm boy's love of the sea, though he could not swim a stroke and was often sick in choppy weather. That was the reason his father, the fisherman's brother, was a farmer and chose to sleep in on the holiday morning at his brother's house. Many of the ones the fisherman had grown up with were regularly seasick and could not swim, but they were unafraid of the water. They could not have dreamed of being anything but fishermen. The fisherman himself could swim like a seal and was never sick, and he would sooner die than be anything else.

He dressed in the cold and dark, and woke the boys gruffly. They tumbled out of bed, their instincts instantly awake while their thoughts still fumbled slumbrously. The fisherman's wife in the adajcent bedroom heard them apparently trying to find their clothes, mumbling sleepily and happily to each other, while her husband went down to the hot kitchen to fry eggs — sunnyside up, she knew, because that was how they all liked them.

Always in the winter she hated to have them go outside, the weather was so treacherous and there were so few others out in case of trouble. To the fisherman these were no more than woman's fears, to be taken for granted and laughed off. When they were first married they fought miserably every fall because she was after him constantly to put his boat up until spring. The fishing was all outside in winter, and though prices were

high the storms made the rate of attrition high on gear. Nevertheless he did well. So she could do nothing with him.

People thought him a hard man, and gave him the reputation
of being all out for himself because he was inclined to brag and
be disdainful. If it was true, and his own brother was one of
those who strongly felt it was, they lived better than others,
and his brother had small right to criticize. There had been times
when in her loneliness she had yearned to leave him for another
man. But it would have been dangerous. So over the years she
had learned to shut her mind to his hard-driving, and take what
comfort she might from his unsympathetic competence. Only
once or twice, perhaps, had she gone so far as to dwell guiltily
on what it would be like to be a widow.

The thought that her boy, because he was small, would not
be insensitive like his father, and the rattle of dishes and smell
of frying bacon downstairs in the kitchen shut off from the rest
of the chilly house, restored the cozy feeling she had had before
she was alone in bed. She heard them after a long while go out
and shut the back door.

Under her window she heard the snow grind dryly beneath
their boots, and her husband's sharp, exasperated commands
to the boys. She shivered slightly in the envelope of her own
warmth. She listened to the noise of her son and nephew talking
elatedly. Twice she caught the glimmer of their lights on the
white ceiling above the window as they went down the path
to the shore. There would be frost on the skiff and freezing
suds at the water's edge. She herself used to go gunning when
she was younger; now, it seemed to her, anyone going out like
that on Christmas morning had to be incurably male. None of
them would think about her until they returned and piled the
birds they had shot on top of the sink for her to dress.

Ripping into the quiet pre-dawn cold she heard the hot snarl
of the outboard taking them out to the boat. It died as abruptly
as it had burst into life. Two or three or four or five minutes
later the big engine broke into a warm reassuring roar. He had
the best of equipment, and he kept it in the best of condition.
The summer drone of the exhaust deepened. Then gradually it
faded in the wind until it was lost at sea, or she slept.

The engine had started immediately in spite of the temperature.

This put the fisherman in a good mood. He was proud of his boat. Together he and the two boys heaved the skiff and outboard onto the stern and secured it athwartships. His son went forward along the deck, iridescent in the ray of the light the nephew shone through the windshield, and cast the mooring pennant loose into darkness. The fisherman swung to starboard, glanced at his compass, and headed seaward down the obscure bay.

There would be just enough visibility by the time they reached the headland to navigate the crooked channel between the islands. It was the only nasty stretch of water. The fisherman had done it often in fog or at night — he always swore he could go anywhere in the bay blindfolded — but there was no sense in taking chances if you didn't have to. From the mouth of the channel he could lay a straight course for Brown Cow Island, anchor the boat out of sight behind it, and from the skiff set their tollers off Devil's Hump three hundred yards to seaward. By then the tide would be clearing the ledge and they could land and be ready to shoot around half-tide.

It was early, it was Christmas, and it was farther out than most hunters cared to go in this season of the year, so that he felt sure no one would be taking possession ahead of them. He had shot thousands of ducks there in his day. The Hump was by far the best hunting. Only thing was you had to plan for the right conditions because you didn't have too much time. About four hours was all, and you had to get it before three in the afternoon when the birds left and went out to sea before nightfall.

They had it figured exactly right for today. The ledge would not be going until after the gunning was over, and they would be home for supper in good season. With a little luck the boys would have a skiff-load of birds to show for their first time outside. Well beyond the legal limit, which was no matter. You took what you could get in this life, or the next man made out and you didn't.

The fisherman had never failed to make out gunning from Devil's Hump. And this trip, he had a hunch, would be above the ordinary. The westerly wind would come up just stiff enough, the tide was right, and it was going to storm by tomorrow morning so the birds would be moving. Things were perfect.

The old fierceness was in his bones. Keeping a weather eye

to the murk out front and a hand on the wheel, he reached over and cuffed both boys playfully as they stood together close to the heat of the exhaust pipe running up through the center of the house. They poked back at him and shouted above the drumming engine, making bets as they always did on who would shoot the most birds. This trip they had the thrill of new guns, the best money could buy, and a man's hunting ground. The black retriever wagged at them and barked. He was too old and arthritic to be allowed in December water, but he was jaunty anyway at being brought along.

Groping in his pocket for his pipe the fisherman suddenly had his high spirits rocked by the discovery that he had left his tobacco at home. He swore. Anticipation of a day out with nothing to smoke made him incredulous. He searched his clothes, and then he searched them again, unable to believe the tobacco was not somewhere. When the boys inquired what was wrong he spoke angrily to them, blaming them for being in some devious way at fault. They were instantly crestfallen and willing to put back after the tobacco, though they could appreciate what it meant only through his irritation. But he bitterly refused. That would throw everything out of phase. He was a man who did things the way he set out to do.

He clamped his pipe between his teeth, and twice more during the next minutes he ransacked his clothes in disbelief. He was no stoic. For one relaxed moment he considered putting about and gunning somewhere nearer home. Instead he held his course and sucked the empty pipe, consoling himself with the reflection that at least he had whiskey enough if it got too uncomfortable on the ledge. Preemptorily he made the boys check to make certain the bottle was really in the knapsack with the lunches where he thought he had taken care to put it. When they reassured him he despised his fate a little less.

The fisherman's judgment was as usual accurate. By the time they were abreast of the headland there was sufficient light so that he could wind his way among the reefs without slackening speed. At last he turned his bow toward open ocean, and as the winter dawn filtered upward through long layers of smoky cloud on the eastern rim, his spirits rose again with it.

He opened the throttle, steadied on his course, and settled

133

down to the two-hour run. The wind was stronger but seemed less cold coming from the sea. The boys had withdrawn from the fisherman and were talking together while they watched the sky through the windows. The boat churned solidly through a light chop, flinging spray off her flaring bow. Astern the headland thinned rapidly till it lay like a blackened sill on the grey water. No other boats were abroad.

The boys fondled their new guns, sighted along the barrels, worked the mechanisms, compared notes, boasted, and gave each other contradictory advice. The fisherman got their attention once and pointed at the horizon. They peered through the windows and saw what looked like a black scum floating on top of gently agitated water. It wheeled and tilted, rippled, curled, then rose, strung itself out and became a huge raft of ducks escaping over the sea. A good sign.

The boys rushed out and leaned over the washboards in the wind and spray to see the flock curl below the horizon. Then they went and hovered around the hot engine, bewailing their lot. If only they had been already set out and waiting. Maybe these ducks would be crazy enough to return later and be slaughtered. Ducks were known to be foolish.

In due course and right on schedule they anchored at mid-morning in the lee of Brown Cow Island. They put the skiff overboard and loaded it with guns, knapsacks, and tollers. The boys showed their eagerness by being clumsy. The fisherman showed his bad temper and abuse which they silently accepted in the absurd tolerance of being boys. No doubt they laid it to lack of tobacco.

By outboard they rounded the island and pointed due east in the direction of a ridge of foam which could be seen whitening the surface three hundred yards away. They set the decoys in a broad, straddling vee opening into the ocean. The fisherman warned them not to get their hands wet, and when they did he made them carry on with red and painful fingers in order to teach them. Once the last roller was bobbing among his fellows, brisk and alluring, they got their numbed fingers inside their oilskins and hugged their warmed crotches. In the meantime the fisherman had turned the skiff toward the patch of foam where as if by magic, like a black glossy rib of earth, the ledge had broken through the belly of the sea.

Carefully they inhabited their slippery nub of the North American continent, while the unresting Atlantic swelled and swirled as it had for eons round the indomitable edges. They hauled the skiff after them, established themselves as comfortably as they could in a shallow sump on top, lay on their sides a foot or so above the water, and waited, guns in hand.

In time the fisherman took a thermos bottle from the knapsack and they drank steaming coffee, and waited for the nodding decoys to lure in the first flight to the rock. Eventually the boys got hungry and restless. The fisherman let them open the picnic lunch and eat one sandwich apiece, which they both shared with the dog. Having no tobacco the fisherman himself would not eat.

Actually the day was relatively mild, and they were warm enough at present in their woollen clothes and socks underneath oilskins and hip boots. After a while, however, the boys began to feel cramped. Their nerves were agonized by inactivity. The nephew complained and was severely told by the fisherman — who pointed to the dog, crouched unmoving except for his white rimmed eyes — that part of doing a man's hunting was learning how to wait. But he was beginning to have misgivings of his own. This could be one of those days where all the right conditions masked an incalculable flaw.

If the fisherman had been alone, as he often was, stopping off when the necessary coincidence of tide and time occurred on his way home from hauling trawls, and had plenty of tobacco, he would not have fidgeted. The boys' being nervous made him nervous. He growled at them again. When it came it was likely to come all at once, and then in a few moments be over. He warned them not to slack off, never to slack off, to be always ready. Under his rebuke they kept their tortured peace, though they could not help shifting and twisting until he lost what patience he had left and bullied them into lying still. A duck could see an eyelid twitch. If the dog could go without moving so could they.

"Here it comes!" the fisherman said tersely at last.

The boys quivered with quick relief. The flock came in downwind, quartering slightly, myriad, black, and swift.

135

"Beautiful —" breathed the fisherman's son.

"All right," said the fisherman, intense and precise. "Aim at singles in the thickest part of the flock. Wait for me to fire and then don't stop shooting till your gun's empty." He rolled up onto his left elbow and spread his legs to brace himself. The flock bore down, arrowy and vibrant, then a hundred yards beyond the decoys it veered off.

"They're going away!" the boys cried, sighting in.

"Not yet!" snapped the fisherman. "They're coming round."

The flock changed shape, folded over itself, and drove into the wind in a tight arc. "Thousands —" the boys hissed through their teeth. All at once a whistling storm of black and white broke over the decoys.

"Now!" the fisherman shouted. "Perfect!" And he opened fire at the flock just as it hung suspended in momentary chaos above the tollers. The three pulled at their triggers and the birds splashed into the water, until the last report went off unheard, the last smoking shell flew unheeded over their shoulders, and the last of the routed flock scattered diminishing, diminishing in every direction.

Exultantly the boys dropped their guns, jumped up and scrambled for the skiff.

"I'll handle that skiff!" the fisherman shouted at them. They stopped. Gripping the painter and balancing himself, he eased the skiff into the water stern first and held the bow hard against the side of the rock shelf the skiff had rested on. "You stay here," he said to his nephew. "No sense in all three of us going into the boat."

The nephew gazed at the grey water rising and falling hypnotically along the glistening edge. It had dropped about a foot since their arrival. "I want to go with you," he said in a sullen tone, his eyes on the streaming eddies.

"You want to do what I tell you if you want to gun with me," answered the fisherman harshly. The boy couldn't swim, and he wasn't going to have him climbing in and out of the skiff any more than necessary. Besides, he was too big.

The fisherman took his son in the skiff and cruised round and round among the decoys picking up dead birds. Meanwhile the other boy stared unmoving after them from the highest part of the ledge. Before they had quite finished gathering the dead birds, the fisherman cut the outboard and dropped to his knees in the skiff. "Down!" he yelled. "Get down!" About a dozen birds came tolling in. "Shoot — shoot!" his son hollered from the bottom of the boat to the boy on the ledge.

The dog, who had been running back and forth whining, sank to his belly, his muzzle in his forepaws. But the boy on the ledge never stirred. The ducks took late alarm at the skiff, swerved aside and into the air, passing with a whirr no more than fifty feet over the head of the boy, who remained on the ledge like a statue, without his gun, watching the two crouching in the boat.

The fisherman's son climbed onto the ledge and held the painter. The bottom of the skiff was covered with feathery bodies with feet upturned and necks lolling. He was jubilant. "We got twenty-seven!" he told his cousin. "How's that?" Nine apiece. Boy —" he added, "what a cool Christmas!"

The fisherman pulled the skiff onto the shelf and all three went and lay down again in anticipation of the next flight. The son, reloading, patted his shotgun affectionately. "I'm going to get me ten next time," he said. Then he asked his cousin, "Whatsamatter — didn't you see the strays?"

"Yeah," the boy said.

"How come you didn't shoot at 'em?"

"Didn't feel like it," replied the boy, still with a trace of sullenness.

"You stupid or something?" The fisherman's son was astounded. "What a highlander?" But the fisherman, though he said nothing, knew that the older boy had had an attack of ledge fever.

"Cripes!" his son kept at it. "I'd at least of tried."

"Shut up," the fisherman finally told him, "and leave him be."

At slack water three more flocks came in, one right after the other, and when it was over, the skiff was half full of clean, dead birds. During the subsequent lull they broke out the lunch and ate it all and finished the hot coffee. For awhile the fisherman sucked away on his cold pipe. Then he had himself a swig of whiskey.

The boys passed the time contentedly jabbering about who

137

shot the most — there were ninety-two all told — which of their friends they would show the biggest ones to, how many each could eat at a meal provided they didn't have to eat any vegetables. Now and then they heard sporadic distant gunfire on the mainland, at its nearest point about two miles to the north. Once far off they saw a fishing boat making in the direction of home.

At length the fisherman got a hand inside his oilskins and produced his watch.

"Do we have to go now?" asked his son.

"Not just yet," he replied. "Pretty soon." Everything had been just perfect. As good as he had ever had it. Because he was getting tired of the boys' chatter he got up, heavily in his hip boots, and stretched. The tide had turned and was coming in, the sky was more ashen, and the wind had freshened enough so that whitecaps were beginning to blossom. It would be a good hour before they had to leave the ledge and pick up the tollers. However, he guessed they would leave a little early. On account of the rising wind he doubted there would be much more shooting. He stepped carefully along the back of the ledge, to work his kinks out. It was also getting a little colder.

The whiskey had begun to warm him, but he was unprepared for the sudden blaze that flashed upward inside him from belly to head. He was standing there looking at the shelf where the skiff was. Only the foolish skiff was not there!

For a second time that day the fisherman felt the deep vacuity of disbelief. He gaped, seeing nothing but the flat shelf of rock. He whirled, started toward the boys, slipped, recovered himself, fetched a complete circle, and stared at the unimaginably empty shelf. Its emptiness made him feel as if everything he had done that day so far, his life so far, he had dreamed. What could have happened? The tide was still nearly a foot below. There had been no sea to speak of. The skiff could hardly have slid off by itself. For the life of him, consciously careful as he inveterately was, he could not now remember hauling it up the last time. Perhaps in the heat of hunting, he had left it to the boy. Perhaps he could not remember which was the last time.

"Christ —" he exclaimed loudly, without realizing it because he was so entranced by the invisible event.

"What's wrong, Dad?" asked his son, getting to his feet.

138

The fisherman went blind with uncontainable rage. "Get back down there where you belong!" he screamed. He scarcely noticed the boy sink back in amazement. In a frenzy he ran along the ledge thinking the skiff might have been drawn up at another place, though he knew better. There was no other place.

He stumbled, half falling, back to the boys who were gawking at him in consternation, as though he had gone insane. "God damn it!" he yelled savagely, grabbing both of them and yanking them to their knees. "Get on your feet!"

"What's wrong?" his son repeated in a stifled voice.

"Never mind what's wrong," he snarled. "Look for the skiff — it's adrift!" When they peered around he gripped their shoulders, brutally facing them about. "Down wind —" He slammed his fist against his thigh. "Jesus!" he cried, struck to madness by their stupidity.

At last he sighted the skiff himself, magically bobbing along the grim sea like a toller, a quarter of a mile to leeward on a direct course for home. The impulse to strip himself naked was succeeded instantly by a queer calm. He simply sat down on the ledge and forgot everything except the marvelous mystery.

As his awareness partially returned he glanced toward the boys. They were still observing the skiff speechlessly. Then he was gazing into the clear young eyes of his son.

"Dad," asked the boy steadily, "what do we do now?"

That brought the fisherman upright. "The first thing we have to do," he heard himself saying with infinite tenderness as if he were making love, "is think."

"Could you swim it?" asked his son.

He shook his head and smiled at them. They smiled quickly back, too quickly. "A hundred yards maybe, in this water. I wish I could," he added. It was the most intimate and pitiful thing he had ever said. He walked in circles round them, trying to break the stall his mind was left in.

He gauged the level of the water. To the eye it was quite stationary, six inches from the shelf at this second. The fisherman did not have to mark it on the side of the rock against the passing of time to prove to his reason that it was rising, always rising. Already it was over the brink of reason, beyond the margins of thought — a senseless measurement. No sense

139

to it.

All his life the fisherman had tried to lick the element of time, by getting up earlier and going to bed later, owning a faster boat, planning more than the day would hold, and tackling just one other job before the deadline fell. If, as on rare occasions he had the grand illusion he ever really had beaten the game, he would need to call on all his reserves of practice and cunning now.

He sized up the scant but unforgivable three hundred yards to Brown Cow Island. Another hundred yards behind it his boat rode at anchor, where, had he been aboard, he could have cut in a fathometer to plumb the profound and occult seas, or a ship-to-shore radio on which in an interminably short time he would have heard his wife's voice talking to him over the air about homecoming.

"Couldn't we wave something so somebody would see us?" his nephew suggested.

The fisherman spun round. "Load your guns!" he ordered. They loaded as if the air had suddenly gone frantic with birds. "I'll fire once and count to five. Then you fire. Count to five. That way they won't just think it's somebody gunning ducks. We'll keep doing that."

"We've only got just two-and-a-half boxes left," said his son.

The fisherman nodded, understanding that from beginning to end their situation was purely mathematical, like the ticking of the alarm clock in his silent bedroom. Then he fired. The dog, who had been keeping watch over the decoys, leaped forward and yelped in confusion. They all counted off, fired the first five rounds by threes and reloaded. The fisherman scanned first the horizon, then the contracting borders of the ledge, which was the sole place the water appeared to be climbing. Soon it would be over the shelf.

They counted off and fired the second five rounds. "We'll hold off a while on the last one," the fisherman told the boys. He sat down and pondered what a trivial thing was a skiff. This one he and the boy had knocked together in a day.

His son tallied up the remaining shells, grouping them symmetrically in threes on the rock when the wet box fell apart. "Two short," he announced. They reloaded and laid the guns on their knees.

140

Behind thickening clouds they could not see the sun going down. The water, coming up, was growing blacker. The fisherman thought he might have told his wife they would be home before dark since it was Christmas day. He realized he had forgotten about it being any particular day. The tide would not be high until two hours after sunset. When they did not get in by nightfall, and could not be raised by radio, she might send somebody to hunt for them right away. He rejected this arithmetic immediately, with a sickening shock, recollecting it was a two-and-a-half hour run at best. Then it occurred to him that she might send somebody on the mainland who was nearer. She would think he had engine trouble.

He rose and searched the shoreline, barely visible. Then his glance dropped to the toy shoreline at the edges of the reef. The shrinking ledge, so sinister from a boat, grew dearer minute by minute as though the whole wide world he gazed on from horizon to horizon balanced on its contracting rim. He checked the water level and found the shelf awash.

Some of what went through his mind the fisherman told to the boys. They accepted it without comment. If he caught their eyes they looked away to spare him or because they were not yet old enough to face what they saw. Mostly they watched the rising water. The fisherman was unable to initiate a word of encouragement. He wanted one of them to ask him whether somebody would reach them ahead of the tide. He would have found it possible to say yes. But they did not inquire.

The fisherman was not sure how much, at their age, they were able to imagine. Both of them had seen from the docks drowned bodies put ashore out of boats. Sometimes they grasped things, and sometimes not. He supposed they might be longing for the comfort of their mothers, and was astonished, as much as he was capable of any astonishment except the supreme one, to discover himself wishing he had not left his wife's dark, close, naked bed that morning.

"Is it time to shoot now?" asked his nephew.

"Pretty soon," he said, as if he were putting off making good on a promise. "Not yet."

His own boy cried softly for a brief moment, like a man, his face averted in an effort neither to give or show pain.

"Before school starts," the fisherman said, wonderfully detached, "we'll go to town and I'll buy you boys anything you want."

With great difficulty, in a dull tone as though he did not in the least desire it, his son said after a pause, "I'd like one of those new thirty-horse outboards."

"All right," said the fisherman. And to his newphew, "How about you?"

The nephew shook his head desolately. "I don't want anything," he said.

After another pause the fisherman's son said, "Yes, he does, Dad. He wants one too."

"All right —" the fisherman said again, and said no more.

The dog whined in uncertainty and licked the boys' faces where they sat together. Each threw an arm over his back and hugged him. Three strays flew in and sat companionably down among the stiff-necked decoys. The dog crouched, obedient to his training. The boys observed them listlessly. Presently, sensing something untoward, the ducks took off, splashing the wave tops with feet and wingtips, into the dusky waste.

The sea began to make up in the mounting wind, and the wind bore a new and deathly chill. The fisherman, scouring the somber, dwindling shadow of the mainland for a sign, hoped it would not snow. But it did. First a few flakes, then a flurry, then storming past horizontally. The fisherman took one long, bewildered look at Brown Cow Island three hundred yards dead to leeward, and got to his feet.

Then it shut in, as if what was happening on the ledge was too private even for the last wan light of the expiring day.

"Last round," the fisherman said austerely.

The boys rose and shouldered their tacit guns. The fisherman fired into the flying snow. He counted methodically to five. His son fired and counted. His nephew. All three fired and counted. Four rounds.

'You've got the one left, Dad," his son said.

The fisherman hesitated another second, then he fired the final shell. Its pathetic report, like the spat of a popgun, whipped away in the wind and was instantly blanketed in falling snow.

Night fell all in a moment to meet the ascending sea. They

142

were now barely able to make one another out through driving snowflakes, dim as ghosts in their yellow oilskins. The fisherman heard a sea break and glanced down where his feet were. They seemed to be wound in a snowy sheet. Gently he took the boys by the shoulders and pushed them in front of him, feeling with his feet along the shallow sump to the place where it triangulated into a sharp crevice at the highest point of the ledge. "Face ahead," he told them. "Put the guns down."

"I'd like to hold mine, Dad," begged his son.

"Put it down," said the fisherman. "The tide won't hurt it. Now brace your feet against both sides and stay there."

They felt the dog, who was pitch black, running up and down in perplexity between their straddled legs. "Dad," said his son, "what about the pooch?"

If he had called the dog by name it would have been too personal. The fisherman would have wept. As it was he had all he could do to keep from laughing. He bent his knees and hoisted the dog with one arm. The dog's belly was soaking wet.

So they waited, marooned in their consciousness, surrounded by a monstrous tidal space which was slowly, slowly closing them out. In this space the periwinkle beneath the fisherman's boots was king. While hovering airborne in his mind he had an inward glimpse of his house as curiously separate, like a June mirage.

Snow, rocks, seas, wind the fisherman had lived by all his life. Now he thought he had never comprehended what they were, and he hated them. Though they had not changed. He was deadly chilled. He set out to ask the boys if they were cold. There was no sense. He thought of the whiskey, and sidled backward, still holding the awkward dog, till he located the bottle under water with his toe. He picked it up squeamishly as though afraid of getting his sleeve wet, worked his way forward and bent over his son. "Drink it," he said, holding the bottle against the boy's ribs. The boy tipped his head back, drank, coughed hotly, then vomited.

"I can't, he told his father wretchedly.

"Try — try—" the fisherman pleaded, as if it meant the difference between life and death.

The boy obediently drank, and again he vomited hotly. He

143

shook his head against his father's chest and passed the bottle forward to his cousin, who drank and vomited also. Passing the bottle back, the boys dropped it in the frigid water between them.

When the waves reached his knees the fisherman set the warm dog loose and said to his son, "Turn around and get up on my shoulders." The boy obeyed. The fisherman opened his oilskin jacket and twisted his hands behind him through his suspenders, clamping the boy's booted ankles with his elbows.

"What about the dog?" the boy asked.

"He'll make his own way all right," the fisherman said. "He can take the cold water." His knees were trembling. Every instinct shrieked and braced like a colossus against the sides of the submerged crevice.

The dog, having lived faithfully as though one of them for eleven years, swam a few minutes in and out around the fisherman's legs, not knowing what was happening, and left them without a whimper. He would swim and swim at random by himself, round and round in the blinding night, and when he had swum routinely through the paralyzing water all he could, he would simply, in one incomprehensible moment, drown. Almost the fisherman, waiting out infinity, envied him his pattern.

Freezing seas swept by, flooding inexorably up and up as the earth sank away inperceptibly beneath them. The boy called out once to his cousin. There was no answer. The fisherman, marvelling on a terror without voice, was dumbly glad when the boy did not call again. His own boots were long full of water. With no sensation left in his straddling legs he dared not move them. So long as the seas came sidewise against his hips, and then sidewise against his shoulders, he might balance—no telling how long. The upper half of him was what felt frozen. His legs, disengaged from his nerves and his will, he came to regard quite scientifically. They were the absurd, precarious axle around which reeled the surged universal tumult. The waves would come on and on; he could not visualize how many tossing reinforcements lurked in the night beyond — inexhaustible numbers, and he wept in supernatural fury at each because it was higher, till he transcended hate and took them, swaying like a convert, one by one as they lunged against him and away aimlessly into their own undisputed, wild realm.

144

From his hips upward the fisherman stretched to his utmost as a man does when spirit reaches out of dead sleep. The boy's head, none too high, must be at least seven feet above the ledge. Though growing larger every minute, it was a small light life. The fisherman meant to hold it there, if need be, through a thousand tides.

By and by the boy, slumped on the head of his father, asked, "Is it over your boots, Dad?"

"Not yet," the fisherman said. Then through his teeth he added, "If I should fall—kick your boots off—swim for it—downwind—to the island...."

"You...?" the boy finally asked.

The fisherman nodded against the boy's belly. "—Won't see each other," he said.

The boy did for the fisherman the greatest thing that can be done. He may have been too young for perfect terror, but he was old enough to know there were things beyond the power of any man. All he could do he did, by trusting his father to do all he could, and asking nothing more.

The fisherman, rocked to his soul by a sea, held his eyes shut upon the interminable night.

"Is it time now?" the boy said.

The fisherman could hardly speak. "Not yet," he said. "Not just yet...."

As the land mass pivoted toward sunlight the day after Christmas, a tiny fleet of small craft converged off shore like iron filings to a magnet. At daybreak they found the skiff floating unscathed off the headland, half full of ducks and snow. The shooting *had* been good, as someone hearing on the nearby mainland the previous afternoon had supposed. Two hours afterward they found the unharmed boat adrift five miles at sea. At high noon they found the fisherman at ebb tide, his right foot jammed cruelly into a glacial crevice of the ledge beside three shotguns, his hands tangled behind him in his suspenders, and under his right elbow a rubber boot with a sock and a live starfish in it. After dragging unlit depths all day for the boys, they towed the fisherman home in his own boat at sundown, and in the frost of evening, mute, laid him on his wharf for his wife to see.

She, somehow, standing on the dock as in her frequent dream, gazing at the fisherman pure as crystal on the icy boards, a small rubber boot still frozen under one clenched arm, saw him exaggerated beyond remorse or grief, absolved of his mortality.

Mr. Tutt

IS NO GENTLEMAN

Judge Quelch was anything but honorable in his quest for the salmon trophy. But Tutt wasn't about to be caught with his pants down ...

by Arthur Train

Mr. Ephraim Tutt had just come out of the clubhouse and was standing rod in hand on the bank of the Santapedia beside his guest, Mr. Bonnie Doon, preparatory to the evening's fishing, when a canoe appeared unexpectedly around the bend a third of a mile downstream.

"By Lazarus, if it ain't Judge Quelch!" Donald McKay expelled a thin brown stream over the bank in the direction of the approaching canoe. "He's got them same two hairy outlaws a-guidin' him he had last season! The gol-blasted old trouble maker!"

Mr. Tutt would have tolerated no such disrespectful allusion to a regular member of the club in good standing from any guide except old Donald, and not from him save and excepting with regard to the aforesaid member of the judiciary. But the

147

judge could hardly be said to be in good standing, except technically, and there was no gainsaying that he was a trouble maker — even a curse!

"Do you suppose he's coming here?" asked Mr. Tutt hopelessly.

"He can't be goin' nowheres else," commented Angus Ogilvy, the old lawyer's bowman. "There's nowheres else for him to go, 'cept to Push-and-be-Damned, and there ain't no fish there."

"He's a slick one," growled old Donald. "He was up here fust thing in May, the minute the season opened, and killed a thirty-two pounder. It gave him his third leg on the trophy — which was all he needed. So he saved the rest of his time in case any one else should go him one better. He's got five days left. He must have heard about Mr. Warburton landin' that thirty-five pound fish on Saturday. That spoiled his chance for the Golden Salmon, so now he's coming' back again."

"That's right!" agreed Mr. Tutt. "The judge had the trophy hog-tied until Saturday. By jumping Jehoshaphat! I'd like to swang-dangle that old fellow!"

"He telephoned up last night to ask who was here," volunteered Angus. "He knows the clubhouse is full. They told him Mr. Warburton was goin' out day after tomorrow. He could have waited perfectly well until next week."

"He's following up that fresh run of fish," alleged Donald shrewdly. "They was at Two Brooks night before last. They'll probably reach here tomorrow."

The canoe, bearing amidships a tall, saturnine man, was rapidly heading for the landing. Mr. Tutt scrambled down to meet it.

"Hello, Judge!" he cried out genially. "How are you? Hope you've had good luck!"

The occupant of the canoe vouchsafed no reply until it had grounded and the bowman had spiked his paddle and leaped out. Then he arose stiffly and stepped ashore.

"I understand that you have a guest," he announced, in a hostile tone, without replying to the old lawyer's greeting. "Of course, you are acquainted with the rule which provides that no guest shall occupy a room in the clubhouse if it is required by a member."

"Of course, I know the rule, Judge," replied Mr. Tutt. "But

148

I had no idea that you wished to stay here until just now when I saw you coming up the river. If you had only telephoned — —"

Judge Quelch turned to his guides.

"Take those duffel bags up to the veranda," he ordered. "We shall be here the best part of a week." Then addressing Mr. Tutt, he added: "The clubhouse is for the members who pay the dues, not for visitors who contribute nothing."

"Mr. Warburton is going out on Tuesday," answered Mr. Tutt, controlling his temper as well as he could. "If you would be willing to use one of the other camps farther up river — Push-and-be-Damned, for instance — until then — —"

"I intend to fish here!" snapped Quelch, making his way up the bank.

"Allow me to present my guest, Mr. Doon," interposed Mr. Tutt. Bonnie stepped forward, but Quelch barely nodded to him.

"The camp at Burnt Hill is vacant, if you and your friend want to go there, or you might try Push-and-be Damned yourself," he shot back, following his dunnage toward the clubhouse. "I have no intention of going anywhere else."

"Very well!" said Mr. Tutt shortly. "I will sleep with the guides until Tuesday. You can occupy my room. I hope you will enjoy it!"

The Golden Salmon is the trophy donated by the Rt. Rev. Lionel Charteris, Bishop of St. Albans, the beloved founder of the Wanic Club, which, as every fisherman knows, owns the best water on Santapedia, one of the great salmon rivers of New Brunswick, if not of the world. Here, on a grassy bluff below the forks overlooking what is known as the Home Pool, stands the low, wide-eaved bungalow where six of the finest gentlemen and grandest sports in the world, including Ephraim Tutt, have spent many of their happiest days — that is, they had spent them there until dear old Bishop Charteris died at the age of eighty-nine and his small estate, including most unfortunately his share in the Wanic Club, had passed into the hands of a relative whom he had never seen, the Honorable Philo Utterbach Quelch.

The Golden Salmon, under the terms of its gift, was to become the property of whichever member should kill the largest fish in the Home Pool in three seasons. It stood in a case of crystal on the mantelpiece of the big fireplace in the sitting room, under

149

the mounted carcass of Leviathan, the famous fifty-pound salmon that the bishop had killed the last season he had spent there, after having hooked it the year before on a Parmachenee Belle and lost it, and after Mr. Tutt had rehooked it the following spring on a Silver Doctor, only to lose it in his turn — which is an entirely different yarn, though true. Very different! For this particular narrative deals with the morals and manners traditional among sportsmen and gentlemen — that is, among real ones, but not to include, of course, the Honorable Philo — curse him — Utterbach Quelch.

Up to the interjection among them by law, so to speak, of the said Utterbach, the half dozen gentlemen now comprising the Wanic membership had fished the Santapedia together in the utmost harmony, eagerly looking forward each year to the moment when the cares of office or of business laid aside, they could resume their sport upon the sunlit reaches of the river and cement their ancient friendships around the camp fire. But with the arrival of the Honorable Utterbach, everything was changed in the twinkling of an eye and a black cloud o'erspread the sunset of their lives. And now, by thunder, the fellow had two legs on the Golden Salmon!

To get the exact picture of the consequences of his eruption upon their peaceful clubhouse, one must comprehend that the Wanic is a rather swell affair. To receive an invitation to cast a fly there is the the dream of every salmon fisherman, but such invitations are in inverse ratio to the eagerness with which they are sought after. The Prince of Wales has fished there — for a goose egg — and so has the Maharajah of Bhurtpore, the King of the Belgians, Will Rogers, Douglas Fairbanks, and a limited number of other potentates, panjandrums and the popular pals thereof; but they are the great exceptions.

An ordinary human being could no more pry himself into the social circle of the Wanic Club than he could into the family dining room at Buckingham Palace. Those old boys have known one another for more than half a century. They went to school together, some of them. Mr. Tutt is the only person ever distinguished with an honorary, or elective, membership. They are all the personification of gentleness and courtesy. It is their pleasure to give way to one another's preferences and to oblige

150

one another in all things, since there is fishing enough for all and to spare.

It had never occurred to them to pay any attention to their legal rights, if they had any, or even to the printed rules of the club, which, to all intents and purposes, had been forgotten ever since they had been drawn up twenty-five years before. Yet no sooner had the Honorable Philo Utterbach Quelch made his appearance than they were rudely awakened to the undeniable fact that a share in a salmon-fishing club is property governed by the laws appertaining to the same, and that the rules and by-laws of such a corporation have a like force and effect.

Quelch was a cadaverous man with a coffin-shaped face, a querulous, rasping voice, and a legal manner, which, perhaps, was only natural considering his profession. Yet a legal manner is a poor manner among sportsmen; as it is too great a regard for the technical niceties of one's rights. He had, moreover, an affliction of some sort which, when he spoke, made him stutter, squawk, strangle and explode so that he could be heard all over the camp; and at night he coughed, hawked and snored so that even the wild beasts, which had come down from the hills to nuzzle the garbage cans, fled back to their fastnesses in terror.

The strange thing about Quelch, like many other unpleasant persons, was that he could be perfectly agreeable when he chose to be so. He was highly cultivated, had read much, traveled widely and was learned in piscatorial as in other branches of the law. But there was something about him which made others dislike him more when he was trying to be affable than when he was being frankly nasty, which was most of the time. For in the woods it is better to be detestable than to be a bore. Quelch was both. The interminable strangulated orations with which he regaled his fellow members upon the veranda after meals, in which he detailed his various exploits in the world of sport, drove his fellow members nearly wild. The news that Quelch was coming was inevitably a signal for the hasty exodus of everyone else, and, in consequence, he usually had the clubhouse to himself.

But this was different — the Golden Salmon was at stake! For a brief space, Mr. Tutt considered accepting the Honorable Quelch's suggestion to move to Burnt Hill or Push-and-be-

151

Damned, but Bonnie Doon had never been salmon fishing before, there was a fresh run on its way up the river, and — curse the fellow! — Old Man Tutt hated to be bullied by a lawyer half a dozen years younger than he was himself, even if he were a judge. So he went over and slept with the guides.

Having thus cooly ousted Mr. Tutt from his room in the clubhouse, Judge Quelch proceeded to make himself at home there, appropriating the seat at the head of the dining table, the best easy-chair next to the fireplace, and the only hammock upon the veranda, acting as if in so doing he was but exercising the prerogatives inherited from his distinguished half uncle. He also indulged in a practice anathema to all campers, preëmpting all the pegs and hooks on the outside of the clubhouse for his personal belongings, distributing his under and over garments everywhere, including a particularly dirty pair of ancient blue overalls, which he hung just outside the door of the living room, so that no one who either went in or out could fail to be reminded of his presence.

Being, therefore, in what was for him a genial frame of mind, he proceeded, after supper, to elucidate, for the edification of his fellow members, the law governing the ownership of wild game.

"There is," he announced, "a great deal of confusion in the minds of most sportsmen as to the rights which they can acquire in what the law calls *ferae naturae,* or wild animals. There are, in fact, no property rights in wild animals, including fish, until the latter are reduced to actual manual possession by the hunter or fisherman, or are so wounded or confined as to be within his absolute control."

"Do you mean to say that the salmon we kill in front of our clubhouse don't belong to any one until they're actually landed?" asked Ives.

Judge Quelch flourished his cigar as if it were a gavel.

"That is precisely what I mean, sir. Ever since the Magna Charta of King John, it has been firmly established that in England the King owns all wild game not legally reduced to possession, and in America that the state in its sovereign capacity exercises the same ownership. That is the reason we all have to take out fishing licenses and pay a fee to the state. Our ownership of the banks of the river gives us only an exclusive right to fish in the waters beside us. While it is true that our right of fishery is enough to enable us to keep off trespassers and appropriate any fish they have killed in our own waters, it would not be sufficient to permit us to follow a poacher who had hooked a fish in front of the clubhouse and to take it away from him after he had killed it in waters other than our own."

Donald McKay, who was whittling at the other end of the veranda, looked up.

"Are you sayin', Judge, that it's the law if a poacher comes on our waters and hooks a salmon, and it runs down stream and he kills it beyond our boundary, we can't take the fish away from him?"

"Exactly. We have only an exclusive privilege of taking the salmon while it is in our water. The moment the fish passes beyond our boundaries we lose that right of fishery and the fish becomes subject to the poacher's superior right of absolute manual possession, although we could, of course, bring an action against him for trespass."

"By Lazarus! That's news to me!" declared Donald. "And it'll be news to a lot of other fellers."

Judge Quelch grinned in what he intended to be a benign fashion, but which merely approximated the smile of a hyena.

"Laymen — including guides like yourself — are not supposed to be familar with the technical rules of law in such matters. There is a fundamental difference between owning a fish outright and having merely the exclusive privilege of trying to catch it on one's own waters."

"They had a funny case like that downriver about a deer," volunteered Donald. "One man wounded it pretty bad, and while it was running, another feller shot it through the heart an' killed it. They had a kind of moot court in the camp and gave it to the feller that wounded it first."

"Entirely wrong!" asserted Quelch authoritatively. "The law is absolutely settled that under such circumstances the animal belonged to the one who killed it — reduced it to actual possession. I can, in fact, cite you an exact precedent — Pierson versus Post, 3 Caines Cases 175, if I remember correctly."

"I'm sure you always remember correctly," said Mr. Tutt.

153

"It was a case about foxes. There had been a hunt, and the hounds were about to make the kill, when a farmer, seeing that the fox was cornered, shot and made off with it. The court held that he was perfectly within his right. I can recall the exact words of the decision: 'An action will not lie against a man for killing and taking a wild animal pursued by and in view of the person who originally found, started, chased it, and was on the point of seizing it. There are innumerable cases on the subject. They cover bear, deer, seals, birds — —"

"Are there any about salmon?" asked Mr. Tutt quietly.

"Er — perhaps not specifically about salmon," conceded Judge Quelch, "but by analogy — —"

"Do you contend that if two men are fishing a stream and one hooks a salmon, the other has a legal right to gaff and take it, on the ground that he was the one to reduce it to actual possession?"

"I most certainly do?" answered the judge. "Most of us know to our cost that our chances of ultimate possession of a salmon on the end of a hundred yards of line are exceedingly precarious, to say the least. The fish belongs to the one who gets him."

"Humph!" snorted the president of the British Columbian Railways. "What would you think of a man who gaffed another man's fish?"

"As a judge," replied Philo, "my task, should such a case come before me, would be soley to interpret and apply the law according to my best lights."

"Don't you agree that there's a great deal of difference between the chances of reducing to possession a deer that has been wounded by a bullet and a salmon which has been solidly hooked, and is attached to a No. I leader on the end of a twenty-four pound test line?" asked Mr. Tutt.

"I do not!" snapped the judge. "The line or leader may break."

"In any case," continued the old lawyer, "I understand your position to be that hooking a salmon gives a fisherman no right to the fish that is superior to any one else's. So that if another fisherman hooked the same fish foul, it would belong to whichever could manage to land him?"

"That is not only my position but it is the law!" affirmed the Honorable Philo.

154

"Don't you think that among sportsmen such a performance would justly be regarded as contemptible?" demanded Warburton.

The Honorable Philo Utterbach Quelch turned a pale orb upon his questioner.

"It is time that sportsmen, so-called, realized that they are governed by the rules of law like everybody else," he remarked.

"So you'd take another man's fish if you hooked him foul?" inquired Mr. Tutt.

"That would depend — on circumstances. I only say that under the law I would have the right to do so, if I chose," replied Quelch.

"But do you think any man calling himself a gentleman would do a thing like that?" persisted Mr. Tutt.

"A gentleman!" repeated Quelch sarcastically. "Will you kindly inform me in what respect a person calling himself a gentleman differs from any one else?"

"The word has had a pretty well defined meaning for several hundred years," mused Mr. Tutt. "You may have heard the phrase 'on my honor as a gentleman,' perhaps?"

"I have heard it, and I fail to see how the honor of a gentleman differs from the honor of any other citizen," sneered Quelch. "Honor is honor, and law is law. Every nation and every religion in the world has a different standard of morals. The only basic test of the rightfulness or wrongfulness of an action is whether that action is legal or illegal."

The president of the Royal Bank of Canada leaned forward.

"The by-laws of practically every club provide that a member may be expelled for conduct unbecoming a gentleman. Why is that, if it means nothing?" he remarked.

"That's all it does mean!" snorted Quelch. "Nothing! Such provisions have no validity in the courts. The member of a club cannot be expelled for anything he had a legal right to do. I'm sure I've no idea of what is meant by a gentleman."

"I can well believe it," murmured Mr. Tutt.

"Hear! Hear!" came from the other end of the veranda.

Quelch's eye swept the circle of disgusted sportsmen.

"Well, come on; tell me! What is a gentleman?" he demanded.

"I don't wonder you ask!" commented Mr. Arbuthnot.

155

"Trying to define a gentleman has been a favorite parlor game so long as I can remember," said Quelch. "It can't be done, for the simple reason that the word is entirely vague, a meaningless term. It belongs in the same category as questions like 'What is art?' and 'What is beauty?' If you ask me — —"

"We do ask you!" Ives shot at him.

"As a man of considerable experience of the world, who has listened to countless litigated disputes, I say that, in the final analysis, the only satisfactory test of a gentleman is whether or not he is willing to infringe the legal rights of others. Any other gauge of human conduct is hopelessly confused. If one applies the purely legal test, everything becomes clear and definite. For example — and I cite this as an excellent and most apropos illustration — when I arrived here, this evening, I found that Mr. Tutt had invited a guest to fish with him — a right derived by him solely from our by-laws; but those very same by-laws provide that no guest can occupy a room in the clubhouse if it is required by a member. Now, I have two legs on the trophy presented to the club by my uncle, Bishop Charteris, and I am entitled to five more days' fishing at the Forks. To attempt to exclude me from the club and to prevent me from securing the trophy, if I can, would certainly not be a gentlemanly course of procedure. But what is the test? The law as expressed in our rules. Should I, out of some mistaken idea of courtesy, waive my rights in this instance, I should not only be unjust to myself but open the door to every sort of abuse. The clubhouse might easily become filled with guests who would prevent the regular members from getting any fish at all. We must uphold the rules. The true gentleman is he who is willing to suffer criticism for the ultimate good of all."

Mr. Tutt produced and lit a stogy.

"What you say — coming, as it does, from the lips of Gamaliel, so to speak — interests me extremely," he remarked. "But I can easily see that questions might arise even under our by-laws which would be very hard to settle by purely legal reasoning and which might have to be determined by an appeal to some less rigid test!"

"Indeed!" remarked the Honorable Quelch. "What, for example?"

"Well," drawled Mr. Tutt, "my very dear old friend, your half-uncle, Bishop Charteris, bequeathed the trophy to whomsoever should kill the biggest salmon in the Home Pool during the three seasons. Now, suppose I hooked a fish in Push-and-be-Damned, say, and it carried me down to the Home Pool and I killed it there — would I come within the requirements?"

"Certainly not!" ejaculated Quelch. "To qualify for the trophy, the fish must be hooked in the Home Pool by the member having the right to fish there at the time."

"And where do you get that?" inquired Ives.

"That is my judicial interpretation of the paragraph of my uncle's will," answered Quelch. "And I am ready to gamble my professional reputation that it would be sustained by any of the higher courts of New Brunswick."

"Suppose I hooked a fish in Push-and-be-Damned and it carried me down to the Home Pool, what would you do if you were fishing there?"

"If I had drawn the Home Pool under the provisions of the by-laws and were fishing it, I should require you to move along."

"Suppose I couldn't? Suppose the salmon wanted to stay there?"

"You'd have no right to remain and spoil my fishing," declared Quelch. "Whoever draws the Home Pool has the right to the undisturbed possession of it. All others are trespassers. In fact," he added, "a proper construction of the by-laws would give me the right to hook and take the fish — in which case it would properly be regarded as having been killed in the Home Pool."

"I merely wanted to know," explained Mr. Tutt. "After all, applying technical legal rules rather simplifies things, as you say .... By jumping Jehoshaphat, it's half past six!"

"Time we were pushing off!" interrupted Norton, adding something under his breath inaudible to the Honorable Philo.

"Did you hear what the judge said, Donald?" asked Mr. Tutt with his gentlest smile as he climbed into the canoe.

"I heard him!" answered Donald, picking up his paddle. "And also his reference to guides in general! Wouldn't it be the gol-blastedest thing if the old scalawag managed to cinch the

157

Golden Salmon?"

"He won't if I can help it!" asserted Mr. Tutt.

The pools at the Wanic Club are drawn by lot each day and, as luck would have it, during the next four days the Honorable Philo, although a redoubtable fisherman, did not improve his position with respect to the Golden Salmon. He still had two legs on it, but no more. Mr. Warburton's thirty-five pound fish remained the largest taken from the Home Pool that year. Then, on the last day of the five upon which he was still entitled to fish, the judge proceeded to draw the Home Pool for both morning and evening. It was a heavy blow to the other members, for the fresh run of fish that had been on their way up the river had just arrived and that particular pool was boiling. Everyone agreed that it would be just Quelch's luck to kill a forty-pound fish at the last minute and carry off the trophy.

The Wanic Club stands at the Forks of the Santapedia. There are six pools in all: The Home Pool just in front of the clubhouse — where a sand pit lying in mid-river divides the current, part of which having flowed past the spit turns upstream in a back eddy, rejoining the rapids again above the bar — the Cocktail, the Corkscrew, and Wildcat on the half-mile stretch below. Above the forks are two others — Push-and-be-Damned, which, being a mile away, has a camp of its own; and lower down, a couple of hundred yards above the Wanic clubhouse, one of the very best pools of all — Donald's Leap — where, in his younger days, Donald McKay had jumped a full twelve feet from the bank to a rock in midstream to gaff a salmon entangled among the driftwood.

The Honorable Philo's last day dawned auspiciously, one of those perfect days for fishing that come but once or twice in a season. The water was neither too high nor too low, the sun was bright and hot, there was enough of a breeze to ruffle the surface without making it difficult to cast. Mr. Tutt had killed two salmon weighing more than thirty pounds each in the Home Pool the evening before, and the wardens had reported that they had seen several big fish, estimated at upwards of forty pounds, moving upstream toward the Forks. And, of course, it had to be the Honorable Philo who drew the Home Pool that day, and, of course, before breakfast he had already killed a thirty-three pounder on a Jock Scot. He came in arrogantly, consuming a trencher of oatmeal, two large platters of corn cakes and maple sirup, and several cups of coffee, after which he proceeded to expatiate magniloquently upon his chances of winning the trophy. Even if he didn't kill the biggest fish that year, he pointed out, his chances were still three to one as against any one else. Clearly, in his opinion, the Golden Salmon was already as good as his.

The limit to the number of fish a member may kill in one day is six, so that Quelch could take but four more and, if he were to capture the trophy, one of these must exceed the weight of Warburton's thirty-five pounder taken the previous week. Now Quelch belonged to that variety of fisherman whose ambition is to kill as many fish as possible. He was inevitably on his pool by five in the morning and kept casting, casting, casting, until darkness rendered it no longer possible to do so. He had even been known to go on fishing when he could no longer see his fly. But if one is not trying to catch more than his competitors, but merely a bigger fish, the greater number he catches without achieving his object the worse it is for him since it reduces his final chances.

"By Lazarus!" exclaimed old Donald as Mr. Tutt emerged from the clubhouse after lunch. "I've just seen something I wouldn't have believed possible, if it weren't fer Angus to corroborate me. I take my oath I saw the judge hook and play a salmon out there, and when he brought him in and saw he was only twenty pounds or so, he had one of his hairy sons-of-guns cut the leader and let him go! Is that within the rules?"

"I suppose so," answered the old lawyer wryly. "A member may kill only six fish, and a fish that is released isn't technically killed even if it dies afterwards."

Donald spat contemptuously. "That's on a par with what he did up to the Headwater Pool last year. You know, all the fish that pass by here go up there to spawn. They're so hungry they'll pretty near jump at the bare hook, let alone a fly. A member is only allowed to stay there two days and kill a dozen fish."

"What did Quelch do?"

"I'll tell ye what he did, and I've made affidavit of it too. He

159

and them two dog-faced boys from Boiestown went up there last September and hooked and landed seventy fish. They kep' twelve of 'em and threw back fifty-eight. You know how much chance for life a salmon has, once he's been hooked and landed. But the judge claimed he was within the rules!

"Donald," he said, "something must be done about this man Quelch."

But luck was with the Judge. All that afternoon, in spite of the protests of the other members, he turned the Home Pool into a piscatorial slaughterhouse, hooking salmon, playing them nearly dead and, because they were not large enough, letting them go. By five o'clock he had hooked nine and kept only four; thus, as he contended still maintaining the legal right to kill two more. He worked like an automaton, standing in his waders on the sand spit and whipping every inch of water from the point where the Santapedia shoots through a flume of rocks in an almost solid column of brown amber into the rapids, across the deep, oily stretches between the bar and the high banks in front of the clubhouse, to where the river broadens into dimpling shallows before part of it swirls onward into the Cocktail and the rest swings into a back eddy that circles around the bar and rejoins the main stream again. Crouched beside his canoe were the two hairy apes from Boiestown, ready to shove off and follow any fish that might seek to escape down river. And still he cast, quartering the pool with every variety of fly in his book, determined before night to land a salmon bigger than Warburton's thirty-five pounder.

Concededly, his chances were good. There were forty-pound fish in the pool and at any moment one of them might take his fly. Ives, Norton and Arbuthnot, who had drawn the Cocktail, the Corkscrew and the Wild Cat, respectively, had given up and were smoking pipes on the veranda. No doubt about it, the fish were all in the Home Pool. Mr. Tutt and Bonnie Doon, with Donald and Angus, had gone up to Donald's Leap and were fishing it from the banks.

A portentous silence hung over the Forks. No sound disturbed the tranquillity of the late afternoon, save the murmur of the river, the occasional splash of a kingfisher or the sound of expectoration from one or the other of Quelch's hairy guides. The shadows began to lengthen and the golden light to creep higher and higher toward the tops of the pines. Dusk was falling fast — that indeterminate translucent veil which, like a mist, screens and magnifies, transforming even the commonest of objects. That, perhaps, is why the late fishing is best, since the gathering darkness helps to deceive the salmon when he sees what he takes to be a fly. Such was the hour, and big with Fate. Now, if ever, Quelch might expect to raise and kill his winning fish.

Suddenly, from far above the Forks, came a distant shouting. Something exciting was going on up there, and it could mean but one thing. Mr. Tutt — or possibly Mr. Doon — had hooked a mighty fish. Instantly the river became alive. The hullabaloo increased, growing momentarily louder, so that the members left the veranda and gathered on the bank to see what was going to happen. The guides and cook came running from the camp and cookhouse.

First, Donald appeared, gaff in hand, jumping from rock to rock, closely followed by Angus and Bonnie Doon. Then, upstream, struggling with all his might, Old Man Tutt came into view, his rod bent in half circle, butt against belly, his reel screeching his line taut as a telegraph wire attached to race horse. Obviously, he had hooked a salmon in Donald's Leap and, do what he would, it was pulling him down the river.

It was a precarious situation, for above the Forks the Santapedia goes sweeping around jagged boulders, over sharp ledges and past tangled piles of logs and driftwood which offer every opportunity for the line to catch and the fish to break away. But although Mr. Tutt had already been dragged a hundred yards, he had, nevertheless, managed to hang fast to his fish, which, accompanied by a chorus of yells from Donald, Angus and Bonnie Doon, was making its way straight for the falls above the Home Pool. Any such view halloo is inevitably the signal for every member to leave what he is doing, no matter where or what, and to come hurrying to watch the kill. But Quelch did not budge. Stolidly he went on with his casting, hardly vouchsafing so much as a look upstream.

They were all there now, Warburton, who had come back to see the finish, Ives, Norton, Arbuthnot, the two wardens, the cook, his helpers, and half a dozen guides were strung along

161

the bluff, for they knew, from the way that Mr. Tutt, Donald and Angus acted, that this was indeed no ordinary fish.

"By Godfrey!" muttered Ives. "That salmon is sure coming down into the Home Pool, and if it does — so help me Quelch! — there's going to be a cat fight before we get through."

"Thar he goes!" shouted Angus hysterically, as a black streak slithered over the falls. "He's a whale! Forty-five pounds if he's an ounce!"

"Fifty, by Lazarus!" yelled old Donald. "I never seen one as big — not even the bishop's!"

"What did you raise him with?" called out the methodical Norton.

"A Griswold Gray. He only riz once — and took it solid!"

"Did you see his tail?"

"Looked like the stern of an ocean liner!"

Mr. Tutt was staggering in midstream, reeling bravely as opportunity offered and struggling to gain the bank above the falls, whence he might hope to exercise some control over the fish at the end of his ninety yards of line. But the current is powerful here, hurling itself like a mill race against the high dune in front of the clubhouse and whirling deep, black and foamflecked along the edge of the pool, so that even a small fish has a good chance of escape. Naturally, the salmon made for this point of least resistance, pulling out more and more line as Mr. Tutt scrambled over the rocks and came running after it along the shore.

"Get a canoe!" ordered Norton, and Donald and Angus plunged down the shelving gravel and, clambering in, pushed off into the center of the pool, ready to follow should the salmon make another break for lower down.

The fish was now hanging directly opposite, about a hundred feet from the sand bar which Quelch was casting. Looking across at Mr. Tutt, he called harshly:

"Get off my water!"

"I can't!" answered the old lawyer, "I'm fast to a salmon."

"Makes no difference! I've the exclusive right to fish in this pool. You're a trespasser! Order your guides ashore!"

Just then Mr. Tutt's line slackened for a moment and a black back rose to sight, only instantly to disappear again. Mr. Tutt

162

reeled frantically.

"I tell you to get off my water!" bellowed Quelch.

"I'm going to land my fish first!"

"You have no right to kill a salmon in this pool!"

"I'm going to, all the same!" replied Mr. Tutt ..."Hey, there Angus! Push out into the shallows!"

"If you kill a salmon here, I shall claim him as mine!" warned Quelch.

"Nonsense!" declared Arbuthnot. "You can't prevent another member from following a fish into your water."

"The courts will decide that!" retorted Quelch.

The black object rose once more to the surface some twenty-odd feet lower down the pool. At the same instant Quelch raised his rod. It was a long cast — forty yards at least — but the judge was an expert and could hit a leaf unerringly at that distance. Ping! His line became taut, his rod whipped into a half circle, and with a leer of elation he began to reel in. Incredible as it seemed, he had succeeded in hooking Mr. Tutt's fish foul at the first cast. An outcry of protest came from the spectators upon the bank.

"That's the dirtiest trick I've ever seen done on a river!" asserted Ives.

"I'm fully within my rights!" retorted Quelch. "No matter who lands this fish, it is mine — and counts for the trophy!"

Both old men were fast to the same salmon — the one by the mouth, the other by the tail — and favored by the swiftness of the current, it was making headway against both of them.

"I hooked this fish!" panted Mr. Tutt.

"That gives you no legal claim. You haven't reduced him to possession! A salmon is *ferae naturae* — —"

"*Ferae naturae* be damned!" bawled the old lawyer, as, at that precise instant, his line parted and his rod straightened so that he nearly fell over backward. A grin of triumph gathered upon the face of the Honorable Utterbach at the realization that the gods had thus unexpectedly intervened in his behalf. All he had to do now was to land his fish, and the trophy would be his; for he felt convinced that he was fast to the biggest salmon of the season, if not of all time. But landing a salmon foul is no easy task, as the Judge well knew. It often means an endurance

163

contest — requiring hours of hard work to tire him out.

So the Honorable Philo sat down carefully on his sand pit, propped his heels against a rock, inserted the butt of his rod in the socket of his leather belt, and dug himself in with his line leading directly into the centre of the pool where the fish was now apparently sulking.

Ives, Warburton, Norton and Arbuthnot had gathered about Mr. Tutt in earnest consultation. Presently Arbuthnot came down to the edge of the landing.

"We have held a meeting of the club members, Judge Quelch," he announced acidly, "and you have been expelled for conduct that was unbecoming a gentleman."

"Rot!" returned the Honorable Philo. "You can't expel me! Besides, your meeting was not properly called. The law will respect my rights, even if you do not!"

He was about to add something more, but his reel began to sing as the salmon made for the end of the pool, so that he scrambled hastily to his feet and followed along the sand pit. Quelch was a good fisherman and knew that even if he could not hold his fish in the swift water, he might be able to steer it into the back eddy; so he let it run the length of the pool and then swung it across the current. It was a daring and clever maneuver — and it succeeded. Back came the salmon upstream into the dead water on the other side of the bar and, with the strain on the line thus relieved, Quelch reeled in until he had shortened his line by fifty or more feet. Making a complete circle around the sand spit, the fish reentered the Home Pool and, taking advantage of the rapids below the falls and the powerful current in front of the clubhouse, made for the lower river, running out the line again until Quelch's reel was all but stripped.

Once more, however, the judge turned him just in the nick of time and nursed his fish into the backwater again, around the head of the spit and into the Home Pool. Already an hour had gone by, it was almost dark, but the salmon seemed as fresh as ever. With every passing minute, the Judge's time was running out and, unless he could land his fish, he would have lost his chance, for that year at least, of capturing the Golden Salmon. The lamps had been lighted in the clubhouse, but, although supper was ready, Tobias, the cook, did not announce it, preferring to stand with the others and watch the fight going on below.

"If he don't land him next trip, it's all over!" declared Norton, as the judge once again steered his quarry into the backwater. "It'll be pitch black inside of ten minutes.

This time, however, it became obvious that the judge meant to bring the struggle to an end, for when the salmon again followed the current of the back eddy into the main pool, he began to reel in with all his strength. Slowly the line shortened.

"Dammit! I believe he's got him!" swore Ives.

One of the hirsute guides had climbed into the canoe and swung it across the end of the spit in order to intercept the salmon, should it make a final rush; the other waded into the water with his gaff held in readiness to strike.

Inch by inch, the salmon came in, not, as usual, turning over so as to exhibit its belly, but with its back flush with the surface.

Quelch walked to the river's edge.

"Now!" he yelled. "Let him have it!"

They all watched breathlessly as, amid a silence like the vacuum between two worlds, the guide reached forward with this gaff and struck. Generally, under such circumstances, the salmon puts up a frantic battle for life, floundering about and scattering the water in every direction. Many a fish has been lost owing to the desperate character of its last minute's struggle. But in this instance nothing of the sort occurred. The gaff encountered no resistance and, with but slight effort, Quelch's guide lifted his quarry from the water. Quickly he dropped it — but not before a chorus of jeers and catcalls had risen from the opposite bank. Shamefacedly he waded backward toward the spit, dragging behind him — a waterlogged pair of overalls! Quelch stared at them stupidly. Gingerly he picked them up by one leg. They were his own!

Slowly, while the crowd upon the bank hugged themselves with delight, the Honorable Utterbach dismounted his rod and got into his canoe.

Arbutnot met him at the landing.

"I call to your attention," said he severely, "that since you arrived in the afternoon, your five days are already up and that you are no longer entitled to remain here. Your room has accordingly been turned over to Mr. Tutt."

"You are correct according to the by-laws," conceded the judge. "I will pack up my things, and after supper — —"

"You are not entitled to supper," interrupted Arbuthnot coldly. "You got here at five o'clock and you have already exceeded your time by two hours. Member or no member, you will move on at once."

The judge turned to his guides.

"Get ready to go to the Push-and-be-Damned," he said shortly. "We'll have supper when we reach camp."

"And be damned!" echoed someone.

Ten minutes later he was gone.

"How did you ever come to think of it, Mr. Tutt?" asked Norton as they all sat around the camp fire that evening.

"Well," admitted the old lawyer as he lit a fresh stogy and tossed the rest of those in his case to the guides, "the fact is I did the very same thing last year at Burnt Hill — with a pair of overalls too. A strong current is very deceptive and will make a small fish act like a big one at any time. I saw Warburton go ashore to land a half-pound chub in front of the clubhouse only last Monday. I figured that if I waited until it was nearly dark, I could make most anything act like salmon."

"I'll say you did!" commented Ives. "You had me fooled to the last second."

"And then, you see," continued Mr. Tutt, "I already had Quelch's assurance as to what he would do under the circumstances. He ran true to form and lived up to his principles — such as they are. I've no doubt he considers himself more sinned against than sinning."

"I caught a wash boiler once down to Henshaw's, and I saw a feller play an old shoe for half and hour at Two Brooks," said old Donald. "I've seen the same sort of thing happen half a dozen times!"

They all smoked in silence for a while. It was broken by Angus.

"And they was his own pants at that!" he chuckled.

The Honorable Utterbach sat disconsolately, after a supper of cold beans, upon the rough porch of Push-and-be-Damned under a leering moon. The two hairy apes from Boiestown lolled at a distance against the veranda, spitting alternately in a disdainful manner at an adjacent stump. Overalls! The Judge's moose lip quivered and something suspiciously like water glistened on his lower lids. Caesar, Alexander, Napoleon — even Bismarck — may have wept, but there is no record of it. And, after all, they were iron men.

The Honorable Utterbach felt very much alone. He was not a man of iron. What could be the trouble? He was a judge, wasn't he? And the law was the law? He had only acted according to his rights. Yes, he had been treated outrageously. Outrageously! And he had lost the Golden Salmon — for that year anyway! Pulling out a huge silk handkerchief, he blew his nose with a blast that might have echoed to the Forks. Then, with his lips still quivering he looked up at the moon.

"Mr. Tutt is no gentleman!" he declared.

THE SPOTTED DEVIL OF
Gummalapur

The maneater had earned a frightening reputation
for his diabolical craftiness. And now, only a few
feet below him, was his next victim.

by Kenneth Douglas Stuart Anderson

The leopard is common to practically all tropical jung-
les, and unlike the tiger, indigenous to the forests of
India; for whereas it has been established that the
tiger is a comparatively recent newcomer from regions
in the colder north, records and remains have shown that the
leopard — or panther, as it is better known in India — has lived
in the peninsula from the earliest times.

Because of its smaller size, and decidedly less strength,
together with its innate fear of mankind, the panther is often
treated with some derision, sometimes coupled with truly
astonishing carelessness, two factors that have resulted in the
maulings and occasional deaths of otherwise intrepid but
cautious tiger-hunters. Even when attacking a human being the
panther rarely kills, but confines itself to a series of quick bites

168

and quicker raking scratches with its small but sharp claws; on the other hand, few persons live to tell that they have been attacked by a tiger.

This general rule has one fearful exception, however, and that is the panther that has turned man-eater. Although examples of such animals are comparatively rare, when they do occur they depict the panther as an engine of destruction quite equal to his far larger cousin, the tiger. Because of his smaller size he can conceal himself in places impossible to a tiger, his need for water is far less, and in veritable demonic cunning and daring, coupled with the uncanny sense of self-preservation and stealthy disappearance when danger threatens, he has no equal.

Such an animal was the man-eating leopard of Gummalapur. This leopard had established a record of some 42 human killings and a reputation for veritable cunning that almost exceeded human intelligence. Some fearful stories of diabolical craftiness had been attributed to him, but certain it was that the panther was held in awe thoughout an area of some 250 square miles over which it held undisputable sway.

Before sundown the door of each hut in every one of the villages within this area was fastened shut, some being reinforced by piles of boxes or large stones, kept for the purpose. Not until the sun was well up in the heavens next morning did the timid inhabitants venture to expose themselves. This state of affairs rapidly told on the sanitary condition of the houses, the majority of which were not equipped with latrines of any sort, the adjacent waste land being used for the purpose.

Finding that its human meals were increasingly difficult to obtain, the panther became correspondingly bolder, and in two instances burrowed its way in through the thatched walls of the smaller huts, dragging its screaming victim out the same way, while the whole village lay awake, trembling behind closed doors, listening to the shrieks of the victim as he was carried away. In one case the panther, frustrated from burrowing its way in through the walls, which had been boarded up with rough planks, resorted to the novel method of entering through the thatched roof. In this instance it found itself unable to carry its prey back through the hole it had made, so in a paroxym of fury had killed all four inhabitants of the hut — a man, his wife

169

and two children — before clawing its way back to the darkness outside and to safety.

Only during the day did the villagers enjoy any respite. Even then they moved about in large, armed groups, but so far no instance had occurred of the leopard attacking in daylight, although it had been very frequently seen at dawn within the precincts of a village.

Such was the position when I arrived at Gummalapur, in response to an invitation from Jepson, the District Magistrate, to rid his area of this scourge. Preliminary conversation with some of the inhabitants revealed that they appeared dejected beyond hope, and with true eastern fatalism had decided to resign themselves to the fact that this shaitan, from whom they believed deliverance to be impossible, had come to stay, till each one of them had been devoured or had fled the district as the only alternative.

It was soon apparent that I would get little or no cooperation from the villagers, many of whom openly stated that if they dared to assist me the shaitan would come to hear of it and would hasten their end. Indeed, they spoke in whispers as if afraid that loud talking would be overheard by the panther, who would single them out for revenge.

That night, I sat in a chair in the midst of the village, with my back to the only house that possessed a twelve-foot wall, having taken the precaution to cover the roof with a deep layer of thorns and brambles, in case I should be attacked from behind by the leopard leaping down on me. It was a moonless night, but the clear sky promised to provide sufficient illumination from its myriad stars to enable me to see the panther should it approach.

The evening, at six o'clock, found the inhabitants behind locked doors, while I sat alone on my chair, with my rifle across my lap, loaded and cocked, a flask of hot tea nearby, a blanket, a water bottle, some biscuits, a torch at hand, and of course my pipe, tobacco and matches as my only consolation during the long vigil till daylight returned.

With the going down of the sun a period of acute anxiety began, for the stars were as yet not brilliant enough to light the scene even dimly. Moreover, immediately to westward of the village lay two abrupt hills which hastened the dusky uncertainty that might otherwise have been lessened by some reflection from the recently set sun.

I gripped my rifle and stared around me, my eyes darting in all directions and from end to end of the deserted village street. At that moment I would have welcomed the jungle, where by their cries of alarm I could rely on the animals and birds to warn me of the approach of the panther. Here all was deathly silent, and the whole village might have been entirely deserted, for not a sound escaped from the many inhabitants whom I knew lay listening behind closed doors, and listening for the scream that would herald my death and another victim for the panther.

Time passed, and one by one the stars became visible, till by 7:15 p.m. they shed a sufficiently diffused glow to enable me to see along the whole village street, although somewhat indistinctly. My confidence returned, and I began to think of some way to draw the leopard towards me, should he be in the vicinity. I forced myself to cough loudly at intervals and then began to talk to myself, hoping that my voice would be heard by the panther and bring him to me quickly.

I do not know if any of my readers have ever tried talking to themselves loudly for any reason, whether to attract a maneating leopard or not. I suppose there must be a few, for I realize what reputation the man who talks to himself acquires. I am sure I acquired that reputation with the villagers, who from behind their closed doors listened to me that night as I talked to myself. But believe me, it is no easy task to talk loudly to yourself for hours on end, while watching intently for the stealthy approach of a killer.

By 9 p.m. I got tired of it, and considered taking a walk around the streets of the village. After some deliberation I did this, still talking to myself as I moved cautiously up one lane and down the next, frequently glancing back over my shoulder. I soon realized, however, that I was exposing myself to extreme danger, as the panther might pounce on me from any corner, from behind any pile of garbage, or from the roof tops of any of the huts. Ceasing my talking abruptly, I returned to my chair, thankful to get back alive.

Time dragged by very slowly and monotonously, the hours

seeming to pass on leaden wheels. Midnight came and I found myself feeling cold, due to a sharp breeze that had set in from the direction of the adjacent forest, which began beyond the two hillocks. I drew the blanket closely around me, while consuming tobacco far in excess of what was good for me. By 2 a.m. I found I was growing sleepy. Hot tea and some biscuits, followed by icy water from the bottle dashed into my face, and a quick raising and lowering of my body from the chair half-a-dozen times, revived me a little, and I fell to talking to myself again, as a means of keeping awake thereafter.

At 3:30 a.m. came an event which caused me untold discomfort for the next two hours. With the sharp wind, banks of heavy cloud were carried along, and these soon covered the heavens and obscured the stars, making the darkness intense, and it would have been quite impossible to see the panther a yard away. I had undoubtedly placed myself in an awkward position, and entirely at the mercy of the beast, should it choose to attack me now. I fell to flashing my torch every half-minute from end to end of the street, a proceeding which was very necessary if I hoped to remain alive with the panther anywhere near, although I felt I was ruining my chances of shooting the beast, as the bright torch-beams would probably scare it away. Still, there was the possibility that it might not be frightened by the light, and that I might be able to see it and bring off a lucky shot, a circumstance that did not materialize, as morning found me still shining the torch after a night-long and futile vigil.

I snatched a few hours' sleep and at noon fell to questioning the villagers again. Having found me still alive that morning — quite obviously contrary to their expectations — and possibly crediting me with the power to communicate with spirits because they had heard me walking around their village talking, they were considerably more communicative and gave me a few more particulars about the beast. Apparently the leopard wandered about its domain a great deal, killing erratically and at places widely distant from one another, and as I had already found out, never in succession at the same village. As no human had been killed at Gummalapur within the past three weeks, it seemed that there was much to be said in favour of staying where I was, rather than moving around, in a haphazard fashion, hoping to come up with the panther. Another factor against wandering about was that this beast was rarely visible in the daytime, and there was therefore practically no chance of my meeting it, as might have been the case with a man-eating tiger. It was reported that the animal had been wounded in its right fore-foot, since it had the habit of placing the pad sidewards, a fact which I was later able to confirm when I actually came across the tracks of the animal.

After lunch, I conceived a fresh plan for that night, which would certainly save me from the great personal discomforts I had experienced the night before. This was to leave a door of one of the huts ajar, and to rig up inside it a very life-like dummy of a human being; meanwhile, I would remain in a corner of the same hut behind a barricade of boxes. This would provide an opportunity to slay the beast as he became visible in the partially-opened doorway, or even as he attacked the dummy, while I myself would be comparitively safe and warm behind my barricade.

I explained the plan to the villagers, who, to my surprise, entered into it with some enthusiasm. A hut was placed at my disposal immediately next to that through the roof of which the leopard had once entered and killed the four inmates. A very life-like dummy was rigged up, made of straw, an old pillow, a jacket, and a saree. This was placed within the doorway of the hut in a sitting position, the door itself being kept half-open. I sat myself behind a low parapet of boxes, placed diagonally across the opposite end of the small hut, the floor of which measured about 12 feet by 10 feet. At this short range, I was confident of accounting for the panther as soon as it made itself visible in the doorway. Furthermore, should it attempt to enter by the roof, or through the thatched walls, I would have ample time to deal with it. To make matters even more realistic, I instructed the inhabitants of both the adjacent huts, especially the women folk, to endeavour to talk in low tones as far into the night as was possible, in order to attract the killer to that vicinity.

An objection was immediately raised, that the leopard might be led to enter one of their huts, instead of attacking the dummy in the doorway of the hut in which I was sitting. This fear was

173

only overcome by promising to come to their aid should they hear the animal attempting an entry. The signal was to be a normal call for help, with which experience had shown the panther to be perfectly familiar, and of which he took no notice. This plan also assured me that the inhabitants would themselves keep awake and continue their low conversation in snatches, in accordance with my instructions.

Everything was in position by 6 p.m., at which time all doors in the village were secured, except that of the hut where I sat. The usual uncertain dusk was followed by bright starlight that threw the open doorway and the crouched figure of the draped dummy into clear relief. Now and again I could hear the low hum of conversation from the two neighbouring huts.

The hours dragged by in dreadful monotony. Suddenly the silence was disturbed by a rustle in the thatched roof which brought me to full alertness. But it was only a rat, which scampered across and then dropped with a thud to the floor nearby, from where it ran along the tops of the boxes before me, becoming clearly visible as it passed across the comparatively light patch of the open doorway. As the early hours of the morning approached, I noticed that the conversation from my neighbours died down and finally ceased, showing that they had fallen asleep, regardless of man-eating panther, or anything else that might threaten them.

I kept awake, occasionally smoking my pipe, or sipping hot tea from the flask, but nothing happened beyond the noises made by the tireless rats, which chased each other about and around the room, and even across me, till daylight finally dawned, and I lay back to fall asleep after another tiring vigil.

The following night, for want of a better plan, and feeling that sooner or later the man-eater would appear, I decided to repeat the performance with the dummy, and I met with an adventure which will remain indelibly impressed on my memory till my dying day.

I was in position again by six o'clock, and the first plan of the night was but a repetition of the night before. The usual noise of scurrying rats, broken now and again by the low-voiced speakers in the neighbouring huts, were the only sounds to mar the stillness of the night. Shortly after 1 a.m. a sharp wind sprang up, and I could hear the breeze rustling through the thatched roof. This rapidly increased in strength, till it was blowing quite a gale. The rectangular patch of light from the partly open doorway practically disappeared as the sky became overcast with storm clouds, and soon the steady rhythmic patter of raindrops, which increased to a regular downpour, made me feel that the leopard, who like all his family are not over-fond of water, would not venture out on this stormy night, and that I would draw a blank once more.

By now the murmuring voices from the neighbouring huts had ceased or become inaudible, drowned in the swish of the rain. I strained my eyes to see the scarcely perceptible doorway, while the crouched figure of the dummy could not be seen at all, and while I looked I evidently fell asleep, tired out by my vigil of the two previous nights.

How long I slept I cannot tell but it must have been for some considerable time. I awoke abruptly with a start, and a feeling that all was not well. The ordinary person in awaking takes some time to collect his faculties, but my jungle training and long years spent in dangerous places enabled me to remember where I was and in what circumstances, as soon as I awoke.

The rain had ceased and the sky had cleared a little, for the oblong patch of open doorway was more visible now, with the crouched figure of the dummy seated at its base. Then, as I watched, a strange thing happened. The dummy seemed to move, and as I looked more intently it suddenly disappeared to the accompaniment of a snarling growl. I realized that the panther had come, seen the crouched figure of the dummy in the doorway which it had mistaken for a human being, and then proceeded to stalk it, creeping in at the opening on its belly, and so low to the ground that its form had not been outlined in the faint light as I had hoped. The growl I had heard was at the panther's realization that the thing it had attacked was not human after all.

Switching on my torch and springing to my feet, I hurdled the barricade of boxes and sprang to the open doorway, to dash outside and almost trip over the dummy which lay across my path. I shone the beam of torchlight in both directions, but nothing could be seen. Hoping that the panther might still be lurking nearby and shining my torch-beam into every corner, I walked slowly down the village street, cautiously negotiated the bend at its end and walked back up the next street, in fear and trembling of a sudden attack. But although the light lit up every corner, every roof-top and every likely hiding-place in the street, there was no sign of my enemy anywhere. Then only did I realise the true significance of the reputation this animal had acquired of possessing diabolical cunning. Just as my own sixth sense had wakened me from sleep at a time of danger, a similar sixth sense had warned the leopard that here was no ordinary human being, but one that was bent upon its destruction. Perhaps it was the bright beam of torchlight that had unnerved it at the last moment; but, whatever the cause, the man-eater had silently, completely and effectively disappeared, for although I searched for it through all the streets of Gummalapur that night, it had vanished as mysteriously as it had come.

Disappointment and annoyance with myself at having fallen asleep were overcome with a grim determination to get even with this beast at any cost.

Next morning the tracks of the leopard were clearly visible at the spot it had entered the village and crossed a muddy drain, where for the first time I saw the pug-marks of the slayer and the peculiar indentation of its right forefoot, the paw of which was not visible as a pug-mark, but remained a blur, due to this animal's habit of placing it on edge. Thus it was clear to me that the panther had at some time received an injury to its foot which had turned it into a man-eater. Later I was able to view the injured foot for myself, and I was probably wrong in my deductions as to the cause of its man-eating propensities; for I came to learn that the animal had acquired the habit of eating the corpses which the people of that area, after a chlorea epidemic within the last year, had by custom carried into the forest and left to the vultures. These easily procured meals had given the panther a taste for human flesh, and the injury to its foot, which made normal hunting and swift movement difficult, had been the concluding factor in turning it into that worst of all menaces to an Indian village — a man-eating panther.

I also realized that, granting the panther was equipped with an almost-human power of deduction, it would not appear in

176

Gummalapur again for a long time after the fright I had given it the night before in following it with my torch light.

It was therefore obvious that I would have to change my scene of operations, and so, after considerable thought, I decided to move on to the village of Devarabetta, diagonally across an intervening range of forest hills, and some eighteen miles away, where the panther had already secured five victims, though it had not been visited for a month.

Therefore, I set out before 11 a.m. that very day, after an early lunch. The going was difficult, as the path led across two hills. Along the valley that lay between them ran a small jungle stream, and beside it I noted the fresh pugs of a big male tiger that had followed the watercourse for some 200 yards before crossing to the other side. It had evidently passed early that morning, as was apparent from the minute trickles of moisture that had seeped into the pug marks through the river sand, but had not had time to evaporate in the morning sun. Holding steadfastly to the job in hand, however, I did not follow the tiger and arrived at Devarabetta just after 5 p.m.

The inhabitants were preparing to shut themselves into their huts when I appeared, and scarcely had the time nor inclination to talk to me. However, I gathered that they agreed that a visit from the man-eater was likely any day, for a full month had elapsed since his last visit and he had never been known to stay away for so long.

Time being short, I hastily looked around for the hut with the highest wall, before which I seated myself as on my first night at Gummalapur, having hastily arranged some dried thorny bushes across its roof as protection against attack from my rear and above. These thorns had been brought from the hedge of a field bordering the village itself, and I had had to escort the men who carried them with my rifle, so afraid they were of the man-eater's early appearance.

Devarabetta was a far smaller village than Gummalapur, and situated much closer to the forest, a fact which I welcomed for the reason that I would be able to obtain information as to the movements of carnivora by the warning notes that the beasts and birds of the jungle would utter, provided I was within hearing.

The night fell with surprising rapidity, though this time a

177

thin sickle of new-moon was showing in the sky. The occasional call of a roosting jungle-cock, and the plaintive call of pea-fowl, answering one another from the nearby forest, told me that all was still well. And then it was night, the faint starlight rendering hardly visible, and as if in a dream, the tortuously winding and filthy lane that formed the main street of Devarabetta. At 8:30 p.m. a sambar hind belled from the forest, following her original short note with a series of warning cries in steady succession. Undoubtedly a beast of prey was afoot and had been seen by the watchful deer, who was telling the other jungle-folk to look out for their lives. Was it the panther or one of the larger carnivora? Time alone would tell, but at least I had been warned.

The hind ceased her belling, and some fifteen minutes later, from the direction in which she had first sounded her alarm, I heard the low moan of a tiger, to be repeated twice in succession, before all became silent again. It was not a mating call that I had heard, but the call of the King of the Jungle in his normal search for food, reminding the inhabitants of the forest that their master was on the move in search of prey, and that one of them must die that night to appease his voracious appetite.

Time passed, and then down the lane I caught sight of some movement. Raising my cocked rifle, I covered the object, which slowly approached me, walking in the middle of the street. Was this the panther after all, and would it walk this openly, and in the middle of the lane, without any attempt at concealment? It was now about thirty yards away and still it came on boldly, without any attempt to take cover or to creep along the edges of objects in the usual manner of a leopard when stalking its prey. Moreover, it seemed a frail and slender animal, as I could see it fairly clearly now. Twenty yards and I pressed the button of my torch, which this night I had clamped to my rifle.

As the powerful beam threw across the intervening space it lighted a village cur, commonly known to us in India as a 'pariah' dog. Starving and lonely, it had sought out human company; it stared blankly into the bright beam of light, feebly wagging a skinny tail in unmistakable signs of friendliness.

Welcoming a companion, if only a lonely cur, I switched off the light and called it to my side by a series of flicks of thumb and finger. It approached cringingly, still wagging its ridiculous

178

tail. I fed it some biscuits and a sandwich, and in the dull light of the star-lit sky its eyes looked back at me in dumb gratitude for the little food I had given it, perhaps the first to enter its stomach for the past two days. Then it curled up at my feet and fell asleep.

Time passed and midnight came. A great horned owl hooted dismally from the edge of the forest, its prolonged mysterious cry of 'Whooo-whooo' seeming to sound a death-knell, or a precursor to that haunting part of the night when the souls of those not at rest returns to the scenes of their earthly activities, to live over and over again the deeds that bind them to the earth.

One o'clock, two and then three o'clock passed in dragging monotony, while I strained my tired and aching eyes and ears for movement or sound. Fortunately it had remained a cloudless night and visibility was comparatively good by the radiance of the myriad stars that spangled the heavens in glorious array, a sight that cannot be seen in any of our dusty towns or cities.

And then, abruptly, the alarmed cry of a plover, or 'Did-you-do-it' bird, as it is known in India, sounded from the nearby muddy tank on the immediate outskirts of the village. 'Did-you-do-it, Did-you-do-it, Did-you-do-it, Did-you-do-it', it called in rapid regularity. No doubt the bird was excited and had been disturbed, or it had seen something. The cur at my feet stirred, raised its head, then sank down again, as if without a care in the world.

The minutes passed, and then suddenly the dog became fully awake. Its ears, that had been drooping in dejection, were standing on end, it trembled violently against my legs, while a low prolonged growl came from its throat. I noticed that it was looking down the lane that led into the village from the vicinity of the tank.

I stared intently in that direction. For a long time I could see nothing, and then it seemed that a shadow moved at a corner of a building some distance away and on the same side of the lane. I focused my eyes on this spot, and after a few seconds again noticed a furtive movement, but this time a little closer.

Placing my left thumb on the switch which would actuate the torch, I waited in the breathless silence. A few minutes passed, five or ten at the most, and then I saw an elongated

179

body spring swiftly and noiselessly on to the roof of a hut some twenty yards away. As it happened, all the huts adjoined each other at this spot, and I guessed the panther had decided to walk along the roofs of these adjoining huts and spring upon me from the rear, rather than continue stalking me in full view.

I got to my feet quickly and placed my back against the wall. In this position the eave of the roof above my head passed over me and on to the road where I had been sitting, for about eighteen inches. The rifle I kept ready, finger on trigger, with my left thumb on the torch switch, pressed to my side and pointing upwards.

A few seconds later I heard a faint rustling as the leopard endeavoured to negotiate the thorns which I had taken the precaution of placing on the roof. He evidently failed in this, for there was silence again. Now I had no means of knowing where he was.

The next fifteen minutes passed in terrible anxiety, with me glancing in all directions in the attempt to locate the leopard before he sprang, while thanking Providence that the night remained clear. And then the cur, that had been restless and whining at my feet, shot out into the middle of the street, faced the corner of the hut against which I was sheltering and began to bark lustily.

This warning saved my life, for within five seconds the panther charged around the corner and sprang at me. I had just time to press the torch switch and fire from my hip, full into the blazing eyes that showed above the wide-opened, snarling mouth. The .405 bullet struck squarely, but the impetus of the charge carried the animal on to me. I jumped nimbly to one side, and as the panther crashed against the wall of the hut, emptied two more rounds from the magazine into the evil, spotted body.

It collapsed and was still, except for the spasmodic jerking of the still-opened jaws and long, extended tail. And then my friend the cur, staunch in faithfulness to his new-found master, rushed in and fixed his feeble teeth in the throat of the dead monster.

And so passed the 'Spotted Devil of Gummalapur', a panther of whose malignant craftiness I had never heard the like before and hope never to have to meet again.

180

When skinning the animal next morning, I found that the injury to the right paw had not been caused, as I had surmised, by a previous bullet wound, but by two porcupine quills that had penetrated between the toes within an inch of each other and then broken off short. This must have happened quite a while before, as a gristly formation between the bones inside the foot had covered the quills. No doubt it had hurt the animal to place his paw on the ground in the normal way, and he had acquired the habit of walking on its edge.

I took the cur home, washed and fed it, and named it 'Nipper'. Nipper has been with me many years since then, and never have I had reason to regret giving him the few biscuits and sandwich that won his staunch little heart, and caused him to repay that small debt within a couple of hours, by saving my life.

Bedtime

S T O R Y

In 1913 two Americans survive a grizzly attack
and banditos to discover a hunter's paradise south
of the border.

by Jack Tooker

ome of the best hunting in North America is to be
found south of the Mexican border along the Sierra
Madre Mountains, from western Chihuahua and extending down to Tepic. It's full of big game, including
some king-size grizzlies. They average larger than our Rocky
Mountain bears. In fact, they resemble our old California grizzly
which was reported to have weighed as much as 1,100 pounds.

Earl Boyles and I had a clash with these Mexican grizzlies in
1913 that I still remember as clearly as if it happened last season.
We hired a guide named Soto and arranged for a hunt in the
wild and rugged country west of Tepehuanes. A branch railway
runs to this little mining town from Durango. We were told that
this part of the country was infested with bandits, which local
officials admitted, and as the government refused to give us any

protection, our guide Soto reluctantly refused to go.

We were cussing our hard luck in the lobby of the hotel in Durango when a stately looking Spaniard came in and registered. I saw Soto perk up. He recognized the man and went over and talked to him. Soon the two went into the dining room, and when they reappeared half an hour later Soto's face had lost its gloom.

He introduced the man as Mr. Garcia, who said immediately, "My friend Mr. Soto tells me you gentlemen want to hunt. Bears are killing many of my cattle and I will furnish you horses from my remuda and supplies from my commissary to hunt on my ranch for as long as you can stay."

He admitted there were bandits, but said they worked mostly along the San Blas trail and on north. We'd hunt south of the trail, and besides, Garcia said he kept on good terms with the outlaws by giving them beef and tobacco — a sort of combined tribute and charity.

"Are there many bears?" we asked.

"Too many!" he said. He went on to explain that Soto had been his foreman for seven years and knew where the bears ranged. Garcia said he was taking out a 12-mule packtrain next morning.

"You mean there are no roads?" I asked.

Garcia shook his head sadly. "Only trails."

The hotel manager helped us get off next morning, and made it a point to warn us about the bandits: We should never trust any of them. If they got the drop on us, they would kill us for our guns and whatever other valuables and money we had.

It took us three days' packing over rough, scenic country to reach the Garcia rancho. There was a large adobe hacienda surrounded by a high rock-and-adobe wall. Walls four feet thick protected the servants' quarters and huge supply buildings. The ponderous doors were locked with huge keys which reminded me of an ancient castle. The place was a fortress.

Bright and early next morning Garcia showed us a cow that had been killed by a grizzly. As we approached the kill a black bear raised up from behind the carcass. Garcia cried out, "Get him! He kill cow!"

Soto was about to shoot when I stopped him. "That little bear didn't kill that cow," I said, "and if you kill him he may disturb

183

all the sign around the carcass. We're after a much bigger bear than that."

The old rancher was disappointed, thinking we'd pardoned a grizzly, but we went on up and found the tracks of a much larger bear, the grizzly that evidently had killed the cow. We showed Garcia the difference between grizzly and black bear tracks and assured him he had made no mistake when he reported a grizzly had done the killing.

He showed us three old-style bear traps built of logs. One had been torn apart and the logs scattered. Garcia said a foreman had found a grizzly in the trap and had made the mistake of shooting him inexpertly with a .30/30 rifle. The wounded bear tore through the logs as if they had been matchsticks. Later they found the foreman dead; the grizzly was gone, leaving a blood trail. That had happened seven months before and there had been no traps set since. Nor any grizzlies killed, for that matter.

In two days' riding we saw lots of tracks and several kills but no bears. Garcia admitted that only a few kills had been made near the ranch house, and Soto agreed that most of the bears were on the southern end of the place — which was 30 or 40 miles away.

It's always been my policy, when after any kind of big game, to go where they are the thickest and if necessary live there for a while. So I had Soto bring in four pack burros and outfit them for a trip south.

We got started about 10 a.m. and began to see game almost immediately. We'd gone perhaps 10 miles through some of the finest country to be found anywhere when 30 or 40 wild turkeys trotted across the trail and stopped in a clearing not more than 60 yards ahead of us. Earl took his rifle from its scabbard and dismounted. The turkeys were so innocent of men they didn't even run when Earl walked toward them. A white gobbler stepped out of the bushes and stretched his long neck, and Earl shot him. Between Monterrey and Tampico I have seen whole flocks of wild white turkeys, but in the Sierra Madres we seldom see more than one or two whites in a hundred.

Soto tied the turkey on one of the packsaddles and we went on. Topping a little ridge, we came to a forest of giant oaks with gray and golden squirrels everywhere and large acorns plentiful.

184

It was typical bear country. A little farther on we flushed a herd of white-tail deer with their stern flags flying the up-go and down-stop signals. Then several more flocks of wild turkeys. We also saw grizzly sign and all sorts of cat tracks.

This oak forest extended for miles and ended in a beautiful green meadow with a brook running through it. Earl remarked he'd seen a lot of hunting country but this was the nearest to paradise he could remember.

Soto called a halt here, saying we could easily reach the site he'd planned for our permanent camp at Cavernas de Agua (Water Caves), which was at the extreme southern end of the range of mountains we were following. He made a fire and put the pot on while Earl and I unpacked the burros and unsaddled our horses, hobbling all the animals and putting bells on them. The bells weren't so much to enable us to find our stock in the morning as to keep the cougars, grizzlies, jaguars, and wolves from killing it.

By the time we got camp in shape and unrolled our sleeping bags, Soto had the turkey in the large Dutch oven and biscuits in the smaller one. Cooked to a turn with just the right amount of chili to give it zest, that turkey was really something to satisfy the inner man.

As night came on we lay among the oak leaves or on our bed rolls smoking and dozing in the flickering light of the fire. It was hardly dark before the wildlife began calling deep in the west fork of the Santiago River not far away. Two jaguars began their peculiar coughlike talk, ending with coarse, vicious growls. Wolves howled their lonely plaint, and a little later some owls flitted in through the firelight as if to see what manner of creatures had invaded their domain.

We rolled into our beds and I was soon asleep, though none of us had forgotten the outlaws. Earl seemed especially nervous. We all slept with our sidearms on.

The last thing I remembered was the faint tinkle of the bells on our saddle and pack animals. Next thing I knew a roar was echoing in my ears and the ground was vibrating around me as if from a small earthquake. When I finally got free of my bedding, I found the horses and burros milling around the camp, apparently having been badly frightened by some beast. It was remarkable that none of us had been stepped on. Whatever caused the panic wasn't to

185

be seen. It probably lost its nerve before all that human scent as it approached the campfire. But within a few minutes the animals calmed down and started working their way back into the timber. We went to sleep again.

It was daylight when I awoke. Earl and Soto were still asleep, and Soto had his head covered and his bare feet sticking out. I tickled his feet, or tried to, but the naked soles of those feet were about half an inch thick and nothing short of a branding iron would have had any effect. But when I uncovered his head he came to life pronto. He'd gone to bed fully dressed, six-shooter and all.

He went to the creek to wash his hands and face while I placed some dry leaves and twigs on the oak-wood coals that were still alive. We soon finished breakfast and were on our way.

Arriving at the caves about 2 p.m., we found ourselves on the edge of a small version of the Grand Canyon. Five tributaries of the Santiago River converged in the distance. There was water in the cave nearest us, and a spring flowed only a few feet from its mouth. Soto said it was the only water for some miles, and that's why he proposed we camp there.

I took a good look at the animal tracks around the spring at the cave's mouth and chose a campsite about 50 yards back from the water. There were wolf, jaguar, lion, lynx, deer, and turkey tracks around the water, and some of the largest grizzly tracks I've ever seen anywhere. For the next day or two we never went near that spring at night, and when we went for water during the day we could expect to see almost anything from wild turkey to grizzly.

Camp was under a big, spreading live-oak tree. While we were setting up, a spike white-tail deer came in for a drink, and we had camp meat. Soto dressed out the deer and hung the carcass about eight feet off the ground on a limb of the oak beside our beds. I should have known better than to permit that. Soto himself was rarely so careless, but he had decided there was so much game in this area the big meateaters wouldn't bother raiding our camp meat.

We spread our sleeping bags across a 14-foot, 18-ounce tarp, folding seven feet of the tarp back over the bags. That made a bed that would stay dry in rain or snow.

We were many miles from the normal range of bandits, yet we

didn't relax our guard. It may have been fear of bandits that got us in trouble that night.

There was pretty moonlight, and I lay awake for a long time listening to the wild animals. I could hear fighting going on and once the bells of the stock tinkled. Then some of our animals wandered through camp between the spring and our beds. I never suspected they were in trouble.

Finally I dropped off to sleep, and awoke some time later to hear the thudding sound a boxer makes punching a heavy bag. I screwed my head around cautiously. A huge bear was clawing and slugging the deer swinging from the tree beside us. The vension would be easy to replace, so I had no intention of disturbing the bear at such dangerously close quarters. Deciding we wouldn't be bothered if we acted seriously, I nudged Earl.

I nudged him twice before he moved, but it didn't occur to me to speak a warning. I should have, because Earl awoke with bandits in mind. Before I knew what he was about, he raised up on his elbow, drew his .45 revolver and shot at the erect silhouette of the bear. I had a feeling right then our goose was cooked.

The grizzly jumped and made a sound like a man's "Oh!" at the impact of the bullet. He probably thought a bee had stung him, but Earl, only half awake, fired again quickly. At the second shot the bear looked our way.

I'd already crawled from under the covers with my rifle, and from a kneeling position I fired at the huge bulk as it came hurtling toward us. The shock of the 8 mm. rifle bullet stopped him momentarily. I saw that Earl was hopelessly tangled in his bedding and I yelled, "Roll up in the canvas!" He did, and that's what saved him.

The bear pounced on him like a dog on a gopher and was soon shaking and mauling both Earl and the canvas. I placed the muzzle of the rifle against the bear's shoulder and fired. The bullet penetrated both shoulders, rendering the great forearms useless. The first shot had torn away the upper part of the heart.

The grizzly fell on his side on top of Earl (who no longer struggled) roaring and growling with rage and trying to turn over to fasten his teeth in whatever was under the canvas. When the grizzly's struggles finally stopped I became aware of Soto

187

standing a little away from me with his six-shooter in hand trembling like a leaf.

Together we rolled the bear off Earl, whom we found alive and miraculously without any broken bones. For that matter, he had no open wounds. His hurts didn't show till morning, but the bedding was so badly soaked with bear blood that sleeping in it was impossible. We made a fire between the campsite and the spring and sat up for the rest of the night. By daylight Earl could hardly move. There was scarcely a place on his body that wasn't bruised black and blue.

We couldn't find the deer carcass that morning. Some animal had evidently come in boldly after we retreated to our new site and carried away the carcass of the deer while we sat by the fire. The only tracks we found other than grizzly prints were of a very large cat.

Then we tackled the grizzly carcass. Soto and I had managed to get it off Earl during the night, but we couldn't budge it off our bed. It was cold and stiff now and the legs stuck out like bedposts. We had to saddle two horses and drag the carcass out of camp with lariat ropes.

At noon only three burros came in for water and I thought immediately of the tinkling bells I'd heard during the night. Backtracking the stock, we found what had taken place. As a rule burros don't help each other, as many animals do, but they are terrible fighters when cornered. Ours had fought a pack of wolves. There'd been a lot of blood spilled and the wolves had killed, eaten, or dragged away most of our pack animals. We found one dead wolf and a crippled one that we killed.

While Earl convalesced, we killed another deer and hung it in a tree well out of camp. The next morning it, too, was gone. We trailed and killed the raider this time — a large jaguar.

It was several days before Earl could walk or ride, and in the meantime Soto showed me the country. There were no kills around the spring but within half a mile of there we found many old kills and some fresh bones. Then he took me southeast nearly a mile from camp to where a steep, narrow trail came up out of the great canyon basin. In some places this trail was so narrow a critter would have had difficulty turning around. If a large animal slipped here it would roll for at least 50 yards.

188

There were bleached bones all over the steep sidehill, as well as some fresh ones. I knew the explanation. We'd had a similar set-up on the west slopes of San Francisco Peaks, just a few miles north of Flagstaff, Arizona. A grizzly there would ambush cattle on the narrow trail and knock them over a deadly dropoff.

"Do these bears do this in daylight?" I asked Soto. He thought they did, but mostly in the evening or early morning.

The trail was crooked and a little brushy point jutted out less than 50 yards from where most of the killing had been done. There was still another place farther down that was completely hidden from our view. It was getting late now and the trail was in shadow. The upper side was just gloomy enough to hide a bear and the wind was right for us also. I saw trees and brush enough to conceal half a dozen grizzlies. Far down the trail we could see a small herd of cattle slowly working their way up to water. They were so far away, I had my doubts they would reach us while it was still light enough to shoot, but we decided to wait anyway.

Earl, back at camp, had said he was going out with his .30/30 rifle and a .22 to try for a deer and young turkey at the spring. Even now Soto and I heard turkeys somewhere above the trail. I got out my wing-bone call and began making turkey talk. They answered and came down on the trail. When they failed to locate the calling turkey, they went on up the trail where we knew Earl would be waiting. We figured that if the turkeys had been unable to locate us, no bear ever could.

The turkeys had only been gone for a few minutes when Earl's .30/30 rifle sounded in the distance. But that wouldn't alarm either the turkeys or a bear for long. Shooting in a country seldom hunted, where thunder showers are frequent, disturbs game little.

Soto and I had just made cigarettes when we heard a slight sound in the bushes above the trail and saw the scrub oak bushes move. No sooner had we ground out our cigarettes than around the curve came a long-horned, spotted steer and three cows. This wasn't the same bunch we'd seen below. These apparently had been on one of the many invisible curves in the trail, and much nearer us.

Just then the lead steer snorted and sprang forward as a

189

grizzly jumped out of the brush and with one smashing blow broke the second animal down in the hindquarters. The last cow reared on her hind legs, spun around like a top, and ran. The second cow was slower in turning and the bear raised up on his hind legs to land a steak maker.

We both shot at that instant. One bullet took effect in the bear's left shoulder, and his cow-killing blow never landed. The cow completed her turn and ran.

The old grizzly roared and wheeled about, looking for his enemy, but finally lost his balance and rolled down the rocky slope to join the crippled cow below. He was dead when we got to him. We shot the maimed cow.

In the ensuing days we killed seven more bears in the vicinity. Earl still carried bruises from his mauling when he got back to Durango. It was the first and last time he ever picked a fight with a grizzly with only a .45 revolver to defend himself. It's dangerous to dream of bandits when there are grizzlies about.

"Bedtime Story", by Jack Tooker appeared in the June 1954 issue of *Outdoor Life*.

D O W N   I N

The Bend

W I T H   R I L E Y

The familiar little tube caught him, swung ahead
— and the opening gun of the goose war of '13
cracked like a well snapped bull whip.

by Nash Buckingham

Nature had at last smeared a layer of frosting upon our slice of the earth's cake, and we duck and goose shooters, full hungry through months of shot and powder fasting, looked on with overjoyed expectancy and were glad in it.

Here it was turning winter again and last January had seen me saying goodbye to my friends, the Rileys, when they left our club at old Beaver Dam, and moved down into the "Bend." I had heard from them occasionally; how little Mike was growing clean out of his boots; how Mr. Riley was supplying the countryside with the finest of delicate catfish; and of the prospects for a big catch of fur. Mrs. Riley wrote of the wild turkeys that were "using" in her backyard cornfield, and of the quail that fed on the pea patch lawn. For, to identify their whereabouts

191

completely, you must know that the woodland abode of my friends was pitched just above O.K. Landing, some seventy-five miles below Memphis, right in a corner pocket of one of Ole Mississippi's gigantic elbows.

I recall distinctly that we were all at Sunday dinner. Grandfather had just stuck his specially whetted blade deep into the red heart of a ponderous rib roast. Grandmother was frantically endeavoring to restrain baby's furious onslaught upon the innocent, but fascinating gravy dish; while Bunk and I viewed this typical home scene with placid expectation and platters held at "ready." Outside, across the expanse of wet blown lawns, a biting north wind, swooping on the heels of a chilling rain, whirled the leaves end over end in a rollicking carnival of winter pranks.

Came then the Melody! Down from the dull grey heights it floated, a wild clangor beating past the barriers of civilization, a vibrant babel above the housetops, chatting o'chill warped stubble fields in the ice gripped northland left behind, voicing a clamorous longing for warmer clime, white and golden gravelly sandbars, luscious rice, pea and corn fields to come.

"Ah — ah-unnncckk — uh — orrrnncckk-un-onk — nonk — uunncckk!

Grandfather's cherished knife edge bent unheeded upon the hidden skewer; grandmother and Baby Dumpling sensing it too, forgot the conquest of the gravy dish and paused to listen, keenly alive to those harbinger calls from the wild goose gabblers. Bunk and I met at the window — to look. There they were, scarce rifle shot above the grove elms, a long moulding, melting V, swinging, wafting into and out of line, strict of discipline in response to guttural flight orders, hoarse of chorus — and on their way!

"Unk-ah-unk-ah — ornck — uk-onk — ehuunnçckk-onk!

"Au revoir, gents," said I, when the flock faded into twinkling specks and almost vanished, beyond the misty park. "I'll see you afore'long, when things get right."

"Me, too, gents," echoed Bunk, "I'll see you too, won't I?" (looking up at me). And back through the lanes of the winds that blow came a faint, defiant, *"UUNNCCKK-ah-ah-ONK!"*

We had climbed a score of times since then, Bunk and I, into the dim vaults of the attic, to delve and potter in our treasure

192

trove of hunting and fishing truck. What evenings those were to be sure! Between us, in mid-floor, the battered old trunk, and beside it, the length and breadth of our gigantic companion of all trips, "buster" the big suitcase. A long sigh from Bunk.

"Now let me see, *IS* that everything?"

"Your waders and heavy socks, righto, check 'em offn' the list!"

"Done done it."

"Quit foolin' with those reels and flies, you make me home-sick."

"My boots and stockings?"

"Uuummpphh!"

"My two fleece-lined overshirts — is that goose call tied on?"

"Those shirts ought to be washed."

"You might have saved their lives two wears ago — too late now."

"You've shipped the shells, all the guns are here!"

"All present or accounted for, Your Fatheadedness!"

"Don't as you value your creamy hide cause me to break a lung strapping that luggage and then shriek out that you've overlooked your toothbrush or cold cream — or pearls. Is that EVERYTHING — answer me, Yes or No!"

"Yeth — Ivory Knob."

Two evenings later we "lit out" for Riley's!

Our first day at the club, shooting ducks, is another story. I could tell you of how I bored deep into the lower cypress brake and made it hot for the big mallards that swarmed and clucked and circled through the tree tops and fluttered down to rich feeding in the loblolly beneath the button willows. I could relate, too, how Bunk drew the New Stand, just behind a wall of buffalo grass in a cove opposite the clubhouse, and boom-banged away to her heart's content. And I can prove her part by showing her as she came up through the cotton patch that afternoon with a clean state limit to show for her work. But our story really opens next day, when Riley himself appeared across the lake, with his quick little horse and roomy fish wagon. Bunk climbed up beside our smiling host while I chucked in the two sacks of wooden profile decoys, the war-bag and shells, and swung atop of it all to hold on as best I could. For us it was a

193

voyage into virgin territory and each turn of the sandy loam and buckshot road held something of interest.

A killing frost had fallen, the sun was brilliant in its path of glorious autumn radiance, abundant, snowy fields were alive with darkies, singing and chatting away while picking at their crops. Rapidly we passed from one plantation to another, swinging gradually all the while toward the southwest. Part of our way led along the sloping bank of a vast cypress stretch, another turn and we penetrated the somnolent shade of the forest itself and out again into the open country. We clattered past comfortable plantation homes, flanked by bulging barns, these in turn sentineled by snug whitewashed darky cabins with grinning, playful pickaninnies rolling poached egg eyes from the doorsteps. The countryside seemed teeming with prospects of good cheer; even to the very fatness of grunting unsuspecting porkers laying on fat against the treachery of their doomsday.

At length we reached the sloping bank of the levee, topped it and entered, so Riley said, the borders of our hunting country. Some two miles farther on, through an intervening community of abandoned bottom land, subject to overflow, we turned a corner and sighted Riley's tent house. And there was Mrs. Riley, as prim and neat and hearty of welcome as ever, and Mike, grown, sure enough, almost like Jack's beanstalk.

"Light down, folks," said Riley, "here's the brown stone front an' please to notice the magnificent grounds an' surpassing view."

Women like things to first be put in order, and this, to Riley and me, couldn't spell "time-out" with goose prospects. So we left the afternoon's setting down to Bunk and Mrs. Riley, while we two, with Mike all in a perspiration to help, set off up the sandbar to explore for territory and get things in readiness for the morrow's fun. Afternoon was well along. We loaded the light but cumbersome bulk of the decoys into Riley's boat, Mike bent to the oars and we set off on a long narrow strip of muddy water, which, slipping in from a recent slight rise had spilled behind the bar, and cut it in half. Riley packed the 22 Hi-power while I lugged my 16 gauge and a pocket full of shells loaded with number two's. For thirty minutes Mike pulled steadily up the shallow cutoff, heading in and landing finally under the slope of a major bar. We stacked the decoys on the beach near the boat and set out on a

194

tramp of discovery. Not a goose in sight! On we paced, until Riley, stopping suddenly, put a warning hand behind his ear. Down wind from the distant head gravels of the bar came a faint *"Ah-euunncckk!"* On went the grinning Riley, until from the height of a sand rise we saw, still far ahead, a few dots that betrayed the sentinels of our strutting enemies — the geese.

Bob," said I, "you know this country and the goose hangouts better'n I do, suppose you take the little needle gun, drift on and sorter circle 'em. I'll drop down behind this snag here, with Mike, and take a chance on some of their royal goosenesses' flagging down into this side track. Sign what says 'Derail Here!' Whatta'ya' think, Old Timer?"

"I think so," vouchsafed Bob, "git down!"

Mike and I "got," and away stalked the weatherbeaten figure of my friend. The huge stranded tree which was to serve us as a blind lay sloping off a dippy sand ridge. Below this dip, snuggled close against the bark of the dismantled willow, I scraped a trough in the soft sand and lay down to wait. In a private nest among the switches Mike cuddled into nothing. On one side I could maintain a far and wide survey of the bar, and by peering underneath the dip, I could also manage to accumulate a pretty fair idea of what was going on toward the river. An eternity seemed to pass. Riley circled far out and disappeared over the east rim of the sand waste. An occasional *"eeuunncckk"* gave hope. They grew more frequent. No sleeping at the switch for the master goose — Riley was spotted to a certainty. What a babel of alarm preceded the wind-blown pop of the Hi-power. He'd landed on 'em! A cloud of black specks beat into the air, mounted the shore line and flapped down wind my way. Not even an eyebrow showed from my hiding place. Then disappointment dropped like a night shadow — surely, but slowly they were swerving off my line.

Another pop from the invisible Riley, another cloud of winking dots headed logward. Hope flamed into hot expectancy. Their hunks and honks came blown in a storm of echoed heart beats. From under my precious log I watched the nearing line and the closer they came, the tighter I squeezed to my dead tree. Cocked, primed and loaded to the muzzle. A faint click of drawn trigger.

Now come on, you great big beautiful geese! What a bedlam of honking!

I saw the puff breasted pilot weaving at their fore and mentally placed him first on the death film. On they swung, right smack dab over the snakelike roots of my treetop. The leader's bulk loomed black between me and the cloud flecked sky; the familiar little tube caught him, swung ahead — and the opening gun of the goose war of 13 cracked like a well snapped bull whip.

Didn't he come tumbling, though! And didn't the rest of the flock take on something scandalous? Such a hovering, clustering consternation and glutters of surprised dismay, I saw Mr. Leader's neck flick backward, saw him wilt with an in and out folding of his powerful wings, and by that time the 16 was warmed to its work and in the heart of the flock, spitting and popping like a live thing. A thunderous wallop right behind me, a blurred vision of Mike's leaping out of the branches, a last despairing shot at a side slanter. Empty! I looked around. The pilot lay breast to sky out front, Mike was retrieving the bird that had almost mashed him in its fall, and while we looked a third goose turned loose all "holts" and plunged to earth — far down the bar. Wasn't it fine and dandy, though! Three burly geese down and out right off the reel — just on chance prospect, too! Ensued quite a period of lying in wait. Mikey moved up to keep me company, and between us we plotted black doings against the geese.

Several small gangs flew high over us and dropped back upon the northern shallows. At length a far-away speck developed into Riley. Our minds were as one on a location for next day. We hiked to the boat, shouldered the decoys. Mike caught up the long handled shovel and for half an hour there went forward a pit digging bee. Into these we piled the decoys and then dropped down the rippling slough to where Mrs. Riley had put a light in the willow gap that marked Sweet Home.

Someone shook the flap of our compartment. We lay quite still. It couldn't be Dixie, the black puppy who roomed in a palatial soap box under our bed and occasionally chased her tail for a soft spot.

Come alive," said Riley, "three forty-five — Mistis' gettin' corrfee." We were fully awake by now and when I threw back the sheath of bedding, I realized that Old B'rer Frost had driv'up an' hitched during the night. My toilet was elaborate, requiring the side of the bed and a world of speed while I put on my boots, cap and goose call. A pocket flashlight showed me the bucket and basin — then I parted the flap of the home tent and looked in upon an exquisite little stove side setting. Riley — with a toehold on the table leg and his face four inches inside his extra special police positive coffee cup. When it comes to general all-round eating ability, I believe that Riley is a diamond in the rough. With proper training and coaching and a year or so in fast company, he would be worth a bet — any old time.

He is not a flashy eater, nor for that matter a tremendous feeder, but he is busy all the time — all the time, he's busy. He has long arms, never wastes a punch and above all is a magnificent judge of distance. And what is even more important, while not wonderfully fast, he is a cracker-jack two handed eater. I have always contended that had Bob ever gone in for playing the "XY-zil-liphone," one of those musical railroad sections with metal cross ties which the musical Zeroes beat with child-size tom-toms, he simply could never have been headed off. At any rate, Mrs. Riley was just shooting a platter of radiant hen-eggs fried "One-eye-to-heaven," and a pan of hot, obese biscuits, when Bunk came along and "throwed in" with us. That was some "deestruction" when Mike finally horned in against the table and added his voice to the eating.

Bob and I are both pupils of the Old School when it comes to applying the K.O. to an opposition of ham, eggs, and burly biscuits. In the fight game there is a punch called the "one-two" — a hard, well sighted left jab with the right coming along just behind it, real snappy — one-two-zip-bing — even so — just like that! The same principle applies when it comes to landing on fried eggs and buttered sofa pillows. Lead with the left blade — split the egg — flop it onto half biscuit — come up with the right — all off! Four or five eggs and two cups of hot kill-chill drip coffee will take anyone a long way up any sandbar on a cold morning.

There was a smudge of grey on the hearth of the East when we filed down through the willow gap and out upon the yielding carpet of the bar. Its wide expanse and the unseen river beyond might have been an ocean stretching away into unknown regions. From below the Bend came the measured chugging exhaust of a packet driving up against the push of sweeping current. We shouldered our guns and strode off toward the boat, Bunk with a hand

197

in the warm pocket of my coat, all alive and excited over the possibilities of her goose hunt. Into our craft we piled with Riley at the oars. Up the shallow slough we thumped, while flock after flock of roosting mallards took wing in roars of protest.

I have come over timberline in the Rockies, when Dawn, parting her blinds, leaned out and pried deep and smiling into spruce toothed gulches and across the vales and mists of placid lakes. I have seen daybreak on the plains, beyond an arid rimless world; I have caught its first gleam upon the birches and golden tamarack tops in the moose bogs of the North; it has crept down to me through vaulted city canyons and melted breeze blown across southern seas. But never yet have I found a day-birth that labors so tranquilly as night's demise upon a sandbar. On and on tugged Riley, full busy with his thoughts and we two, listening to the ripple of the boat's wash, dreamed dreams of a wonderful shoot and flocks of brainless obliging geese, who just would decoy. We spoke in whispers while the daub of grey smouldered into an ash of rose and flamed a threat of sunrise.

And in the heart of day's opal belt, a great star, diamond blue, burned its defiant, steadfast spotlight. The giant steamboat, rounding a bend, loomed glittering and monstrous as she cleaved a way ahead. Scarcely had our little boat grated hard aground upon hidden shoals, before we were halted by the same sonorous, warning *"Ah — uunncckk!"*

It required probably five minutes' swift work to set up the decoys, a neat array of confidence goose "come-ons" they were, too. Bunk, neck deep in her pit, looked on eagerly, offering suggestions as to pose and poise in such cases as wronged her sense of style in decoys.

"There," gulped Bob, shoving his last bird into the powdery sand, "all slantin' inta the wind, if them geese don't decoy to 'em they've gotta be devilish wise — that's all I gotta say." Then he and I dropped down into our double pit and prepared for business. First we put the long handled shovel across the pit mouth and made a gun rack of it, then we shrouded our guns in an old coat. Bunk, meanwhile had arranged a rack of her own, fashioned from a dead drift limb and protected her gun by means of a triumphant tan stocking pulled down over the muzzle and fastened about the stock with a rubber band. The sun was well up now, revealing

198

the vast frost tinted bar, the drab river still steaming off its vapor bath, and the bleak, forest clad outlines of the high Arkansas shore. A light breeze puffed out of the north. "They'll hav' ta swing aroun' to decoy," said Bob, "an' them what don't 'll come beatin' up — wind — lookee yonder — there's a big bunch gettin' off the water 'cross yonder up the bay."

We heard their rising clamor and shrank watchfully into the pits. Out came my goose call and a loud, awkward squawk supposed to be sufficiently succinct of purpose awoke the reaches of the bar.

"They're swinging, they're swinging,"murmured Bob — then — "you be peeper — we'll keep down an' open up on 'em when you holler 'NOW !'" With that both he and Bunk were effaced from the scene pro tem.

My awkward call had proved a stray bullet gone home, for the flock pivoted over the Mississippi shore line willows and headed down the bar — straight for our trap. Talk about your deer stand when the hounds bay behind some poor fagged out, scared to death buck! Talk about chattering teeth on a cold morning and the seductive brilliancy of military rag-time! Why — there is no excitement on earth like a pit, a bunch of decoys and a herd of bugling geese preparing to do business on a sight unseen basis. The rim of my pit dike and the tip of my cap were a hopeless merger and the big honkers had cupped their wings and were sliding along low almost over the decoys. Off flashed the gun cover and just as I pitched the 16 gauge to my shoulder, the lead goose threw a shadow into my pit. Up sprang I, with a shout of "NOW."

And up sprang Riley and Bunk. Fellow Goose Shooters, I am here to state that for the space of twenty seconds there was something doing in that immediate vicinity. I'll admit, frankly, that I tried to kill all the geese in the world; that my gun hung after the two first shots and that I added quite a little to the complete uproar by proclaiming bitterly against it. Bob bounced both barrels of number twelve off a particularly unfortunate goose, and little Bunk took her time and nailed a fine fat fellow, too. But my shots had felled two birds and what with all the shooting and excitement and falling geese, it looked as though the rebellion was over for the time being. The disrupted flock beat it off down wind, sorely

199

stricken and thrown into hideous confusion. Was Milady delighted? She was dancing in her pit when I scrambled out to retrieve — chanting something about "Goosey-goosey Gander, where shall I wander," and making so infernally much noise that I reminded her of the other rhyme about the "Little man who had a little gun and his bullets were made of lead, lead, lead!" I stored the slain honkers in a frost encased cavity beside a neighboring snag and rejoined Bob in our pit.

The latter was just lighting his pipe a bit later and remarking that it took something pretty strong to make his tongue crawl, when Bunk, with watchful orbs turned south, hollered "I spy." Sure enough, five geese emerged from the atmosphere in that direction and hunched luggingly up toward us. Once again the call gained their attention to the general direction of our whereabouts. With set wings they deliberately volplaned directly at our wooden sleuths. I was just on the point of giving the signal when up shot Mr. Leader and barely out of range he led his flock of four craftily around the other way. But our wooden heads were there with the foolish powders and having given them the "once over," in swung Messrs. Geese. We should have got all five of them, but I made a mess of my first bird, and spent all my time on him while Riley and Bunk were plastering several loads of number two's all over the face of the sky, some of them taking effect in the person of a singularly fat goose who "took the count." Following a lengthy post-mortem the two victims were put into our cold storage lockup and the scene took on its customary attitude of peace.

During the next four hours only one goose showed up and when he finally circled on off up the river we rose in a body and voted him the foxiest guy that ever lived. He flew around and over and all but under our decoys. He scrutinized them from every direction, read both sides of them and read 'em on the edge. "Not a friend in the crowd," muttered Bob as Herr Goose finally came to a decision and went his way!

The sun was probably just past overhead when Bunk suggested that we come out of the pits and set about a little relaxation in the shape of lunch. Now it is a fact, and a well proven one, that the very best method of getting a rise out of laggardly ducks or geese is to just dare to emerge from one's blind and get gay with the one full of sausage and biscuit and the other laden with coffee, put an end to all goose sense we might, or might not have had. So out we wormed, and pretty pronto Bunk had a little blaze snapping beside the far end of our refrigerator snag and the coffee bucket doing a get-warm stunt.

Riley had just settled himself comfortably against the log, bitten a half moon out of a sausage sandwich and observed that Bernard Shaw made him sick, when Bunk let loose a muffled shriek and pointed due west — toward the river. There, just skimming the tree tops, came a long, wide line of geese making a sneak on our bar. Consternation reigned supreme — and then reigned some more. Cries of "To the pits; Kick out the fire, Douse the glim, Never mind me, save the women and children," rent the crisp autumnal air. Bunk jerked the coffee can aside just as I made a kick at the blaze; Riley shoved the sausage bucket under a long log and off to the hides we raced, diving into them finally, not a moment too soon.

Had they seen us! The goose call, muffled to a pleasing tone, besought our unexpected visitors to overlook appearances and do business with us.

Widely they circled — once again — far down wind — then a twisting circle and back they headed — wings cupped. But discretion proved the better part of valor — off they veered and lit probably a hundred and fifty yards beyond the outskirts of our "come ons." Gradually we arose, peeked and stretched our strained and cramped limbs. The infernal villains! Their big bow-legged scout goose waddled a bit to the fore and set his sharp eyes full upon us. His retainers picked about, cleared their throats or fell to napping. "If I just had that rifle I'd sho' knock two or three of those rascals up to about 800," said Riley.

We were standing up by this time, fully visible, but the geese didn't seem to be apprehensive — just looked, saw our profile decoy and wondered! We fell to chatting in undertones and Riley was just telling us what a magnificent goose bar lay a bit above, when something, either ashore or at any rate beyond the geese, set Watcheye, the scout to running his warning scale. Down we dodged and up went they, swinging our way, too! Would they this time? The only one near enough for a shot. I think all three guns had the old chap spotted for three shots

201

sounded, timed almost as one, and down he came like a ton of brick! Thirteen full pounds he dragged the fish scales to that night. Then we crawled out and resumed lunch, after which I set off up the bar, carrying three folding decoys and having exploration in my mind.

A mile farther along the waste of gradually rising sand brought me to where the island bar meandered out into the gravelly river spits. The district was littered with flood deposit and stranded snags. A deep haze settled about me — afternoon was just about to turn over for another nap. I waded out into the shallows and set down my three folding decoys — for what reason I'm sure I don't know, and was just wondering, in addition, why I had lugged them and a box of shells all the way up the bar.

Picked up again! Then and there came the goose alarm and, I, looking wildly about for shelter, espied a jumble of heavy boards lodged fantastically about a tree root close by. In two jumps I was into the nest, stretched out full length, watching and waiting. There they came, two of them, as straight up to the bar as a plumb line could have caught them. A hundred yards off they caught my decoys, veered a bit and setting their wings at seeing so congenial a little crowd of friends, swung glidingly in. And I let them do the ridiculous. Just as their bandy legs were wiggling in preparatory ground maneuvers — then I sat up and rolled the bones. "Seven-eleven, I yelled — Oh, you Gander! *Bamm-bamm-wop-floppity-floppity-baum-woop!*"

It was just like shooting fish, even if I did have to throw in a third shot, and retrieving those two burlies within ten feet of each other was a genuine pleasure. But no more geese came along and my patience finally frazzled out.

Riley had gone to the boat for something when I came back to the pits and Bunk was coiled up in her big coat and two gunny sacks — fast asleep in her pit. We had a reunion a bit later on when Bob returned and Bunk came out of her nap. "Time t'was sumpthin' doin' with them bullies," said Riley, cutting an eye at the "low descending sun!" But time waited not for us goose hunters, and half an hour toiled off without hide or hair of gooseflesh. "This ain't no way," fumed Bob, "Aw — come on, geese!" And as if in answer to his call, and

202

our prayer, the biggest flock of the day came lugging in from the northeast — the rascals had evidently been feeding over the way. They circled once — then, strange to say, split all asunder; some flew east, some went west, but some flew over the shooter's nest — and got in awful bad — awful bad. Three of their number went to glory amid a popping of ballistite, honks of dismay and general all around hullabaloo.

When it was all over, Bob and I decided that the time to leave had arrived — there were the decoys to take up and sack, transport to the boat, and heaviest of all, some several geese. Our backs groaned in anticipatory labor. Bunk was loaded with the guns and her coat and trudged off — the same willing, strong little huntress who always does her share. But it took us two trips to load in the geese and decoys, the former carried strung on the stout handle of the shovel.

Evening was dipping gold tipped sun ladles into the glowing tureen of the west when we dropped down the quiet slough. Across the flaming shadow flecked glass of the great river, above and beyond the gaunt heights of the forest, a trail of smoke curled from the cook fires of some labor camp. Little Mike met us when our craft slid in upon the near bar; we resumed a new division of the spoils — and set out again. Our footsteps were noiseless, we talked little, just walked and watched and walked and were busy with our thoughts. Myriad flocks of ducks winged in zizzing flight to faraway night roosts. A startling honk rasped from shadows beyond the bar shallows on our left. Instinctively we dropped to our knees — graven images upon the sands, in the twinkling of an eye.

"Yonner," hissed Riley, "the pilot goose, see 'im swinging down the slough under the trees, giv' 'em a call." I did and to our surprise the spy turned sharply on his great pinions and beat straight across the powdery waves of sand to where we crouched. In a moment, it seemed his bulk reared sharp and clean cut above the willow tops and when the ballistite shoved that ounce of 2's into him, he simply shook himself like a wet dog and plugged ahead. But there were others where those 2's came from, and the third strike put him plump onto the bar, stricken sorely and with Mike fair atop of him almost as soon as he was struck. And even while we bent over him, tying his

203

warm plumpness into the fold, a hissing of wings came down to us and his friends in whose interests he had attempted the survey of the bar, slid past into security.

It was plum pitch dark when we threw down our burdens before the glow and savory welcome of the tent house. No moon was riding high to show a glim, only a deep and brooding black and awesome stillness down there in the faraway Bend.

The air was sharp with gathering frost. We hung the geese high, washed up and combed our locks; slid into easy slippers and waited for Mrs. Riley to bid us "slide up and pounce upon it." And when she did, Brethren of the Outdoor Cult, me an' Bunk an' Riley did *SOME* pouncing. Who wouldn't have — listen to this! Ever eat any fresh water sturgeon — of the fall run? Being loyal to the Stars and Bars, if any one had ever slipped up behind me and shouted suddenly in my ear — "What's the best fish on earth?" I would have yelled "cat," quite as naturally as getting up in the morning. But here was a fish, I hate to admit, but it's true, that had a catfish cornered and with all escape cut off. No bones, save a tiny fern-like back one, just pure white, flaky, sweet meat that sorter ate itself. There were baked spuds, good browned beans, hot rolls picked smoking dreamily from the oven, hot chocolate and some home made tomato chutney that ate right where you held it. After supper, with the dishes washed and everything made snug, we sat around in the cozy comfort of the tent home and talked of many things.

We of the city know little of the world whose people dwell so closely in touch with and wrest their bread from nature. We travel our streets, talk business, rates, drive our automobiles, harp upon our sales and losses, our pleasures and the wear and tear of it all. With us, it is a concrete reckoning; a world of stunning human competition. For them, it is a peaceful striving for nature's yield. Their streets are the aisles of the forest, the paths and trails of the rugged hills; their rates are figured in the cunning of their brains — the jump of a trap, the bat of an eye, the fall of a trigger. Tranquil solvers of world problems — producers, exterminators; furriers by right of conquest of His Majesty, the Universe! We talked that night of the summer agone, of the day's fun; we went over the trap line of memory!

204

In the quiet lapses, while the old stove purred and hissed, there came from the willow brake hard by the nestling undertone of roosting wildfowl chatter, or through the moonless depth of the jungle there wound down to us the faraway note of some 'coon hunter's horn.

Finally Mikey rolled his bedding onto the floor and at this signal Bunk and I arose and stumbled into our tent. The light just sorter flickered out — blinking pitiful winks — and all was still.

This story first appeared in the April, 1914 issue of Outdoor World & Recreation.

RACE AT

This compelling story by one of America's greatest
writers reminds us that the pleasure of the hunt
lies in the pursuit, not in the kill.

by William Faulkner

I was in the boat when I seen him. It was jest dust-dark;
I had jest fed the horses and clumb back down the
bank to the boat and shoved off to cross back to camp
when I seen him, about half a quarter up the river,
swimming; jest his head above the water, and it no more than
a dot in that light. But I could see that rocking chair he toted
on it and I knowed it was him, going right back to that canebrake
in the fork of the bayou where he lived all year until the day
before the season opened, like the game wardens had give him
a calendar, when he would clear out and disappear, nobody
knowed where, until the day after the season closed. But here
he was, coming back a day ahead of time, like maybe he had
got mixed up and was using last year's calendar by mistake.
Which was jest too bad for him, because me and Mister Ernest

would be setting on the horse right over him when the sun rose tomorrow morning.

So I told Mister Ernest and we et supper and fed the dogs, and then I holp Mister Ernest in the poker game, standing behind his chair until about ten o'clock, when Roth Edmonds said, "Why don't you go to bed, boy?"

"Or if you're going to set up," Willy Legate said, "why don't you take a spelling book to set up over? He knows every cuss word in the dictionary, every poker hand in the deck and every whisky label in the distillery, but he can't even write his name. Can you?" he says to me.

"I don't need to write my name down," I said. "I can remember in my mind who I am."

"You're twelve years old," Walter Ewell said. "Man to man now, how many days in your life did you ever spend in school?"

"He ain't got time to go to school," Willy Legate said. "What's the use in going to school from September to middle of November, when he'll have to quit then to come in here and do Ernest's hearing for him? And what's the use in going back to school in January, when in jest eleven months it will be November fifteenth again and he'll have to start all over telling Ernest which way the dogs went?"

"Well, stop looking into my hand, anyway," Roth Edmonds said.

"What's that? What's that?" Mister Ernest said. He wore his listening button in his ear all the time, but he never brought the battery to camp with him because the cord would bound to get snagged ever time we run through a thicket.

"Willy says for me to go to bed!" I hollered.

"Don't you never call nobody 'mister'?" Willy said.

"I call Mister Ernest 'mister'," I said.

"All right," Mister Ernest said, "Go to bed then, I don't need you."

"That ain't no lie," Willy said. "Deaf or no deaf, he can hear a fifty-dollar raise if you don't even move your lips."

So I went to bed, and after a while Mister Ernest come in and I wanted to tell him again how big them horns looked even half a quarter away in the river. Only I would'a' had to holler, and the only time Mister Ernest agreed he couldn't hear was

207

when we would be setting on Dan, waiting for me to point which way the dogs was going. So we jest laid down, and it wasn't no time Simon was beating the bottom of the dishpan with the spoon, hollering, "Raise up and get your four-o'clock coffee!" and I crossed the river in the dark this time, with the lantern, and fed Dan and Roth Edmondziz horse. It was going to be a fine day, cold and bright; even in the dark I could see the white frost on the leaves and bushes — jest exactly the kind of day that big old son-of-a-gun laying up there in that brake would like to run.

Then we et, and set the stand-holder across for Uncle Ike McCaslin to put them on the stands where he thought they ought to be, because he was the oldest one in camp. He had been hunting deer in these woods for about a hundred years, I reckon, and if anybody would know where a buck would pass, it would be him. Maybe with a big old buck like this one, that had been running the woods for what would amount to a hundred years in a deer's life, too, him and Uncle Ike would sholy manage to be at the same place at the same time this morning — provided, of course, he managed to git away from me and Mister Ernest on the jump. Because me and Mister Ernest was going to git him.

Then me and Mister Ernest and Roth Edmonds sent the dogs over, with Simon holding Eagle and the other old dogs on leash because the young ones, the puppies, wasn't going nowhere until Eagle let them, nohow. Then me and Mister Ernest and Roth saddled up, and Mister Ernest got up and I handed him up his pump gun and let Dan's bridle go for him to git rid of the spell of bucking he had to git shut of ever morning until Mister Ernest hit him between the ears with the gun barrel. Then Mister Ernest loaded the gun and give me the stirrup, and I got up behind him and we taken the fire road up toward the bayou, the four big dogs dragging Simon along in front with his single-barrel britchloader slung on a piece of plow line across his back, and the puppies moiling along in ever'body's way. It was light now and it was going to be jest fine; the east already yellow for the sun and our breaths smoking in the cold still bright air until the sun would come up and warm it, and a little skim of ice in the ruts, and ever leaf and twig and switch and even the frozen clods frosted over, waiting to sparkle like a rainbow when the sun finally come up and hit them. Until all my insides felt light and strong as a balloon, full of that light cold strong air, so that it seemed to me like I couldn't even feel the horse's back I was straddle of — jest the hot strong muscles moving under the hot strong skin, setting up there without no weight atall, so that when old Eagle struck and jumped, me and Dan and Mister Ernest would go jest like a bird, not even touching the ground. It was jest fine. When that big old buck got killed today, I knowed that even if he had put it off another ten years, he couldn't't'a' picked a better one.

And sho enough, as soon as we come to the bayou we seen his foot in the mud where he had come up out of the river last night, spread in the soft mud like a cow's foot, big as a cow's, big as a mule's, with Eagle and the other dogs laying into the leash rope now until Mister Ernest told me to jump down and help Simon hold them. Because me and Mister Ernest knowed exactly where he would be — a little canebrake island in the middle of the bayou, where he could lay up until whatever doe or little deer the dogs had happened to jump could go up or down the bayou in either direction and take the dogs on away, so he could steal out and creep back down the bayou to the river and swim it, and leave the country like he always done the day the season opened.

Which is jest what we never aimed for him to do this time. So we left Roth on his horse to cut him off and turn him over Uncle Ike's standers if he tried to slip back down the bayou, and me and Simon, with the leashed dogs, walked on up the bayou until Mister Ernest on the horse said it was fur enough; then turned up into the woods about half a quarter above the brake because the wind was going to be south this morning when it riz, and turned down toward the brake, and Mister Ernest give the word to cast them, and we slipped the leash and Mister Ernest give me the stirrup again and I got up.

Old Eagle had done already took off because he knowed where that old son-of-a-gun would be laying as good as we did, not making no racket atall yet, but jest boring on through the buck vines with the other dogs trailing along behind him, and even Dan seemed to know about that buck, too, beginning to souple up and jump a little through the vines, so that I taken my holt on Mister Ernest's belt already before the time had come for Mister Ernest to touch him. Because when we got strung out, going fast behind a deer, I wasn't on Dan's back much of the time nohow, but mostly jest strung out from my holt on Mister Ernest's belt, so that Willy Legate said that when we was going through the woods fast, it looked like Mister Ernest had a boy-size pair or empty overalls blowing out of his hind pocket.

So it wasn't even a strike, it was a jump. Eagle must'a' walked right up behind him or maybe even stepped on him while he was laying there still thinking it was day after tomorrow. Eagle jest throwed his head back and up and said, "There he goes," and we even heard the buck crashing through the first of the cane. Then all the other dogs was hollering behind him, and Dan give a squat to jump, but it was against the curb this time, not jest the snaffle, and Mister Ernest let him down into the bayou and swung him around the brake and up the other bank. Only he never had to say, "Which way?" because I was already pointing past his shoulder, freshening my holt on the belt jest as Mister Ernest touched Dan with that big old rusty spur on his nigh heel, because when Dan felt it he would go off jest like a stick of dynamite, straight through whatever he could bust and over or under what he couldn't, over it like a bird or under it crawling on his knees like a mole or a big coon, with Mister Ernest still on him because he had the saddle to hold on to, and me still there because I had Mister Ernest to hold on to; me and Mister Ernest not riding him, but jest going along with him, provided we held on. Because when the jump come, Dan never cared who else was there neither; I believe to my soul he could'a' cast and run them dogs by hisself, without me or Mister Ernest or Simon or nobody.

That's what he done. He had to; the dogs was already almost out of hearing. Eagle must 'a' been looking right up that big son-of-a gun's-tail until he finally decided he better git on out of there. And now they must 'a' been getting pretty close to Uncle Ike's standers, and Mister Ernest reined Dan back and held him, squatting and bouncing and trembling like a mule having his tail roached, while we listened for the shots. But

210

never none come, and I hollered to Mister Ernest we better go on while I could still hear the dogs, and he let Dan off, but still there wasn't no shots, and now we knowed the race had done already passed the standers, like that old son-of-a-gun actually was a hant, like Simon and the other field hands said he was, and we busted out of a thicket, and sho enough there was Uncle Ike and Willy standing beside his foot in a soft patch.

"He got through us all," Uncle Ike said. "I don't know how he done it. I just had a glimpse of him. He looked big as an elephant, with a rack on his head you could cradle a yellin' calf in. He went right on down the ridge. You better get on, too; that Hog Bayou camp might not miss him."

So I freshened my holt and Mister Ernest touched Dan again. The ridge run due south; it was clear of vines and bushes so we could go fast, into the wind, too, because it had riz now, and now the sun was up, too; though I hadn't had time to notice it, bright and strong and level through the woods, shining and sparking like a rainbow on the frosted leaves. So we would hear the dogs again any time now, but still holding Dan back to a canter, because it was either going to be quick, when he got down to the standers from that Hog Bayou camp eight miles below ourn, or a long time, in case he got by them, too. And sho enough, after a while we heard the dogs; we was walking Dan now to let him blow a while, and we heard them, the sound coming faint up the wind, not running now, but trailing because the big son-of-a-gun had decided a good piece back, probably, to put an end to this foolishness, and picked hisself up and soupled out and put about a mile between hisself and the dogs — until he run up on them other standers from that camp below. I could almost see him stopped behind a bush, peeping out and saying, "What's this? What's this? Is this whole durn country full of folks this morning?" Then looking back over his shoulder at where old Eagle and the others was hollering along after him while he decided how much time he had to decide what to do next.

Except he almost shaved it too fine. We heard the shots; it sounded like a war. Old Eagle must'a' been looking right up his tail again and he had to bust on through the best way he could. "Pow, pow, pow, pow" and then "Pow, pow, pow,

211

pow," like it must 'a' been three or four ganged right up on
him before he had time even to swerve, and me hollering, "No!
No! No! No!" because he was ourn. It was our beans and oats
he et and our brake he laid in; we had been watching him every
year, and it was like we had raised him, to be killed at last on
our jump, in front of our dogs, by some strangers that would
probably try to beat the dogs off and drag him away before we
could even git a piece of the meat.

"Shut up and listen," Mister Ernest said. So I done it and we
could hear the dogs; not just the others, but Eagle, too, not
trailing no scent now and not baying no downed meat neither,
but running hot on sight long after the shooting was over. I
jest had time to freshen my holt. Yes, sir, they was running on
sight. Like Willy Legate would say, if Eagle jest had a drink of
whisky he would ketch that deer; going on, done already gone
when we broke out of the thicket and seen the fellers that had
done the shooting, five or six of them, squatting and crawling
around, looking at the ground and the bushes, like maybe if
they looked hard enough, spots of blood would bloom out on
the stalks and leaves like frogstools or hawberries, with old
Eagle still in hearing and still telling them that what blood they
found wasn't coming out of nothing in front of him.

"Have any luck, boys?" Mister Ernest said.

"I think I hit him," one of them said. "I know I did. We're
hunting blood now."

"Well, when you find him, blow your horn and I'll come
back and tote him in to camp for you," Mister Ernest said.

So we went on, going fast now because the race was almost
out of hearing again, going fast, too, like not jest the buck, but
the dogs, too, had took a new leash on life from all the excitement
and shooting.

We was in strange country now because we never had to run
this fur before, we had always killed before now; now we had
come to Hog Bayou that runs into the river a good fifteen miles
below our camp. It had water in it, not to mention a mess of
down trees and logs and such, and Mister Ernest checked Dan
again, saying, "Which way?" I could just barely hear them, off
to the east a little, like the old son-of-a-gun had given up the
idea of Vicksburg or New Orleans, like he first seemed to have,

212

and had decided to have a look at Alabama, maybe, since he was already up and moving; so I pointed and we turned up the bayou hunting for a crossing, and maybe we could'a' found one, except that I reckon Mister Ernest decided we never had time to wait.

We come to a place where the bayou had narrowed down to about twelve or fifteen feet, and Mister Ernest said, "Look out, I'm going to touch him" and done it; I didn't even have time to freshen my holt when we was already in the air, and then I seen the vine — it was a loop of grapevine nigh as big as my wrist, looping down right across the middle of the bayou — and I thought he seen it, too, and was jest waiting to grab it and fling it up over our heads to go under it, and I know Dan seen it because he even ducked his head to jump under it. But Mister Ernest never seen it until it skun back along Dan's neck and hooked under the head of the saddle horn, us flying on through the air, the loop of the vine gitting tighter and tighter until something somewhere was going to have to give. It was the saddle girth. It broke, and Dan going on and scrabbling up the other bank bare nek-kid except for the bridle, and me and Mister Ernest and the saddle, Mister Ernest still setting in the saddle holding the gun, and me still holding onto Mister Ernest's belt, hanging in the air over the bayou in the tightened loop of that vine like in the drawed-back loop of a big rubber-banded slingshot, until it snapped back and shot us back across the bayou and flang us clear, me still holding onto Mister Ernest's belt and on the bottom now, so that when we lit I would'a' had Mister Ernest and the saddle both on top of me if I hadn't clumb fast around the saddle and up Mister Ernest's side, so that when we landed, it was the saddle first, then Mister Ernest, and me on top, until I jumped up, and Mister Ernest still laying there with jest the white rim of his eyes showing.

"Mister Ernest!" I hollered, and then clumb down to the bayou and scooped my cap full of water and clumb back and throwed it in his face, and he opened his eyes and laid there on the saddle cussing me.

"God dawg it," he said. "Why didn't you stay behind where you started out?"

"You was the biggest!" I said. "You would'a' mashed me flat!"

213

"What do you think you done to me?" Mister Ernest said. "Next time, if you can't stay where you start out, jump clear. Don't climb up on top of me no more. You hear?"

"Yes, sir," I said.

So he got up then, still cussing and holding his back, and clumb down to the water and dipped some in his hand onto his face and neck and dipped some more up and drunk it, and I drunk some, too, and clumb back and got the saddle and the gun, and we crossed the bayou on the down logs. If we could jest ketch Dan; not that he would have went them fifteen miles back to camp, because, if anything, he would have went on by hisself to try to help Eagle ketch that buck. But he was about fifty yards away, eating buck vines, so I brought him back, and we taken Mister Ernest's galluses and my belt and the whang leather loop off Mister Ernest's horn and tied the saddle back on Dan. It didn't look like much but maybe it would hold.

"Provided you don't let me jump him through no more grapevines without hollering first," Mister Ernest said.

"Yes sir," I said. "I'll holler first next time — provided you'll holler a little quicker when you touch him next time, too." But it was all right; we jest had to be a little easy getting up. "Now which-a-way?" I said. Because we couldn't hear nothing now, after wasting all this time. And this was new country, sho enough. It had been cut over and growed up in thickets we couldn't 'a' seen over even standing up on Dan.

But Mister Ernest never even answered. He jest turned Dan along the bank of the bayou where it was a little more open and we could move faster again, soon as Dan and us got used to that homemade cinch strop and got a little confidence in it. Which jest happened to be east, or so I thought then, because I never paid no attention to east then because the sun — I don't know where the morning had went, but it was gone, the morning and the frost, too — was up high now, even if my insides had told me it was past dinnertime.

And then we heard him. No, that's wrong; what we heard was shots. And that was when we realized how fur we had come, because the only camp we knowed about in that direction was the Hollyknowe camp, and Hollyknowe was exactly twenty-eight miles from Van Dorn, where me and Mister Ernest

214

lived — jest the shots, no dogs nor nothing. If old Eagle was still behind him and the buck was still alive, he was too wore out now to even say, "Here he comes."

"Don't touch him!" I hollered. But Mister Ernest remembered that cinch strop, too, and he jest let Dan off the snaffle. And Dan heard them shots, too, picking his way through the thickets, hopping the vines and logs when he could and going under them when he couldn't. And sho enough, it was jest like before — two or three men squatting and creeping among the bushes, looking for blood that Eagle had done already told them wasn't there. But we never stopped this time, jest trotting on by with Dan hopping and dodging among the brush and vines dainty as a dancer. Then Mister Ernest swung Dan until we was going due north.

"Wait!" I hollered. "Not this way."

But Mister Ernest jest turned his face back over his shoulder. It looked tired, too, and there was a smear of mud on it where that ere grapevine had snatched him off the horse.

"Don't you know where he's heading?" he said. "He's done done his part, give everybody a fair open shot at him, and now he's going home, back to that brake in our bayou. He ought to make it exactly at dark."

And that's what he was doing. We went on. It didn't matter to hurry now. There wasn't no sound nowhere; it was that time in the early afternoon in November when don't nothing move or cry, not even birds, the peckerwoods and yellowhammers and jays, and it seemed like I could see all three of us — me and Mister Ernest and Dan — and Eagle, and the other dogs, and that big old buck, moving through the quiet woods in the same direction, headed for the same place, not running now but walking, that had all run the fine race the best we knowed how, all three of us now turned like on a agreement to walk back home, not together in a bunch because we didn't want to worry or tempt one another, because what we had all three spent this morning doing was no play-acting jest for fun, but was serious, and all three of us was still what we was — that old buck that had to run, not because he was skeered, but because running was what he done the best and was proudest at; and Eagle and the dogs that chased him, not because they

215

hated or feared him, but because that was the thing they done the best and was proudest at; and me and Mister Ernest and Dan, that run him not because we wanted his meat, which would be too tough to eat anyhow, or his head to hang on the wall, but because now we could go back and work hard for eleven months making a crop, so we would have the right to come back here next November — all three of us going back home now, peaceful and separate, but still side by side, until next year, next time.

Then we seen him for the first time. We was out of the cut-over now; we could even 'a' cantered, except that all three of us was long past that, and now you could tell where west was because the sun was already halfway down it. So we was walking, too, when we come on the dogs — the puppies and one of the old ones — played out, laying in a little wet swag, panting, jest looking up at us when we passed but not moving when we went on. Then we come to a long open glade, you could see about half a quarter, and we seen the three other old dogs and about hundred yards ahead of them Eagle, all walking, not making no sound; and then suddenly, at the fur end of the glade, the buck hisself getting up from where he had been resting for the dogs to come up, getting up without no hurry, big, big as a mule, tall as a mule, and turned without no hurry still, and the white underside of his tail for a second or two more before the thicket taken him.

It might 'a' been a signal, a good-bye, a farewell. Still walking, we passed the other three old dogs in the middle of the glade, laying down, too, now jest where they was when the buck vanished, and not trying to get up neither when we passed; and still that hundred yards ahead of them, Eagle, too, not laying down, because he was still on his feet, but his legs was spraddled and his head was down; maybe jest waiting until we was out of sight of his shame, his eyes saying plain as talk when we passed, "I'm sorry, boys, but this here is all."

Mister Ernest stopped Dan. "Jump down and look at his feet," he said.

"Ain't nothing wrong with his feet," I said. "It's his wind has done give out."

"Jump down and look at his feet," Mister Ernest said.

216

So I done it, and while I was stooping over Eagle I could hear the pump gun go, "Snick-cluck. Snick-cluck. Snick-cluck" three times, except that I never thought nothing then. Maybe he was jest running the shells through to be sho it would work when we seen him again or maybe to make sho they was all buckshot. Then I got up again, and we went on, still walking; a little west of north now, because when we seen his white flag that second or two before the thicket hid it, it was on a beeline for that notch in the bayou. And it was evening, too, now. The wind had done dropped and there was a edge to the air and the sun jest touched the tops of the trees now, except jest now and then, when it found a hole to come almost level through onto the ground. And he was taking the easiest way, too, now, going straight as he could. When we seen his foot in the soft places he was running for a while at first after his rest. But soon he was walking, too, like he knowed, too, where Eagle and the dogs was.

And then we seen him again. It was the last time — a thicket, with the sun coming through a hole onto it like a searchlight. He crashed jest once; then he was standing there broadside to us, not twenty yards away, big as a statue and red as gold in the sun, and the sun sparking on the tips of his horns — they was twelve of them — so that he looked like he had twelve candles branched around his head, standing there looking at us while Mister Ernest raised the gun and aimed at his neck, and the gun went, "Click. Snick-cluck. Click. Snick-cluck. Snick-cluck" three times, and Mister Ernest still holding the gun aimed while the buck turned and give one long bound, the white underside of his tail like a blaze of fire, too, until the thicket and the shadows put it out; and Mister Ernest laid the gun slow and gentle back across the saddle in front of him, saying quiet and peaceful, and not much louder than jest breathing, "God dawg. God dawg."

Then he jogged me with his elbow and we got down, easy and careful because of that ere cinch strop, and he reached into his vest and taken out one of the cigars. It was busted where I had fell on it, I reckon, when we hit the ground. He throwed it away and taken out the other one. It was busted, too, so he bit off a hunk of it to chew and throwed the rest away. And

217

now the sun was gone even from the tops of the trees and there wasn't nothing left but a big red glare in the west.

"Don't worry," I said. "I ain't going to tell them you forgot to load your gun. For that matter, they don't need to know we ever seed him."

"Much oblige," Mister Ernest said. There wasn't going to be no moon tonight neither, so he taken the compass off the whang leather loop in his buttonhole and handed me the gun and set the compass on a stump and stepped back and looked at it. "Jest about the way we're headed now," he said, and taken the gun from me and opened it and put one shell in the britch and taken up the compass, and I taken Dan's reins and we started, with him in front with the compass in his hand.

And after a while it was full dark; Mister Ernest would have to strike a match ever now and then to read the compass, until the stars come out good and we could pick out one to follow, because I said, "How fur do you reckon it is?" and he said, "A little more than one box of matches." So we used a star when we could, only we couldn't see it all the time because the woods was too dense and we would git a little off until he would have to spend another match. And now it was good and late, and he stopped and said, "Get on the horse."

"I ain't tired," I said.

"Get on the horse," he said. "We don't want to spoil him."

Because he had been a good feller ever since I had knowed him, which was even before the day two years ago when maw went off with the Vicksburg roadhouse feller and the next day pap didn't come home neither, and on the third one Mister Ernest rid Dan up to the door of the cabin on the river he let us live in, so pap could work his piece of land and run his fish line, too, and said, "Put that gun down and come on here and climb up behind."

So I got in the saddle even if I couldn't reach the stirrups, and Mister Ernest taken the reins and I must 'a' went to sleep, because the next thing I knowed a buttonhole of my lumberjack was tied to the saddle horn with that ere whang cord off the compass, and it was good and late now and we wasn't fur, because Dan was already smelling water, the river. Or maybe it was the feed lot itself he smelled, because we struck the fire

218

road not a quarter below it, and soon I could see the river, too, with the white mist laying on it soft and still as cotton. Then the lot, home; and up yonder in the dark, not no piece akchully, close enough to hear us unsaddling and shucking corn prob'ly, and sholy close enough to hear Mister Ernest blowing his horn at the dark camp for Simon to come in the boat and git us, that old buck in his brake in the bayou; home, too, resting, too, after the hard sun, waking hisself now and then, dreaming of dogs behind him or maybe it was the racket we was making would wake him, but not neither of them for more than jest a little while before sleeping again.

Then Mister Ernest stood on the bank blowing until Simon's lantern went bobbing down into the mist; then we clumb down to the landing and Mister Ernest blowed again now and then to guide Simon, until we seen the lantern in the mist, and then Simon and the boat, only it looked like ever time I set down and got still, I went back to sleep, because Mister Ernest was shaking me again to git out and climb the bank into the dark camp, until I felt a bed against my knees and tumbled into it.

Then it was morning, tomorrow; it was all over now until next November, next year, and we could come back. Uncle Ike and Willy and Walter and Roth and the rest of them had come in yestiddy, soon as Eagle taken the buck out of hearing and they knowed that the deer was gone, to pack up and be ready to leave this morning for Yoknapatawpha, where they lived, until it would be November again and they could come back again.

So, as soon as we et breakfast, Simon run them back up the river in the big boat to where they left their cars and pickups, and now it wasn't nobody but jest me and Mister Ernest setting on the bench against the kitchen wall in the sun; Mister Ernest smoking a cigar — a whole one this time that Dan hadn't had no chance to jump him through a grapevine and bust. He hadn't washed his face neither where that vine had throwed him into the mud. But that was all right, too; his face usually did have a smudge of mud or tractor grease or beard stubble on it, because he wasn't jest a planter; he was a farmer, he worked as hard as ara one of his hands and tenants — which is why I knowed from the very first that we would git along, that I wouldn't have no trouble with him and he wouldn't have no trouble with me,

219

from that very first day when I woke up and maw had done gone off with that Vicksburg roadhouse feller without even waiting to cook breakfast, and the next morning pap was gone, too, and it was almost night the next day when I heard a horse coming up and I taken the gun that I had already throwed a shell into the britch when pap never come home last night, and stood in the door while Mister Ernest rid up and said, "Come on. Your paw ain't coming back neither."

"You mean he give me to you?" I said.

"Who cares?" he said. "Come on. I brought a lock for the door. We'll send the pickup back tomorrow for whatever you want."

So I come home with him and it was all right, it was jest fine — his wife had died about three years ago — without no women to worry us or take off in the middle of the night with a durn Vicksburg roadhouse jake without even waiting to cook breakfast. And we would go home this afternoon, too, but not jest yet; we always stayed one more day after the others left because Uncle Ike always left what grub they hadn't et, and the rest of the homemade corn whiskey he drunk and that town whiskey of Roth Edmondziz he called Scotch that smelled like it come out of a old bucket of roof paint; setting in the sun for one more day before we went back home to git ready to put in next year's crop of cotton and oats and beans and hay; and across the river yonder, behind the wall of trees where the big woods started, that old buck laying up today in the sun, too — resting today, too, without nobody to bother him until next November.

So at least one of us was glad it would be eleven months and two weeks before he would have to run that fur that fast again. So he was glad of the very same thing we was sorry of, and so all of a sudden I thought about how maybe planting and working and then harvesting oats and cotton and beans and hay wasn't jest something me and Mister Ernest done three hundred and fifty-one days to fill in the time until we could come back hunting again, but it was something we had to do, and do honest and good during the three hundred and fifty-one days, to have the right to come back into the big woods and hunt for the other fourteen; and the fourteen days that old buck run in front of dogs wasn't jest something to fill his time until the three hundred and fifty-one when he didn't have to, but the running and the risking

220

in front of guns and dogs was something he had to do for fourteen days to have the right not to be bothered for the other three hundred and fifty-one. And so the hunting and the farming wasn't two different things atall — they was jest the other side of each other.

"Yes," I said. "All we got to do now is put in that next year's crop. Then November won't be no time away atall."

"You ain't going to put in the crop next year," Mister Ernest said. "You're going to school."

So at first I didn't even believe I had heard him. "What?" I said. "Me? Go to school?"

"Yes," Mister Ernest said. "You must make something out of yourself."

"I am," I said. "I'm doing it now. I'm going to be a hunter and a farmer like you."

"No," Mister Ernest said. "That ain't enough any more. Time was when all a man had to do was just farm eleven and a half months, and hunt the other half. But not now. Now just to belong to the farming business and the hunting business ain't enough. You got to belong to the business of mankind."

"Mankind?" I said.

"Yes," Mister Ernest said. "So you're going to school. Because you got to know why. You can belong to the farming and hunting business and you can learn the difference between what's right and what's wrong, and do right. And that used to be enough — just to do right. But not now. You got to know why it's right and why it's wrong, and then be able to tell the folks that never had no chance to learn it; teach them how to do what's right, not just because they know it's right, but because they know now why it's right because you just showed them, told them, taught them, why. So you're going to school."

"It's because you been listening to that darn Will Legate and Walter Ewell!" I said.

"No," Mister Ernest said.

"Yes!" I said. "No wonder you missed that buck yestiddy, taking ideas from the very fellers that let him git away, after me and you had run Dan and the dogs durn right clean to death! Because you never even missed them! You never forgot to load that gun! You had done already unloaded it a purpose! I heard you!"

221

"All right, all right," Mister Ernest said. "Which would you rather have? His bloody head and hide on the kitchen floor yonder and half his meat in a pickup truck on the way to Yoknapatawpha County, or him with his head and hide and meat still together over yonder in that brake, waiting for next November for us to run him again?"

"And git him, too," I said. "We won't even fool with no Willy Legate and Walter Ewell next time."

"Maybe," Mister Ernest said.

"Yes," I said.

"Maybe," Mister Ernest said. "The best word in our language, the best of all. That's what keeps mankind going on: Maybe. The best days of his life ain't the ones when he said 'Yes' beforehand: they're the ones when all he knew to say was 'Maybe.' He can't say 'Yes' until afterward because he not only don't know it until then, he don't want to know 'Yes' until then ... Step in the kitchen and make me a toddy. Then we'll see about dinner."

"All right," I said. I got up. "You want some of Uncle Ike's corn or that town whiskey of Roth Edmondziz?"

"Can't you say Mister Roth or Mister Edmonds?" Mister Ernest said.

"Yes, sir," I said. "Well, which do you want? Uncle Ike's corn or that ere stuff of Roth Edmondziz?"

The Giant

OF THE SOUTH SEAS

The author of over 70 books and one-time holder
of nine world records for saltwater gamefish duels
a gigantic marlin on the South Seas.

by Zane Grey

ime is probably more generous and healing to an angler
than to any other individual. The wind, the sun, the
open, the colors and smells, the loneliness of the sea
or the solitude of the stream work some kind of magic.
In a few days my disappointment at losing a wonderful fish was
only a memory, another incident of angling history.

On the 15th of last May, which was the seventh day of clear,
hot, sunny weather, I stayed in my camp near Tahiti, in the
South Seas, to do some neglected writing, and let Cappy run
out alone off the east end, where we had not scouted for several
weeks. He returned to report a rather choppy sea, but he had
raised two marlin, one of which was a good-sized fish that came
for his bait three times, to refuse it, no doubt because it was
stale. Tuna, a small species, were numerous, and there was

223

some bonito showing.

"Same old story," averred the Captain (Captain Laurie Mitchell). "If I'd had a fresh bait I'd have hooked that bird. A lunker, too. All of 500 pounds."

Just what had transpired in my mind I was not conscious of then. It all came to me afterward, and it was that this game was long, and some day one of us might capture a giant Tahitian marlin. We would go on trying.

That night the dry spell broke. The rain roared on the pandanus roof, most welcome and dreamy of sounds. Morning disclosed dark, massed, broken clouds, red-edged and purple-centered, with curtains of rain falling over the mountains. This weather was something like March come back again for a day! Wondrous South Seas!

I took down a couple of new feather gigs — silver-headed with blue eyes — just for good luck. They worked. We caught five fine bonito in the lagoon, right off the point where my cottage stands. Jimmy, one of my natives, held up five fingers: "Five bonito, Good!" he ejaculated, which voiced all our sentiments.

Cappy had gone up the lagoon toward the second pass, and we tried to catch him so as to give him a fresh bait. As usual, however, Cappy's natives were running the wheels off his launch, and we could not catch him. The second pass looked sort of white and rough to me. Cappy went out, however, through a smooth channel. Presently we saw a swell gather and rise, to close the channel and mount to a great, curling, white-crested wave which broke all the way across. Charley, who had the wheel, grinned up at me. "No good!" We turned inshore and made for the third pass, some miles on, and got through that wide one without risk. Afterward Cappy told me his guide, Areiareia, knew exactly when to run through the second pass.

We headed out. A few black noddies skimmed the dark sea, and a few scattered bonito broke the surface. As usual — when we had them — we put out a big bonito on my big tackle and an ordinary one on the other. As my medium tackle holds 1,000 yards of 39-thread Swastika line it will seem interesting to anglers to speak of it as medium. The big outfit held 1,500 yards of line — 1,000 of 39-thread and 500 yards of 42 for backing; and this

224

story will prove I needed a Hardy rod and reel, and the great Swastika line.

Off the east end there was a brightness of white and blue, where the clouds broke, and in the west there were trade wind clouds of gold and pearl, but for the most part a gray canopy overspread mountain and sea. All along the saw-toothed front of this range inshore the peaks were obscured and the canyons filled with down-drooping veils of rain.

What a relief from the late days of sun and wind and wave! This was the kind of sea I loved to fish. The boat ran easily over a dark, low, lumpy swell. The air was cool, and as I did not have on any shirt the fine mist felt pleasant to my skin. John Loef was at the wheel. Bob Carney sat up on top with Jimmy and Charley, learning to talk Tahitian. The teasers and heavy baits made a splashing, swishy sound that could be heard above the boil and gurgle of water from the propellers. We followed some low-skimming boobies for a while, and then headed for Captain M.'s boat, several miles farther out. A rain squall was obscuring the white, tumbling reef and slowly moving toward us. Peter Williams sat at my right hand, holding the line which had the larger bonito. He had both feet up on the gunwale. I noticed that the line on this reel was white and dry. I sat in the left chair, precisely as Peter, except that I had on two pairs of gloves with thumbstalls in them. I have cut, burned, and skinned my hands too often on a hard strike to go without gloves. They are a nuisance to wear all day, when the rest of you, almost, is getting pleasantly caressed by sun and wind, but they are absolutely necessary to an angler who knows what he is doing.

Peter (saltwater guide from New Zealand) and I were discussing plans for our great round-the-world trip next year, boats, camp equipment, and what not. And, although our gaze seldom strayed from the baits, the idea of raising a fish was the furthest from our minds. We were just fishing, putting in the few remaining hours of this Tahitian trip, and already given over to the hopes and anticipations of the new one. That is the comfortable way to make a trip endurable — to pass from the hard reality of the present to the ideal romance of the future.

Suddenly I heard a sounding, vicious thump of water. Peter's

225

feet went up in the air.

"Ge-suss!" he bawled.

His reel screeched. Quick as thought, I leaned over to press my gloved hand on the whizzing spool of line. Just in time to save the reel from overrunning!

Out where Peter's bait had been showed a whirling, closing hole in the boiling white-green water. I saw a wide purple mass shooting away so close under the surface as to make the water look shallow. Peter fell out of the chair at the same instant I leaped up to straddle his rod. I had the situation in hand. My mind worked swiftly and coolly. It was an incredibly wonderful strike. The other boys piled back to the cockpit to help Peter get my other bait and the teasers in.

Before this was even started the fish ran out 200 yards of line, then, turning to the right, he tore off another hundred. All in a very few seconds! Then a white splash, high as a tree, shot up, out of which leaped the most magnificent of all the leaping fish I ever saw.

"Giant marlin!" screamed Peter. What had happened to me I did not know, but I was cold, keen, hard, tingling, motivated to think and do the right thing. This glorious fish made a leap of 30 feet at least, low and swift, which yet gave me time to gauge his enormous size and species. Here at last on the end of my line was the great Tahitian swordfish! He looked monstrous. He was pale, shiny gray in color, with broad stripes of purple. When he hit the water he sent up a splash like the flying surf on the reef.

By the time he was down I had the drag on and was winding the reel. Out he blazed again, faster, higher, longer, whirling the bonito round his head.

"Hook didn't catch!" yelled Peter, wildly. "It's on this side, He'll throw it."

I had instinctively come up mightily on the rod, winding with all speed, and I had felt the tremendous, solid pull. The big Pflueger hook had caught before that, however, and the bag in the line, coupled with his momentrum, had set it.

"No, Peter! He's fast," I replied. Still I kept working like a windmill in a cyclone to get up the slack. The monster had circled in these two leaps. Again he burst out, a plunging leap which took him under a wall of rippling white spray. Next instant such a terrific jerk as I had never sustained nearly unseated me. He was away on his run.

"Take the wheel, Peter," I ordered, and released the drag. "Water! Somebody pour water on this reel! Quick!"

The white line melted, smoked, burned off the reel. I smelled the scorching. It burned through my gloves. John was swift to plunge a bucket overboard and douse reel, rod, and me with water. That, too, saved us.

"After him, Pete!" I called, piercingly. The engines roared, and the launch danced around to leap in the direction of the tight line.

"Full speed!" I added.

"Aye, sir," yelled Peter, who had been a sailor before he became a whaler and a fisherman.

Then we had our race. It was thrilling in the extreme, and, though brief, it was far too long for me. A thousand yards from us — over half a mile — he came up to pound and beat the water into a maelstrom.

"Slow up!" I sang out. We were bagging the line. Then I turned on the wheel drag and began to pump and reel as never before in all my life. How precious that big spool — that big reel handle! They fairly ate up the line. We got back 500 yards of the 1,000 out before he was off again. This time, quick as I was, it took all my strength to release the drag, for when a weight is pulling hard it releases with extreme difficulty. No more risk like that!

He beat us in another race, shorter, at the end of which, when he showed like a plunging elephant, he had about 750 yards of line.

"Too much — Peter!" I panted. "We must — get him closer! Go to it!"

So we ran down upon him. I worked as before, desperately, holding on my nerve, and, when I got 500 yards back again on the reel, I was completely winded, and the hot sweat poured off my naked arms and breast.

"He's sounding! Get my shirt — harness!"

Warily I let go with one hand and then with the other, as John and Jimmy helped me on with my shirt, and then with the leather harness. With that hooked on to my reel and the great strain transferred to my shoulders, I felt that I might not be torn asunder.

"All set. Let's go," I said grimly. But he had gone down, which gave me a chance to get back my breath. Not long, however, did he remain down. I felt and saw the line rising.

"Keep him on the starboard quarter, Peter. Run up on him now. Bob, your chance for pictures!"

I was quick to grasp that the swordfish kept coming to our left, and repeatedly on that run I had Peter swerve in the same direction, so as to keep the line out on the quarter. Once we were almost in danger. But I saw it. I got back all but 100 yards of line. Close enough. He kept edging in ahead of us, and once we had to turn halfway to keep the stern toward him. But he quickly shot ahead again. He was fast, angry, heavy. How his tail pounded the leader. The short, powerful strokes vibrated all over me.

"Port — port, Peter," I yelled, and even then, so quick was the swordfish, that I missed seeing two leaps directly in front of the boat, as he curved ahead of us. But the uproar from Bob and the others was enough for me.

As the launch sheered around, however, I saw the third of that series of leaps — and if anything could have loosed my chained emotion on the instant, that unbelievably swift and savage plunge would have done so. But I was clamped. No more dreaming! No more bliss! I was there to think and act. And I did not even thrill.

By the same tactics the swordfish sped off a hundred yards of line, and by the same we recovered them and drew close to see him leap again, only 200 feet off our starboard, a little ahead, and of all the magnificent fish I have ever seen he excelled. His power to leap was beyond credence. Captain M.'s big fish, that broke off two years before, did not move like this one. True, he was larger. Nevertheless, this swordfish was so huge that when he came out in dazzling, swift flight, my crew went simply mad. This was the first time my natives had been flabbergasted. They were as excited, as carried away, as Bob and John. Peter, however, stuck at the wheel as if he were after a wounded whale which might any instant turn upon him. I did not need to warn Peter not to let that fish hit us. If he had he would have made splinters out of that launch. Many an anxious glance did I cast toward Cappy's boat, two or three miles distant. Why did he not come? The peril was too great for us to be alone at the mercy of that beautiful brute, if he charged us either by accident or design. But Captain could not locate us, owing to the misty atmosphere, and missed seeing this grand fish in action.

How sensitive I was to the strain on the line! A slight slackening directed all my faculties to ascertain the cause. The light at the moment was bad, and I had to peer closely to see the line. He had not slowed up, but he was curving back and to the left again — the cunning strategist!

"Port, Peter — port!" I commanded.

We sheered, but not enough. With the wheel hard over, one engine full speed ahead, the other in reverse, we wheeled like a top. But not swift enough for that Tahitian swordfish.

The line went under the bow.

"Reverse!" I called, sharply.

We pounded on the waves, slowly caught hold, slowed, started back. Then I ordered the clutches thrown out. It was a terrible moment, and took all my will not to yield to sudden blank panic.

When my line ceased to pay out, I felt that it had been caught on the keel. And as I was only human, I surrendered for an instant to agony. But no! That line was new, strong. The swordfish was slowing. I could yet avert catastrophe.

"Quick, Pete. Feels as if the line is caught," I cried, unhooking my harness from the reel.

Peter complied with my order. "Yes, by cripes! It's caught. Overboard, Jimmy! Jump in! Loose the line!"

The big Tahitian in a flash was out of his shirt and bending to dive.

"No! Hold on, Jimmy!" I yelled. Only a moment before I had seen sharks milling about. "Grab him, John!"

They held Jimmy back, and a second later I plunged my rod over the side into the water, so suddenly that the weight of it and the reel nearly carried me overboard.

"Hold me — or it's all — day!" I panted, and I thought that if my swordfish had fouled on keel or propellers I did not care if I did fall in.

229

"Let go my line, Peter," I said, making ready to extend the rod to the limit of my arms.

"I can feel him moving, sir," shouted Peter, excitedly. "By jingo! He's coming! It's free! It wasn't caught!"

That was such intense relief I could not recover my balance. They had to haul me back into the boat. I shook all over as one with the palsy, so violently that Peter had to help me get the rod in the rod socket of the chair. An instant later came the strong, electrifying pull on the line, the scream of the reel. Never such sweet music! He was away from the boat — on a tight line! The feeling was so great that it propelled me instantaneously back into my former state of hard, cold, calculating, and critical judgment, and iron determination.

"Close shave, sir," said Peter, cheerily. "It was like when a whale turns on me, after I've struck him. We're all clear, sir, and after him again."

The gray pall of rain bore down on us. I was hot and wet with sweat, and asked for a raincoat to keep me from being chilled. Enveloped in this I went on with my absorbing toil. Blisters began to smart on my hands, especially one on the inside of the third finger of my right hand, certainly a queer place to raise one. But it bothered me, hampered me. Bob put on his rubber coat and, protecting his camera more than himself, sat out on the bow waiting.

My swordfish, with short, swift runs, took us five miles farther out, and then, welcome to see, brought us back, all this while without leaping, though he broke water on the surface a number of times. He never sounded after that first dive. The bane of an angler is a sounding fish, and here in Tahitian waters, where there is no bottom, it spells catastrophe. The marlin slowed up and took to milling, a sure sign of a rattled fish. Then he rose again, and it happened to be when the rain had ceased. He made one high, frantic jump about 200 yards ahead of us, and then threshed on the surface, sending the bloody spray high. All on board were quick to see that sign of weakening, of tragedy — blood.

Peter turned to say, coolly: "He's our meat, sir."

I did not allow any such idea to catch in my consciousness. Peter's words, like those of Bob and John, and the happy jargon of the Tahitians, had no effect upon me whatever.

230

It rained half an hour longer, during which we repeated several phases of the fight, except slower on the part of the marlin. In all he leaped fifteen times clear of the water. I did not attempt to keep track of his threshings.

After the rain passed I had them remove the rubber coat, which hampered me, and settled to a slower fight. About this time the natives again sighted sharks coming around the boat. I did not like this. Uncanny devils! They were the worst of these marvelous fishing waters. But Peter said: "They don't know what it's all about. They'll go away."

They did go away long enough to relieve me of dread, then they trooped back, lean, yellow-backed, white-finned wolves.

"We ought to have a rifle," I said. "Sharks won't stay to be shot at, whether hit or not."

It developed that my swordfish had leaped too often and run too swiftly to make an extremely long fight. I had expected a perceptible weakening and recognized it. So did Peter, who smiled gladly. Then I taxed myself to the utmost and spared nothing. In another hour, which seemed only a few minutes, I had him whipped and coming. I could lead him. The slow strokes of his tail took no more line. Then he quit wagging.

"Clear for action, Pete. Give John the wheel. I see the end of the double line. There!"

I heaved and wound. With the end of the double line over my reel I screwed the drag up tight. The finish was in sight. Suddenly I felt tugs and jerks at my fish.

"Sharks!" I yelled, hauling away for dear life.

Everybody leaned over the gunwale. I saw a wide, sheery mass, greenish silver, crossed by purple bars. It moved. It weaved. But I could drag it easily.

"Manu! Manu!" shrilled the natives.

"Heave!" shouted Peter, as he peered down.

"By God! They're on him!" roared Peter, hauling on the leader. "Get the lance, boat hook, gaffs — anything. Fight them off!"

Suddenly Peter let go the leader and, jerking the big gaff from Jimmy, he lunged out. There was a single enormous roar of water and a sheeted splash. I saw a blue tail so wide I thought I was crazy. It threw a 6-foot yellow shark into the air!

"Rope his tail, Charley," yelled Peter. "Rest of you fight the

231

tigers off."

I unhooked the harness and stood up to lean over the gunwales. A swordfish rolled on the surface, extending from forward of the cockpit to two yards or more beyond the end. His barred body was as large as that of an ox. And to it sharks were clinging, tearing, out on the small part near the tail. Charley looped the great tail, and that was a signal for the men to get into action.

One big shark had a hold just below the anal fin. How cruel, brutish, ferocious! Peter made a powerful stab at him. The big lance head went clear through his neck. He gulped and sank. Peter stabbed another underneath, and still another. Jimmy was tearing at sharks with the long-handled gaff, and when he hooked one he was nearly hauled overboard. Charley threshed with his rope; John did valiant work with the boat hook, and Bob frightened me by his daring fury, as he leaned far over to hack with the cleaver.

We keep these huge cleavers on board to use in case we are attacked by an octopus, which is not a far-fetched fear at all. It might happen. Bob is lean and long and powerful. Also he was mad. Whack! He slashed a shark that let go and appeared to slip up into the air.

"On the nose, Bob. Split his nose. That's the weak spot on a shark," yelled Peter.

Next shot Bob cut deep into the round stub nose of this big, black shark — the only one of that color I saw — and it had the effect of dynamite. More sharks appeared under Bob, and I was scared so stiff I could not move.

"Take that! And that!" sang out Bob, in a kind of fierce ecstasy. "You will try to eat our swordfish — dirty, stinking pups! Aha! On your beak, huh! Zambesi! Wow, Pete, that sure is the place."

"Look out, Bob! For God's sake — look out!" I begged, frantically, after I saw a shark almost reach Bob's arm.

Peter swore at him. But there was no keeping Bob off those cannibals. Blood and water flew all over us. The smell of sharks in any case was not pleasant, and with them spouting blood, and my giant swordfish rolling in blood, the stench that arose was sickening. They appeared to come from all directions, especially from under the boat. Finally I had to get into the thick of
232

it, armed only with a gaff handle minus the gaff. I did hit one a stunning welt over the nose, making him let go. If we had all had lances like the one Peter was using so effectively, we would have made short work of them. One jab from Peter either killed or disabled a shark. The crippled ones swam about belly up or lopsided, and stuck up their heads as if to get air. Of all the bloody messes I ever saw, that was the worst.

"Makes me remember — the war!" panted Peter, grimly.

And it was Peter who whipped the flock of ravenous sharks off. Chuck! went the heavy lance, and that was the end of another. My heart apparently had ceased to function. To capture that glorious fish, only to see it devoured before my eyes!

"Run ahead, Johnny, out of this bloody slaughter hole, so we can see," called Peter.

John ran forward a few rods into clear water. A few sharks followed, one of which did so to his death. The others grew wary; they swam around.

"We got 'em licked! Say, I had the wind up me," said Peter. "Who ever saw the like of that? The bloody devils!"

Bob took the lance from Peter, and stuck the most venturesome of the remaining sharks. It appeared then that we had the situation in hand again. My swordfish was still with us, his beautiful body bitten here and there, his tail almost severed, but not irreparably lacerated. All around the boat wounded sharks were lolling with fins out, sticking ugly heads up, to gulp and dive.

There came a let-down then, and we exchanged the natural elation we felt. The next thing was to see what was to be done with the monster, now we had him. I vowed we could do nothing but tow him to camp. But Peter made the attempt to lift him on the boat. All six of us, hauling on the ropes, could not get his back half out of the water. So we tied him fast and started campward.

Halfway in we espied Cappy's boat. He headed for us, no doubt attracted by all the flags the boys strung up. There was one, a red and blue flag that I had never flown. Jimmy tied this on his bamboo pole and tied that high on the mast. Cappy bore quickly down on us, and ran alongside, he and all of crew vastly excited.

"What is it? Lamming big broadbill?" he yelled back.

233

My fish did resemble a broadbill in his long, black beak, his widespread flukes, his purple color, shading so dark now that the broad bars showed indistinctly. Besides, he lay belly up.

"No, Cappy. He's a giant Tahitian striped marlin, one of the kind we've tried so hard to catch," I replied, happily.

"By gad! So he is. What a monster! I'm glad, old man. My word, I'm glad! I didn't tell you, but I was discouraged. Now we're sitting on top of the world again."

"Rather," replied Peter, for me. "We've got him, Captain, and he's some fish. But the damn sharks nearly beat us."

"So I see. They are bad. I saw a number. Well, I had a 400-pound swordie throw my hook at me, and I've raised two more, besides a sailfish. Fish out here again. Have you got any fresh bonito?"

We threw our bait into his boat and headed for camp again. Cappy waved, a fine, happy smile on his tanned face, and called: "He's a walloper, old man. I'm sure glad."

"I owe it to you, Cap," I called after him.

We ran for the nearest pass, necessarily fairly slowly with all that weight on our stem. The boat listed half a foot and tried to run in a circle. It was about 1 o'clock, and the sky began to clear. Bob raved about what pictures he would take.

"Oh, boy, what a fish! If only Romer had been with us! I saw him hit the bait, and I nearly fell off the deck. I couldn't yell. Wasn't it a wonderful fight? Everything just right. I was scared when he tried to go under the boat."

"So was I, Bob," I replied, remembering that crucial moment. "I wasn't," said Peter. "The other day when we had the boat out at Papeete I shaved all the rough places off her keel. So I felt safe. What puts the wind up me is the way these Tahitian swordfish can jump. Fast? My word! This fellow beat any small marlin I ever saw in my life."

I agreed with Peter and we discussed this startling and amazing power of the giant marlin. I put forward the conviction that the sole reason for their incredible speed and ferocity was that evolution, the struggle to survive, was magnified in these crystal-clear waters around Tahiti. We talked over every phase of the fight, and that which pleased me most was the old whaler's tribute:

"You were there, sir. That cool and quick! On the strike that dry line scared me stiff. But afterward I had no doubt of the result."

We were all wringing wet, and some of us as bloody as wet. I removed my wet clothes and gave myself a brisk rub. I could not stand erect, and my hands hurt — pangs I endured gratefully.

We arrived at the dock about 3 o'clock, to find all our camp folk and a hundred natives assembled to greet us. Up and down had sped the news of the flags waving.

I went ashore and waited impatiently to see the marlin hauled out on the sand. It took a dozen men, all wading, to drag him in. And when they at last got him under the tripod, I approached, knowing I was to have a shock and prepared for it.

But at that he surprised me in several ways. His color had grown darker and the bars showed only palely. Still they were there, and helped to identify him as one of the striped species. He was bigger than I had ever hoped for. And his body was long and round. This roundness appeared to be an extraordinary feature for a marlin spearfish. His bill was three feet long, not slender and rapier-like, as in the ordinary marlin, or short and bludgeon-like, as in the black marlin. It was about the same size all the way from tip to where it swelled into his snout, and slightly flattened on top — a superb and remarkable weapon. The fact that the great striped spearfish Captain Mitchell lost in 1928 had a long, curved bill, like a rhinoceros, did not deter me from pronouncing this of the same species. Right there I named this species, "Great Tahitian Striped Marlin." Singularly, he had a small head, only a foot or more from where his beak broadened to his eye, which, however, was as large as that of a broadbill swordfish. There were two gill openings on each side, a feature I never observed before in any swordfish, the one toward the mouth being considerably smaller than the regular gill opening. From there his head sheered up to his humped back, out of which stood an enormous dorsal fin. He had a straight-under maxillary. The pectoral fins were large, wide, like wings, and dark in color. The fin-like appendages under the back of his lower jaw were only about six inches long and quite slender. In other spearfish these are long, and in sailfish sometimes exceed two feet and more. His body, for eight feet, was as symmetrical and round as that of a good, big stallion. According to my deduction, it was a male fish. He carried this roundness

235

back to his anal fin, and there further accuracy was impossible because the sharks had torn out enough meat to fill a bushel basket. His tail was the most splendid of all the fish tails I ever observed. It was a perfect bent bow, slender, curved, dark purple in color, finely ribbed, and expressive of the tremendous speed and strength the fish had exhibited.

This tail had a spread of 5 feet 2 inches. His length was 14 feet 2 inches. His girth was 6 feet 9 inches. And his weight, as he was, 1,040 pounds.

Every drop of blood had been drained from his body, and this with at least 200 pounds of flesh the sharks took would have fetched his true and natural weight to 1,250 pounds. But I thought it best to have the record stand at the actual weight, without allowance for what he had lost. Nevertheless, despite my satisfaction and elation, as I looked up at this appalling shape, I could not help but remember the giant marlin Captain had lost in 1928 which we estimated at 22 or 23 feet, or the 20-foot one I had raised at Tautira, or the 28-foot one the natives had seen repeatedly alongside their canoes. And I thought of the prodigious leaps and astounding fleetness of this one I had caught. "My heaven!" I breathed. "What would a bigger one do?"

"Giant of the South Seas" first appeared in the November 1930 issue of *Outdoor Life*. Reprinted by permission of Loren Grey.

T H E
Intruder

After all those years, his hallowed spot was at last discovered. He tore his eyes away from the trout and glowered at the intruder.

by Robert Traver

It was about noon when I put down my fly rod and sculled the little cedar boat with one hand and ate a sandwich and drank a can of beer with the other, just floating and enjoying the ride down the beautiful broad main Escanaba River. Between times I watched the merest speck of an eagle tacking and endlessly wheeling far up in the cloudless sky. Perhaps he was stalking my sandwich or even, dark thought, stalking me. . . The fishing so far had been poor; the good trout simply weren't rising. I rounded a slow double bend, with high gravel banks on either side, and there stood a lone fisherman — the first person I had seen in hours. He was standing astride a little feeder creek on a gravel point on the left downstream side, fast to a good fish, his glistening rod hooped and straining, the line taut, the leader vibrating and sawing the

237

water, the fish itself boring far down out of sight.

Since I was curious to watch a good battle and anxious not to interfere, I eased the claw anchor over the stern — *plop* — and the little boat hung there, gurgling and swaying from side to side in the slow deep current. The young fisherman either did not hear me or, hearing, and being a good one, kept his mind on his work. As I sat watching he shifted the rod to his left hand, shaking out his right wrist as though it were asleep, so I knew then that the fight had been a long one and that this fish was no midget. The young fisherman fumbled in his shirt and produced a cigarette and light and lit up, a real cool character. The fish made a sudden long downstream run and the fisherman raced after him, prancing through the water like a yearling buck, gradually coaxing and working him back up to the deep slow water across from the gravel bar. It was a nice job of handling and I wanted to cheer. Instead I coughed discreetly and he glanced quickly upstream and saw me.

"Hi," he said pleasantly, turning his attention back to his fish.

"Hi," I answered.

"How's luck?" he said, still concentrating.

"Fairish," I said. "But I haven't anything quite like you seem to be on to. How you been doin' — otherwise, I mean?"

"Fairish," he said. "This is the third good trout in this same stretch — all about the same size."

"My, my," I murmured, thinking ruefully of the half-dozen barely legal brook trout frying away in my sun-baked creel. "Guess I've just been out floating over the good spots."

"Pleasant day for a ride, though," he said, frowning intently at his fish.

"Delightful," I said wryly, taking a slow swallow of beer.

"Yep," the assured young fisherman went on, expertly feeding out line as his fish made another downstream sashay. "Yep," he repeated, nicely taking up slack on the retrieve, "that's why I gave up floating this lovely river. Nearly ten years ago, just a kid. Decided then 'twas a hell of a lot more fun fishing a hundred yards of her carefully than taking off on these all-day floating picnics."

I was silent for a while. Then: "I think you've got something there," I said, and I meant it. Of course he was right, and I was simply out joy-riding past the good fishing. I should have

238

brought along a girl or a camera. On this beautiful river if there was no rise a float was simply an enforced if lovely scenic tour. If there was a rise, no decent fisherman ever needed to float. Presto, I now had it all figured out. . .

"Wanna get by?" the poised young fisherman said, flipping his cigarette into the water.

"I'll wait," I said. "I got all day. My pal isn't meeting me till dark — 'way down at the old burned logging bridge."

"Hm. . . trust you brought your passport — you really are out on a voyage," he said. "Perhaps you'd better slip by, fella — by the feel of this customer it'll be at least ten-twenty minutes more. Like a smart woman in the mood for play, these big trout don't like to be rushed. C'mon, just bear in sort of close to me, over here, right under London Bridge. It won't bother us at all."

My easy philosopher evidently didn't want me to see how really big his fish was. But being a fisherman myself I knew, I knew. "All right," I said, lifting the anchor and sculling down over his way and under his throbbing line. "Thanks and good luck."

"Thanks, chum," he said, grinning at me. "Have a nice ride and good luck to you."

"Looks like I'll need it," I said, looking enviously back over my shoulder at his trembling rod tip. "Hey," I said, belatedly remembering my company manners, "want a nice warm can of beer?"

Smiling: "Despite your glowing testimonial, no thanks."

"You're welcome," I said, realizing we were carrying on like a pair of strange diplomats.

"And one more thing, please," he said, raising his voice a little to be heard over the burbling water, still smiling intently at his straining fish. "If you don't mind, please keep this little stretch under your hat — it's been all mine for nearly ten years. It's really something special. No use kidding you — I see you've spotted my bulging creel and I guess by now you've got a fair idea of what I'm on to. And anyway I've got to take a little trip. But I'll be back — soon I hope. In the meantime try to be good to the place. I know it will be good to you."

"Right!" I shouted, for by then I had floated nearly around the downstream bend. "Mum's the word." He waved his free hand and then was blotted from view by a tall doomed spruce leaning far down out across the river from a crumbling water-blasted bank. The last thing I saw was the gleaming flash of his rod, the long taut line, the strumming leader. It made a picture I've never forgotten.

That was the last time ever that I floated the Big Escanaba River. I had learned my lesson well. Always after that when I visited this fabled new spot I hiked in, packing my gear, threading my way down river through a pungent needled maze of ancient deer trails, like a fleeing felon keeping always slyly away from the broad winding river itself. My strategy was two-fold: to prevent other sly fishermen from finding and deflowering the place, and to save myself an extra mile of walking.

Despite the grand fishing I discovered there, I did not go back too often. It was a place to hoard and save, being indeed most good to me, as advertised. And always I fished it alone, for a fisherman's pact had been made, a pact that became increasingly hard to keep as the weeks rolled into months, the seasons into years, during which I never again encountered my poised young fisherman. In the morbid pathology of trout fishermen such a phenomenon is mightily disturbing. What had become of my fisherman? Hadn't he ever got back from his trip? Was he sick or had he moved away? Worse yet, had he died? How could such a consummate young artist have possibly given up fishing such an enchanted spot? Was he one of that entirely mad race of eccentric fishermen who cannot abide the thought of sharing a place, however fabulous, with *one* other fisherman?

By and by, with the innocent selfishness possessed by all fishermen, I dwelt less and less upon the probable fate of my young fisherman and instead came smugly to think it was I who had craftily discovered the place. Nearly twenty fishing seasons slipped by on golden wings, as fishing seasons do, during which time I, fast getting no sprightlier, at last found it expedient to locate and hack out a series of abandoned old logging roads to let me drive within easier walking distance of my secret spot. The low cunning of middle age was replacing the hot stamina of youth. . . As a road my new trail was strictly a spring-breaking bronco-buster, but at least I was able to sit and ride, after a fashion, thus saving my aging legs for the real labor of love to follow.

Another fishing season was nearly done when, one afternoon,

240

brooding over that gloomy fact, I suddenly tore off my lawyer-mask and fled my office, heading for the Big Escanaba, bouncing and bucking my way in, finally hitting the Glide — as I had come to call the place — about sundown. For a long time I just stood there on the high bank, drinking in the sights and pungent river smells. No fish were rising, and slowly, lovingly, I went through the familiar ritual of rigging up; scrubbing out a fine new leader, dressing the tapered line, jointing the rod and threading the line, pulling on the tall patched waders, anointing myself with fly dope. No woman dressing for a ball was more fussy. . . Then I composed myself on my favorite fallen log and waited. I smoked a slow pipe and sipped a can of beer, cold this time, thanks to the marvels of dry ice and my new road. My watching spot overlooked a wide bend and commanded a grand double view: above, the deep slow velvet glide with its little feeder stream where I first met my young fisherman; below, a sporty and productive broken run of white water stretching nearly a half-mile. The old leaning spruce that used to be there below me had long since bowed in surrender and been swept away by some forgotten spring torrent. As I sat waiting the wind had died, the shadowing waters had taken on the brooding blue hush of evening, the dying embers of sundown suddenly lit a great blazing forest fire in the tops of the tall spruces across river from me, and an unknown bird that I have always called simply the "lonely" bird sang timidly its ancient haunting plaintive song. I arose and took a deep breath like a soldier advancing upon the enemy.

The fisherman's mystic hour was at hand.

First I heard and then saw a young buck in late velvet slowly, tentatively splashing his way across to my side, above me and beyond the feeder creek, ears twitching and tall tail nervously wig-wagging. Then he winded me, freezing in midstream, giving me a still and liquid stare for a poised instant; then came charging on across in great pawing incredibly graceful leaps, lacquered flanks quivering, white flag up and waving, bounding up the bank and into the anonymous woods, the sounds of his excited blowing fading and growing fainter and then dying away.

In the meantime four fair trout had begun rising in the smooth tail of the glide just below me. I selected and tied on a favorite

241

small dry fly and got down below the lowest riser and managed to take him on the first cast, a short dainty float. Without moving I stood and lengthened line and took all four risers, all nice firm brook trout upwards of a foot, all the time purring and smirking with increasing complacency. The omens were good. As I relit my pipe and waited for new worlds to conquer I heard a mighty splash above me and wheeled gaping at the spreading magic ring of a really good trout, carefully marking the spot. Oddly enough he had risen just above where the young buck had just crossed, a little above the feeder creek. Perhaps, I thought extravagantly, perhaps he was after the deer. . . I waited, tense and watchful, but he did not rise again.

I left the river and scrambled up the steep gravelly bank and made my way through the tall dense spruces up to the little feeder creek. I slipped down the bank like a footpad, stealthily inching my way out to the river in the silted creek itself, so as not to scare the big one, *my* big one. I could feel the familiar shock of icy cold water suddenly clutching at my ankles as I stood waiting at the spot where I had first run across my lost fisherman. I quickly changed to a fresh fly in the same pattern, carefully snubbing the knot. Then the fish obediently rose again, a savage easy engulfing roll, again the undulant outgoing ring, just where I had marked him, not more than thirty feet from me and a little beyond the middle and obliquely upstream. Here was, I saw, a cagey selective riser, lord of his pool, and one who would not suffer fools gladly. So I commanded myself to rest him before casting. "Twenty-one, twenty-two, twenty-three ..." I counted.

The cast itself was indecently easy and, finally releasing it, the little Adams sped out on its quest, hung poised in mid-air for an instant, and then settled sleepily upon the water like a thistle, uncurling before the leader like the languid, outward folding of a ballerina's arm. The fly circled a moment, uncertainly, then was caught by the current. Down, down it rode, closer, closer, then — clap! — the fish rose and kissed it, I flicked my wrist and he was on, and then away he went roaring off downstream, past feeder creek and happy fisherman, the latter hot after him.

During the next mad half-hour I fought this explosive creature up and down the broad stream, up and down, ranging at least a hundred feet each way, or so it seemed, without ever once seeing him. This meant, I figured, that he was either a big brown or a brook. A rainbow would surely have leapt a dozen times by now. Finally I worked him into the deep safe water off the feeder creek where he sulked nicely while I panted and rested my benumbed rod arm. As twilight receded into dusk with no sign of his tiring I began vaguely to wonder just who had latched on to whom. For the fifth or sixth time I rested my aching arm by transferring the rod to my left hand, professionally shaking out my tired wrist just as I had once seen a young fisherman do.

Nonchalantly I reached in my jacket and got out and tried to light one of my rigidly abominable Italian cigars. My fish, unimpressed by my show of aplomb, shot suddenly away on a powerful zigzag exploratory tour upstream, the fisherman nearly swallowing his unlit cigar as he scrambled up after him. It was then that I saw a lone man sitting quietly in a canoe, anchored in midstream above me. The tip of his fly rod showed over the stem. My heart sank: after all these years my hallowed spot was at last discovered.

"Hi," I said, trying to convert a grimace of pain into an amiable grin, all the while keeping my eye on my sulking fish. The show must go on.

"Hi," he said.

"How you doin'?" I said, trying to make a brave show of casual fish talk.

"Fairish," he said, "but nothing like you seem to be on to."

"Oh, he isn't so much," I said, lying automatically if not too well. "I'm working a fine leader and don't dare to bull him." At least that was the truth.

The stranger laughed briefly and glanced at his wrist watch. "You've been on to him that I know of for over forty minutes — and I didn't see you make the strike. Let's not try to kid the Marines. I just moved down a bit closer to be in on the finish. I'll shove away if you think I'm too close."

"Nope," I answered generously, delicately snubbing my fish away from a partly submerged windfall. "But about floating this lovely river," I pontificated, "there's nothing in it, my friend. Absolutely nothing. Gave it up myself eighteen-twenty years ago.

243

Figured out it was better working one stretch carefully than shoving off on those floating picnics. Recommend it to you, comrade."

The man in the canoe was silent. I could see the little red moon of his cigarette glowing and fading in the gathering gloom. Perhaps my gratuitous pedagogical ruminations had offended him; after all, trout fishermen are a queer proud race. Perhaps I should try diversionary tactics. "Wanna get by?" I inquired silkily. Maybe I could get him to go away before I tried landing this unwilling porpoise. He still remained silent. "Wanna get by?" I repeated. "It's perfectly O.K. by me. As you can see — it's a big roomy river."

"No," he said dryly. "No thanks." There was another long pause. Then: "If you wouldn't mind too much I think I'll put in here for the night. It's getting pretty late — and somehow I've come to like the looks of this spot."

"Oh," I said in a small voice — just "Oh" — as I disconsolately watched him lift his anchor and expertly push his canoe in to the near gravelly shore, above me, where it grated halfway in and scraped to rest. He sat there quietly, his little neon cigarette moon glowing, and I felt I just had to say something more. After all I didn't *own* the river. "Why sure, of course, it's a beautiful place to camp, plenty of pine knots for fuel, a spring-fed creek for drinking water and cooling your beer," I ran on gaily, rattling away like an hysterical realtor trying to sell the place. Then I began wondering how I would ever spirit my noisy fish car out of the woods without the whole greedy world of fishermen learning about my new secret road to this old secret spot. Maybe I'd even have to abandon it for the night and hike out ... Then I remembered there was an uncooperative fish to be landed, so I turned my full attention to the unfinished and uncertain business at hand. "Make yourself at home," I lied softly.

"Thanks," the voice again answered dryly, and again I heard the soft chuckle in the semidarkness.

My fish had stopped his mad rushes now and was busily boring the bottom, the long leader vibrating like the plucked string of a harp. For the first time I found I was able gently to pump him up for a cautious look. And again I almost swallowed my still unlit stump of cigar as I beheld his dorsal fin cleaving the water nearly a foot back from the fly. He wallowed and

244

shook like a dog and then rolled on his side, then recovered and fought his way back down and away on another run, but shorter this time. With a little pang I knew then that my fish was done, but the pang quickly passed — it always did and again I gently, relentlessly pumped him up, shortening line, drawing him in to the familiar daisy hoop of landing range, kneeling and stretching and straining out my opposing aching arms like those of an extravagant archer. The net slipped fairly under him on the first try and, clenching my cigar, I made my pass and lo! lifted him free and dripping from the water. "Ah-h-h ..." He was a glowing superb spaniel-sized brown. I staggered drunkenly away from the water and sank to the ground, panting like a winded miler.

"Beautiful, *beautiful*," I heard my forgotten and unwelcome visitor saying like a prayer. "I've dreamed all this — over a thousand times I've dreamed it."

I tore my feasting eyes away from my fish and glowered up at the intruder. He was half standing in the beached canoe now, one hand on the side, trying vainly to wrest the cap from a bottle, of all things, seeming in the dusk to smile uncertainly. I felt a sudden chill sense of concern, of vague nameless alarm.

"Look, chum," I said, speaking lightly, very casually, "is everything all O.K.?"

"Yes, yes, of course," he said shortly, still plucking away at his bottle. "There. . . I — I'm coming now."

Bottle in hand he stood up and took a resolute broad step out of the canoe, then suddenly, clumsily he lurched and pitched forward, falling heavily, cruelly, half in the beached canoe and half out upon the rocky wet shore. For a moment I sat staring ruefully, then I scrambled up and started running toward him, still holding my rod and the netted fish, thinking this fisherman was indubitably potted. "No, no, no!" he shouted at me, struggling and scrambling to his feet in a kind of wild urgent frenzy. I halted, frozen, holding my sagging dead fish and the intruder limped toward me, in a curious sort of creaking stiffly mechanical limp, the uncorked but still intact bottle held triumphantly aloft in one muddy wet hand, the other hand reaching gladly toward me.

"Guess I'll never get properly used to this particular battle stripe," he said, slapping his thudding and unyielding right leg.

245

"But how are you, stranger?" he went on, his wet eyes glistening, his bruised face smiling. "How about our having a drink to your glorious trout — and still another to reunion at our old secret fishing spot?"

From *Trout Madness*, 1960, by John D. Voelkner (Robert Traver), published by St. Martin's Press & Peregrine Smith Books. Permission of Peregrine Smith Books.

I DON'T WANT TO SHOOT AN Elephant

In no other form can seven ounces make a grown man turn against society, abstain from his wife, and flop down into the broomstraw and cry.

by Havilah Babcock

I don't want to shoot an elephant. I don't want to stalk a Rocky Mountain goat, be treed by a Cape buffalo, or bag a white rhinoceros. I don't want to do anything big. What I want to hunt weighs seven ounces, not seven tons.

The dictionary calls him *Colinus viriginianus*, but various frustrated citizens have been known to call him other things. By habit and habitat he is an Unreconstructed Rebel, if ever there was one. In the South, where gunning for him is both a pastime and a passion, he is still called partridge by everybody who voted for Grover Cleveland. (These old boys are still shooting birds down here.) You Yankees, who can name things better than you can hit them, insist on "bobwhite quail." Well, that sets him apart. But he doesn't depend on the English language to get that done. He sets himself apart.

On paper, bobwhite is an easy mark. In fact, it is difficult to see how anybody could miss him. A country boy with a home-made gravel shooter could mow him down. On paper, that is. He squats and holds beautifully when a dog points him. You have all the time in the world to get there, check your gun, maneuver into position, marshal your forces, dig your heels into the ground like an embattled golfer in a sand trap, and call your wife by long distance.

He is the only animated target in the world that will wait indefinitely for you, the most accommodating of all game birds. You can leisurely bring your $350 gun into position, with your 700 scientifically tested shot pellets. Six times that many if you wish, for the law affords Bob no such three-shot protection as it affords ducks, doves and other pampered migrants.

When he does get up — at your invitation and convenience, mind you — he doesn't fly fast. He really doesn't. Bobwhite's speed is the great American hallucination. Beside a souped-up mourning dove in high gear, he hangs motionless in the air. Besides a green-winged teal in business for himself, he flies backward. And when you shoot him, you don't have to hunt for him or pick him up. Your faithful dog looks after such chores. If you miss him, he is most accommodating and considerate: he doesn't fly far. Within two or three hundred yards he goes down again, obligingly giving you another chance. Such a bird could never survive, you would say.

This beautiful picture I have painted is all true, yet it is the biggest lie in history, which demonstrates the falsity of the mathematical axiom that things-equal-to-same-thing-are-equal-to-each-other. Don't let trigonometry kid you!

In spite of the bargain that bobwhite offers to the gunner, he remains the most hunted, the most shot at and the most missed game bird in America. And I might add a fourth distinction: he is more fun to hunt than any other. How comes this paradoxical paradox? one might ask.

To begin with, what else so small can upset a man so much? What other target, either animate or inanimate? Seven ounces of avoirdupois could be wrapped up in no other shape or form that would possess such power to befog and confound the

248

senses, or to disconcert and disorganize the human nervous system. In no other shape or form can seven ounces make a grown man turn against society, abstain from his wife and flop down into the broomstraw and cry. How comes this phenomenal phenomenon? Because, in short, Bob is a psychologist. The other animals are merely physiologists.

Nature, the head of the parts department, provided all animals with some defense against their enemies. And being a crafty and impartial dame, she doubtless figured she was giving each such defense as he required. To none did she give more than was needed, for superfluities and surpluses exist only in human affairs. Some she endowed with a prodigious birth rate, so that they could reproduce faster than they could be digested. (I can sure think of clubs I'd rather belong to!)

Others she blessed with a repugnant odor or unpalatable flesh, so that few things would stoop low enough to eat them. Still others she endowed with great bulk to withstand attack, or great speed to outstrip it. Some she equipped with deadly fang or raking talon, or maybe an impenetrable coat of mail. If they couldn't run, Nature gave them a gun. And she distributed sensory perceptions — plus a sort of radar equipment — as they seemed needed in particular cases.

Nature did not equip bobwhite with the foregoing armaments and defenses, but she probably figured she had given him all he required. I think so too, although his primary defense against man is a bit on the unique side. For Bob's frontline defense is the clamor of his takeoff — the racket he makes when he rings your doorbell. This is his coat of mail. Various words have been used to describe this sound — explode, whirr, buzz, clatter and what not. None is adequate.

There is no word in the language that can accurately describe it, as there is none that can reproduce the sound of a bass striking against a top water plug. It is one of Nature's inimitable accompaniments. Suffice it to say that there is no other sound, unless it be the angry singing of a concealed rattler, that can so unman and disarm a gunner. If you haven't heard it, on a crisp morning with a gun in your hand, you are one of the earth's unfortunates.

It's an odd thing. You know it's going to happen. You fortify your resolutions and screw up your courage to the sticking point.

Yet when a bevy explodes under your feet and the air is suddenly filled with pirouetting targets, your manly defenses crumple. A moment later it is but a ghastly memory. Everything in nature is tranquil again — except your surging blood pressure. Then you hold a post-mortem and shamefacedly confess to yourself that at least half of them would have been easy shots if you hadn't completely gone to pieces. You swear you will not be guilty of such unmitigated folly again. You won't, until the next time.

I have seen corporation heads get so rattled that they didn't have sense enough to release the safety. I have seen upstanding and self-contained citizens enthusiastically dump both barrels into the trunk of a sweet gum or loblolly, while the birds sailed leisurely down Main Street. I once took a psychiatrist hunting with me. The eruption of a covey under his feet left his bedside manner somewhat less than intact. In fact, I was lucky to emerge unperforated.

I have known honest men who blamed their guns, their shells and their blameless dogs, men who swore on the spot to change churches and vote the Republican ticket thereafter.

"I wear myself out trying to decide which bird to shoot at," a companion once complained. "It's making those decisions that breaks a fellow down. It's like a woman standing undecided in a shop full of hats, like a man running rampant in a girls' dormitory, like the master of a harem — — "

"Aren't your comparisons getting rather far afield?" I said. "Let's stick to birds. It's safer."

"Anyway, you know what I mean?"

I did.

"I always shoot better when only a segment of a covey gets up," puzzled another companion. "And when a single gets up, I always get a double. Does that make sense to you?"

"May I assure you," I grinned, "that your logic is unassailable, and that you are a perfectly normal person."

A hunter never completely overcomes the impact of an exploding bevy. I ought to know. It still upsets me after thirty years. If it didn't, I would quit hunting. Who wants to do what he *can* do? The only way to shoot well is to hunt so much that a bird becomes unimportant to you. That sounds crazy, but it's true.

I once contrived a way to offset the disconcerting clamor of

Bob's exit. An ingenious trick it looked, and I was immoderately proud of it. In high school at the time, I had just read how the wily Ulysses sealed the ears of his crew with wax to protect them from the seductive songs of the sirens. (And left his own unsealed, the dirty dog!) Very well, I would emulate Ulysses by stuffing my own ears with cotton. But it was no good. I could still hear them thundering away in my mind.

I play golf on occasion, fish a great deal, work faithfully in my garden and teach school a little. Just how little I hope the university never finds out. And I do a lot of other things that I am willing to put in the paper. But what I really live for is bird hunting. For nine months of the year I am a doting grandfather, a reasonably faithful husband and a fairly upright citizen. The other three months I am not worth a damn.

And I'll tell you what I think is a fact: if I saw a big covey of birds deploy nicely in the broomstraw, and on the way toward them I chanced to espy Jane Russell, Ava Gardner and Gina Lollobrigida attired only in their upswept hairdos, I would keep right on after those singles! I think. Now, after I had run out of shells ... Such exemplary conduct is, I admit, somewhat speculative on my part. I might add that I have not thus far been confronted with such a situation.

I hunted so much last season that my classes became very popular. My students and I often met, going out and coming in. One morning, after arriving at my classroom, I decided to go bird hunting; so I wrote on the blackboard: "Mr. Babcock will not meet his classes today." Twenty minutes later I came back for my car keys, which I had inadvertently left on the desk. The class had come and departed, but some smart aleck had erased the "c" in "classes," making it read: "Mr. Babcock will not meet his lasses today." So I erased the "l" and left.

Funny thing about bird hunting. I abominate pavements and rigorously abstain from walking for the sake of walking. Can't imagine anything worse. Yet, I often walk fifteen miles a day while hunting, and count it a great privilege. And give a repeat performance the next day. This puzzles my wife no end.

For some reason, indoor exercise doesn't agree with me. Such disbursements of energy as carpet beating, furniture moving, or papering the living room would probably leave me a candidate

251

for hospitalization. Furthermore, if somebody hired me to carry a 7-pound log on my shoulder for fifteen miles, it would cost him $100. That's a minimum figure. Matter of fact, don't think I could do it. I have a theory that exercise doesn't do you any good unless you enjoy it. How do you feel about this theory? The dividing line between work and exercise may be very thin, but, mister, it is very real.

Not that Alice objects to my bird hunting, although I go and come at unconscionable hours. Down through the years I have evolved a modus operandi for coming in late without getting bawled out. Here is my recipe for effecting a belated entrance into my menage. If I get back late, she is mad as a wet hen. If I get back *very* late, she is worried — and grateful for my coming in at all. So I stay through the *mad* into the *worried* period. Let your wife contemplate the prospect of widowhood awhile, and when you do get in she will bake a cake and hire a band.

When I'm bird hunting, I don't want conditions too perfect. For instance I like a tree standing here and there to furnish a decent alibi when I need one. Miss a rise in the wide open, and you haven't a leg to stand on. I want a companion who talks, but not too much, a companion who shoots well, but not too well. I want birds that fly fast, but not too fast. And I want a dog that is good, but not too good. I want nothing to do with a dog so perfect that he undermines my self-respect. Nor a smart aleck. A fellow once tried to sell me a Phi Beta Kappa. "This dog is so smart," he said, "that he barks whenever you miss a bird."

"Keep your damned dog," I growled.

Bird hunting gets into a man's blood worse than the seven-year itch. I've never known a bird hunter to quit. They die sometimes, but never quit. And they do all sorts of whimsical and extravagant things. A New England manufacturer often calls me long-distance and says: "Get yourself a comfortable rocking chair and let's talk bird hunting awhile. I'm paying for the call." A furniture maker and an insurance executive often long-distance me for quarter of an hour — just to talk about bird hunting.

A crony of mine, a nationally known industrial chemist, who has hunted with me every opening day for twenty-five years, thinks nothing of flying from Denver or Milwaukee and back for a two-day hunt. It's an old story with us. Yet the night before the opening is invariably a sleepless one. We always get up too early, drive ninety miles to the Low Country and sit in our car until daybreak. We lean back in the cozy darkness, light our pipes, and chat about the "snows of yesteryear" until the *thump! thump!* of a dog's tail in the trunk brings us back to reality. And we think we are having a good time.

When day finally cracks, we let our dogs out. They proceed at once to select a spot, and leisurely address themselves to the transaction of such business as they deem prudent before a long day's hunt gets underway. "The sign of a good dog," we always laugh. Then we take off our caps, bow our heads and say in unison:

"O Lord, who looketh down on the frailities of man with charity and understanding, we thank Thee for bringing us safely through another year unto this pleasant day, and for the privilege of being abroad on Thy bountiful earth. Let no ungenerous thoughts find lodgment in our hearts, nor gluttony. And please let no mischance befall us this day, nor those we love. Amen!"

Then we load our guns, let out what even the most critical historians would accept as a Rebel yell, grinningly shake hands, and begin the hunt.

May the great Keeper of the Gates, in his infinite goodness, find a little space for idiots like us.

Change of Idols

A compelling account of a troubled teenager,
whose longing and uncertainty are erased by one
sweep of a huge salmon's tail.

by John Taintor Foote

or as long as he could remember, there had been times when it was no fun to go home after school or play was over. At such times the whole house seemed to whisper, "Dad isn't in his study. He isn't in the fly-tying room. He isn't out in the garage fooling with the car. No use to look; he's gone!"

With him had gone — as David knew from a fascinated watching of the packing of duffel bags and suitcases — shooting clothes in the fall, fishing clothes in the spring. Also, of course, warm brown leather gun cases or shiny aluminum rod cases, depending on the season. Sometimes the rod cases would be long and made of leather. That meant it was salmon. The smaller aluminum cases meant trout.

His father always whistled while he packed — a funny whistle through his teeth. No tune. It was like a bird's song with a faint hiss woven through it. The whistle was constant. It was an accompaniment to putting guns or rods in their cases, reels into small chamois bags, flies and leaders in their respective aluminum boxes. David noticed that the whistle changed when the rod cases and leaders were long and the flies bigger and much more brilliant. Salmon! the whistle was slower, lower, more reverent when it was salmon.

David was imitating the more lilting whistle as he came into the house one blazing afternoon in late August. He had just trimmed Bud Ellsworth three sets to one and dad was home and mother would probably forget the rule about eating between meals — she almost always did. He put his racket in a press, laid it on a shelf in the hall closet and moved soundlessly in his sneakers into the living room.

His mother was stretched on a couch with many pillows. Her jade-colored gown seemed like a shimmering green river flowing past islands of orange and yellow and robin's-egg blue.

"Hi, muz! How about a noggin of milk with some cheese sandwiches on the side?"

Her eyes traveled up his long gaunt body. His tennis shirt, wet through, clung to his angular torso. He was nothing but hollows and ridges. Along his ribs he suggested a corduroy road.

"How on earth can you eat as much as you do and keep on looking like Mahatma Gandhi?"

"It all goes to brain."

"Really?" How do you account for your school reports?"

"Aw, are you going to start that again, when I could eat one of those pillows?"

She eyed him for a moment.

"You should put on a sweater when you're as hot as that. Go take a shower and change. I'll tell Mary to put something for you on a tray in dad's study. He wants to see you."

"Oke," said David. He bounded upstairs, shedding his wet shirt as he went. In ten minutes he was bathed, dressed and heading for the study by leaps, jig steps, short runs and slides. He found his father seating a reel on a long rod. Milk and sandwiches were on the encyclopedia stand. Two kinds of sandwiches — cheese and ham. Swell!

255

"Hi, pop! He poured a glass of milk and seized a sandwich.

"Hello, son. Sit down?"

Son! Gosh! It should have been "Dave" or "long fellow" or "Skeezicks." Was it the darned old school reports again?

"Yes sir," he said.

His father laid the rod carefully down on a flat-topped desk and lit a cigarette. He watched David take alternative gulps of milk and bites of sandwich, then brushed away a wan haze of cigarette smoke that hung between them.

"Every man should learn to play as well as work."

"Yes, sir," agreed David, with some difficulty. It was a cheese-sandwich moment at the time.

"There are a lot of ways to play. Contract and golf seem to be the most popular just now. The sanest way — because it's closest to nature — is shooting and fishing. Mostly you'll find sportsmen lean, clean birds who mind their own business and don't talk too much. That's what streams and lakes and fields and woods and marshes do to a man. In addition to that, they're keener than the rest. They'll drive a hundred miles to fight a spring-trout stream with snow coming down and no trout coming up; or sit in a duck blind for eight hours when it's not far from zero.

"The reason why sportsmen are keener than golfers or polo players or bridge sharks or stamp collectors is this: The urge to shoot and fish is atavistic. You know what atavistic means?"

David considered while he took a swallow of milk and applied school methods to the situation.

"Has it anything to do with being active?"

"Good God! Look it up!"

" 'Pertaining to atavism,' " David read aloud from the dictionary a moment later.

"Well, look up atavism!"

" 'The reversion or tendency to revert to the ancestral type of a species. The —' "

"Never mind the rest! You'll see what I'm getting at. Hunting and fishing were vital to our remote ancestors. And I think that when a man tries to make a good trout take his fly or works a duck call to bring a smart old drake mallard down to his blind, he's tense and thrilled and keen as a brier, because somewhere

256

inside him is a fellow with a bone fishhook and a spear or a sling who's got to bring home fish and game or his wife and kids will starve. That's clear, isn't it?"

David, who had returned to his milk and sandwiches, nodded, gulped and spoke:

"Yes, sir."

His father stared at him unseeingly for a moment, then looked at the beautiful rod, with its gunmetal reel attached, lying across the desk. His eyes came back to David.

"You're going to shoot and fish, of course. If you'd been raised in real country as I was, you'd have been at it long ago. New York and Southampton don't give a kid much chance. Well, we're going out in the back yard now and I'm going to show you a little something about how to handle a salmon rod. Tonight I'll teach you to tie a fly on a leader."

"That'll be swell, dad!"

His father picked up the rod and balanced it.

"That's a light fourteen-footer. I think you can swing it. But before we take it outside, I might as well tell you something. I'm going up to Nova Scotia with your Uncle Jim. The Margaree has a late run of salmon. We leave week after next. We're taking you with us. You'll miss some school, but I think it will be worth it."

"Gee! Gosh! Hot dog! Oh, boy!"

Every day after that, for nearly two weeks, David spent the better part of each afternoon in the back yard with the fourteen-foot rod, under his father's critical eye. Most of the time he practiced casting, but when his shoulders and back began to ache, his father played fish. Picking up the end of the line, he would dash down the garden walk.

"Don't try to stop me. Let me make my run. Rest the butt just below your belt. Hold the rod with your left hand well above the reel and keep the rod up. Just let me run on the click. Look out, I'm coming back! Don't let me pull it down that way! The rod'll fight for you if you let it."

It was interesting for a day or so, David thought. Then he began to miss his tennis. He was glad when at last they stood on the front porch saying good-by to his mother.

She kissed him. "Good-by, darling. Have a good time!" She looked at his father. "Now I suppose there'll be two of them in the family!" She turned and disappeared through the front door.

They got into the loaded car and drove away. David looked back at the rambling white house with its moss-colored roof and its dark-green shutters. Mother might be looking out a window! ... She wasn't.

"They just can't understand," mused his father. "They call it killing things!" How you feeling, Dave?"

"Swell," said David.

Uncle Jim was waiting at the pier, surrounded by rod cases and duffel bags. They watched the car being swung from the pier to the steamer's hold before going aboard to inspect their cabins. Then David inspected the ship from engine room to bridge. He heard the shattering bellow of the whistle, saw that the pier was moving along the main saloon windows, and rushed on deck. His father and Uncle Jim were smoking by the rail.

"Well, here we go, Davy." His uncle's big hand closed, lightly, on David's scrawny arm.

"Is it much fun to catch a salmon, Uncle Jim?"

"Fun!" His uncle knocked out his pipe against the rail and looked at his father. "You answer that one!"

"Well, son," said his father, "the day will come when a grouse getting up in a thicket will make your heart gallop like a fire horse. You'll crouch in a blind and shake when a bunch of canvasbacks are circling you. You'll feel something happen to your spinal cord when a big brown or rainbow trout rolls up and takes your dry fly. But tops, absolute tops, is the rise of a salmon and what happens after that. Don't call it fun. It's — it's — I've done my stuff. Now you take over, Jim."

His uncle tapped his pipe against his palm and thought for a moment.

"It's a mixture of glory hallelujah and the Battle of Gettysburg," he decided at last.

They ran into a storm twelve hours out. David developed a slightly greenish pallor and — this was serious — lost all interest in food. Placid Halifax harbor seemed like heaven. He crept miserably down the gangplank, but by the time the car was swung from the ship and loaded, he began to think of ham and eggs — lots of ham and eggs and, well, yes — plenty of French-

258

fried potatoes to go with them.

He got ham and eggs for supper that night at Mrs. Gerard's, two hundred and ninety miles northeast of Halifax, on the upper Margaree. There was also smoked salmon, baked beans with plenty of catchup, bread and butter — four slices — with sugar spread carefully over all, and apple sauce. Also there was Miriam Gerard. She had waited on them at table. Her shoulder had brushed David's once as she served him.

He drifted to sleep that night with the roar of the Margaree in his ears, wondering if she would be such a knockout in daylight.

She was! He saw that at a glance when she came in with the coffee for breakfast. Gosh, what hair! Like golden fire! She looked at him. David dropped his eyes hastily and began to butter a flapjack. If he was the kind of a guy that bothered about girls ˙— but, of course, he wasn't. It was funny, though, how he felt when she stood beside him with more flapjacks. Her shoulder didn't touch his, but somehow you knew, without looking, it was a girl.

"Well, are you full, long fellow?"

"Yes, dad."

"Miriam, will you ask your mother if she'll have dinner at night and lunch at noon? We don't want our heavy meal in the middle of the day.

"Yes, sir."

"And, oh, yes. May we keep our rods on the front porch?"

"Yes, sir. They always do."

"Thank you. Let's get going, you two."

While they were getting into their waders, Uncle Jim addressed him:

"Better watch your step, Dave; that's some gal."

David flushed.

"I don't bother with girls," he said.

His father and uncle exchanged winks.

There followed a morning in which David dropped from the peak of thrilled expectancy to a pit of aching boredom. He had waded into the swift mystery of the first pool in the stretch they had assigned to him with his knees knocking together. His father and uncle watched him work out line and make his first cast. The fly shot out and across and dropped to the surface without too much splash and with no curve in the leader. Nothing happened. He looked at his father and got a nod of approval. He made another cast, and another. Ten minutes later he realized that his father and uncle were gone. They had left him alone in a salmon pool with a salmon rod. He was casting as well as he ever had in the back yard and now his fly was dropping into golden water that frothed around boulders and then slid rapidly on. At any cast a salmon might take that fly! A salmon! He cast and cast and cast, taking a step downriver after each cast, as dad had told him to do.

He grew conscious of his father standing on the bank. He beckoned and David waded slowly in to him, bracing himself against the current and planting his felt-soled wading shoes carefully on the rough bottom.

"River's too warm, Dave. We won't do much until we get a rise of water. I haven't given you a gaff because you might catch your leader with it. If you hook a fish, remember everything I've told you. Play him until he's finished, then take hold of him just above the tail and drag him out on a bar."

David nodded.

"Uncle Jim's just below you. I'm going down below him. Keep plugging away; there's always a chance. Hope you get one."

His father strode off downstream.

David waded out into the current and started casting again. An hour went by. Another hour. His shoulders began to ache. His arms ached. His back ached. Cast, recover, one step downstream! Cast, recover, one step downstream! He seemed to have been doing it all his life. And what for? There weren't any fish in the darned old river. Cast, recover — Ouch! Gosh! His back was broken. David waded out and sat on a log.

That was where they found him at lunchtime. Uncle Jim had a four-pound grilse.

"Saw him lying in a shallow run. Floated a dry fly over him and teased him up. Got to have rain! Got to!"

Well, he hadn't caught a fish, but, boy, was he hungry! Scrambled eggs, fried potatoes, sardines, beet salad, biscuits, milk, canned peaches, and Miriam to look at. He still looked away whenever she looked at him. He didn't know why.

After lunch he told his father about his back.

"You're using new muscles. Better not take it too fast! Suppose you rest this afternoon."

"All right, I'll read. Mother put in some books."

He selected *Men of Iron* and took it to a faded canvas hammock on the front porch. He was sharing Myles Falworth's cold horror as the grim Earl of Mackworth appeared, suddenly, in the privy garden, when the screen door opened and closed with a bang.

"Hello."

"Hello," said David.

"Why ain't you fishin'?"

"I strained my back."

"What you readin'?" She came to the hammock.

"Men of Iron."

She slid into the hammock beside him.

"Is it good?" She made no effort to resist the pull of gravity toward the center of the hammock.

"Swell," said David hoarsely.

He had never dreamed that anything could be so soft and warm. A penetrating electric warmth that flowed into him and through him like a tide.

"How old are you?"

"Sixteen," he managed to say.

"That's funny. I'm sixteen too. Sweet sixteen and never been kissed." She gave David a languishing look, their faces inches apart.

Something was expected of him — he knew that — but he sat there rigid, the blood pounding his ears. He was in the grip of the bashfulness of the adolescent male, which transcends girlish modesty mountains high.

"You're from New York, ain't you?"

The moment was over! Oh, why hadn't he kissed her?

He nodded, speechless.

"What's it like?"

"Just buildings and traffic cops and taxicabs. It isn't much."

"What's your house like?"

She was still burning against his side like a delicious fire.

"It isn't a house. It's an apartment. Our house is in Southampton."

261

"I thought you lived in New York."

"We do, in winter. We live in Southampton in the summer."

"What's that like?"

"Just houses and a little burg and the beach. It isn't much."

"Are the houses nice?"

"They're all right, I guess. Some of them have tennis courts."

"Are all the boys in New York like you?"

"How do you mean?"

"Oh" — she moved a hand into one of his — "sort of slow." Once more she was looking into his eyes.

Another chance! He'd not act like a dumb bunny this time. His lips traveled the few inches separating them from her enticing, slightly opened mouth.

His nose and mouth buried themselves in her hair. The scent of it was devastating. A gentle delicate girl odor, more urgently commanding than all the perfumes of the world.

"Miri-a-am! Miri-a-am!"

"Comin-n-g! There's ma! Lemme go!"

"Aw, please! Before you go!"

The fingers that were entwined with his tightened convulsively. Her lips met his, clung to them. The screen door opened and banged shut. She was gone!

There remained a trembling youngster, no longer concerned with the doings of Myles Falworth. He was gazing into a new, ecstatic world that he had just discovered in a faded hammock.

So that was what it was all about! He waited as long as he could. Then he got to his feet. He couldn't stand it in the hammock, without her, any longer. He must get away by himself and think it over. He stumbled down the steps and headed for the Margaree. He plowed through some willows and came to the upper pool that he had fished that morning. He sat down on a boulder, dropped his head in his hands and stared at the slicks and troubled swirls of the amber river — red gold in the afternoon sun. Red gold like Miriam's hair!

His father and uncle found him there as they came upriver at dusk.

His father chuckled as they stopped to take in that slender figure, brooding at the water's edge.

"Too lame to fish, but he can't keep away from it. It's in the blood, Jim." He raised his voice: "Hi, fisherman! Time out to eat!"

David got stiffly to his feet, picked his way through river boulders and joined them.

"Catch anything?"

"Nary a fish," said his uncle. "Anyway. I'm not skunked." He poked David's father with his elbow.

"Huh, I don't catch minnows! ... Guess what we're going to have for dinner, Skeezicks? Turkey! I saw it in the kitchen."

"Gosh!" said David. But for some reason he wasn't hungry.

He was careful not to look at Miriam at dinner, although he wanted to. He wanted to see how she would look at him, now that they shared the secret of the hammock.

After dinner he went out on the porch and sat on the steps. He avoided the hammock. He didn't want her to find him in it if she came out. It would look too much as though he were just waiting there to neck her.

She didn't come out. He went quietly around the house and looked through the kitchen window. She was wiping dishes as her mother washed them. There was a screen on the window and the kitchen wasn't very light. He couldn't see her face well, but her sleeves were rolled up and he watched the gleam of her white arms under the dim lamplight. He felt his mouth go dry.

He went back and sat on the porch again. She would come to him when she was through in the kitchen, he guessed.

His father called him and he went in. They wanted him to play dominoes. He played dominoes until it was time for bed.

He looked at her at breakfast. She made a mouth at him. A delicious, funny mouth. He laughed out loud before he thought.

"Let us in on it, fisherman!" said his uncle.

"Can't," said David.

He stole another glance at Miriam, who departed for the kitchen with a luxurious roll of the hips.

His father's eyes followed her through the door. He took one look at David's face and lifted his eyebrows at his brother.

David began his casting that morning with the utmost care. Miriam was no longer in his mind. He was handling his rod with more ease than ever before. He was checking his back-cast when the rod tip was almost straight above him, not tilted far back as when he first began. As a result of this and the leverage

263

of his right and left hands traveling in opposite directions, but in full coordination, the line was rolling out over the water with an ease that was delightful. Now, how about the leader? He saw with pride that it straightened perfectly with every cast. Say, this was fun! It continued to be fun for an hour. Then it became a dumb business without rhyme or reason. He sat down to rest.

He scowled at the river for a time, then turned his eyes to the mountains, rising on the other side, along which the Margaree hurried, fretting, to the sea. His eyes lifted to the tops of the mountains. Great, billowing, whipped-cream clouds were hanging over them, shutting off the steady blue of the sky. The clouds shut off the sun from time to time. When this happened, a shadow would come racing up the river to put out the tiny fires in the dancing rapids and dull the gleam of the pools.

And now David really began to hear the voice of the river — a steady chuckling roar. He had not been conscious of it while fishing. As he listened, his ill humor left him. That sound seemed to fill every crevice of his brain, leaving no room for thought. He sat there in a sort of dream, submerged in the sound of the river, vaguely aware of its steady, though varied march.

A covey of partridges nodded past him through the willows. A mink came in an arching gallop along the shore, to stop dead at his moveless figure. It plunged like a brown flash into the river, its whiskers bristling with horror. David grinned. It was kind of nice here. Peaceful!

It was not peaceful long. Warm arms came from behind him to clasp themselves about this neck. A hot cheek was pressed against his own.

He rolled off his boulder and pulled her down behind him among some smaller stones. His long arms tightened about her. As he pressed against her, she sank back, bringing him with her, until her head came to rest on a water-smoothed, sun-baked stone. He felt the grip of her arms become firmer around his shoulders, then suddenly they relaxed. Her hands flew to his chest. He was being pushed violently from her.

"Oh, Miriam, don't!"

"Get away! Get away, quick! You're soaking wet!"

Then David remembered his waders. They were still dripping.

He slid, contritely, away from her.

Miriam sat up with a jerk and looked at the skirt of her blue print dress, now a vast dark stain.

"God!" she said. "What'll I tell ma?"

David turned white. Now he was in for it! Darn the waders! Darn this fishing where there weren't any fish! Dad was a nut. And Uncle Jim, too. Boys had told him about girls' mothers finding out!

"Maybe it'll dry in the sun," he suggested wanly. "Maybe if you'd kind of spread it out and — "

"Do you think I can stay here till it dries? I sneaked away just for a minute. She'll be looking for me by this time, mebbe. What did you want to come wallowing all over me in them wet pants for, anyway?"

David looked at her, bewildered. She had pulled him down against her. Well, girls were like that, he supposed, when they knew you were crazy about them.

"I'm sorry," he said.

"Well, it's done now." She stared, frowning, at the havoc he had wrought. Her face swiftly cleared. "I know what I'll do. I'll say I dropped a rock in the river and it splashed me." She put a hand on his shoulder and got to her feet. "Gimme a kiss 'fore I go, sweetie!"

David sprang up and obeyed with alacrity.

He watched her out of sight, wishing he dared go to the house with her. As it was, he had to fuss around in the darned ole river until dad and Uncle Jim came. He sighed and picked up his rod.

The week that followed was a trial. It remained hot, with cloudless skies. Now and then, his father or Uncle Jim, by means of much patience and a deeper guile than David knew, would bring home a salmon. The largest one weighed twelve pounds. He looked huge to David, but his father said, "Wait till, you see a real fish! Wait till you have hold of one that'll go twenty pounds or better."

Fat chance, thought David. By now he was fed up for life with salmon fishing. He hated the thought of that silly, futile casting in the hot sun. He snorted when he remembered that he had been crazy to leave a world that contained tennis courts

265

for this dumb business.

But then, there was Miriam! She was worth the trip. She dazzled him by day. She haunted him by night. He lived in a feverish daze — uplifted one minute, downcast the next. His appetite fell off. He grew thinner than ever. He had all but stopped fishing. He would tell his father that he had a headache or that he wanted to read. Then he would wait in the hammock on the chance of a too-swift embrace.

Miriam was of the earth, earthy, but she was also a born coquette. It pleased her to toy with this rich man's son who thought fishing was hard work. She had known affairs of the heart since she was fourteen. That was why ma was always watching her. Ma was becoming different about this boy from New York, though. That was funny! Ma would even say, "Why don't you take a nice walk through the woods with that poor, lonesome young fella?" Well, she'd handle it to suit herself, thank you.

There was a bank of clouds one morning beyond the mountains to the east — dark clouds. David's father and uncle watched them with keen, interested faces as they got into waders and wading shoes.

"Looks like the real thing, Jim — at last!"

"Let's kneel and pray."

"Not coming, David?"

"I don't believe I will, dad. Think I'll stay here and read for a while."

His father looked at him steadily, opened his mouth to speak, closed it again. "Just as you like." He turned away, put on his worn fishing jacket, took his rod from its row of pegs and followed David's uncle down the steps. Presently he caught up with him.

"So that's a son of mine?"

"Sa-a-y," drawled his brother, "What were you doing at his age?"

"I'll tell you what I was doing," said David's father grimly. "I was walking four miles to Jackson's Pond to fish for bullheads with a cane pole."

"Sure. And you were catching bullheads, weren't you?"

"Certainly. What of it?"

"What if you'd hoofed it to Jackson's Pond every day for a week and never got a nibble?"

David's father rubbed his chin thoughtfully.

"Well, I dunno about that."

"Well, I know. You'd have quit! And now you expect that boy, who never had a fish on a line in his life, to pound a dead river in the hot sun, day after day — and like it."

"That isn't it. It's simply that he wants to stay here and hang around that cheap, little, hip-swinging — "

"Wh-o-a! Back up, fella! This father business has got you down. That's just about the niftiest little trick I ever saw. At his age she'd have had me jumping through hoops and rolling over and playing dead. Slander Dave if you like — he's your offspring — but lay off that gal. I don't dare look at her much or Dave and I would be rivals."

David's father chuckled. He sobered suddenly.

"I'm worried. Of course she's attractive — too attractive! What's going on back there while we're fishing? She hasn't any more morals than a cat — you can see that at a glance."

"There you go again! Thank God I'm not a father! Just who managed your girling for you when you were Dave's age? Of course, after he's twenty-one you've lost control. Why don't you put him in a monastery till then? That would let you fish in peace."

"Perhaps you're right — I don't know. I've always tried to make him work out things for himself. But I know I'm worried. I'm worried plenty. My God, what would his mother say?"

"Well, I'll tell you what I'll do. I'll just bet you fifty dollars those clouds don't mean a rain that'll raise the river, say, six inches, in the next twenty-four hours. If I lose I'll be tickled pink. If I win I'll have the fifty bucks."

"Where do I come in?"

"You? Why, you'll have something to think about besides Dave."

"All right, you're on," said David's father.

Back at the house, David seated himself on the porch steps and waited. It seemed an age before he was rewarded. At last the screen door banged. She dashed across the porch and kissed him, hurriedly.

He seized her hands.

"Listen, Miriam! Let's get away from here. Let's go where no one will bother us. Will you? Please, oh, please!"

"Can't, sweetie; it's wash day."

"What about late this afternoon?"

"Me go anywhere this afternoon! You ain't never done a wash."

"Well, tomorrow morning."

"Ironing tomorrow morning."

David, sick with disappointment, let go her hands.

"It's always something! Some rotten, silly excuse!"

She leaned down and smiled into his face.

"Awful mad?"

"Listen! If you'll be good today I'll get ma to do the ironing and we'll go to the fox farm tomorrow morning."

Silence from David.

"They're silver foxes. Hundreds of 'em. They're pretty as pictures."

"What do I care about darned ole foxes?" he asked sulkily.

"It's only three miles."

"I don't care. I don't want to go!"

She suddenly kneeled beside him with eyes that had lost their bright provoking look. They had grown dark and unseeing. With a quick, possessive gesture she gathered his head in her arms. Then she kissed his cheeks, his eyelids, his throat, his mouth.

"Don't be a little donkey," she whispered. "There's a short cut — *through the woods.*"

That was a long day. He tried reading. No good! He tried skipping stones across the river. Worse! By late afternoon the bank of dark clouds had become a black canopy covering the entire sky. When bedtime came he undressed and lay staring straight above him. Then the thought of the way she had kissed him drove him to turning and tossing and pounding his pillow.

At last he quieted. His drifting to sleep was retarded by a sudden steady roar. Rain on the roof. It was pouring. What if it rained tomorrow! No going to the woods! He didn't see how he could stand it. He heard his father call to Uncle Jim: "I'm going to buy a nice two-piece trout rod with that fifty dollars, old-timer!"

Rods! That's all they thought about. Just goofy!

268

David sank into slumber with the rain still beating on the roof. He wakened with a start next morning, feeling that something was going to happen that day — something wonderful. Now he remembered! He heard no sound of rain. He got out of bed and went to the window. The trees were still dripping, but the rain had ceased. There was a gray sky high up with low smoky clouds below. It was much colder. So cold that he began to shiver. That was too bad. He wanted it to be a nice warm day.

He saw Uncle Jim coming from the direction of the river and heard him call to his father:

"Up about eight inches! Just colored enough! I saw fish traveling! Let's get this eating over in a hurry!"

At breakfast his father and Uncle Jim simply gobbled their bacon and eggs, swallowed their coffee and pushed back their chairs.

"Make it snappy, Davy! Something doing today!"

"I'm not going fishing, Uncle Jim," said David. He felt himself blushing.

His father, who was striding out of the room, halted and turned.

"Why not?"

"I've promised Miriam to go with her this morning to see some silver foxes at a fox farm."

"You can do that some other day. Come and get into your waders."

"But, Dad —"

"Did you hear me?"

No use! When he spoke like that, you just had to keep still. David followed them to the front porch, white with rage and disappointment.

"You've had a discouraging time with your fishing, son. It's been tough. When a river is as warm as this has been, salmon don't move and seldom take a fly. A good rise of water stirs them up. Every pool will have taking fish in it today. I don't want you to miss it. Now stop sulking! By night you'll know why I'm making you come with us."

"Yes, sir," said David.

They left him at the head of his stretch of river.

"Tie on a fair-sized Thunder and Lightning, Dave," his uncle

269

called as they were leaving. "It's a good fly in this kind of water."

David selected a Thunder and Lightning from his fly box and tied it on. He found that his fingers were trembling a little. The river was different. Under gray skies and with dark pines still glistening with rain, crowding either bank, this higher, more deeply muttering river was more mysterious, more forbidding. Anything might be concealed in such a river, waiting for his fly.

He began to cast. Presently his excitement died. The same old thing! Cast for hours and get nothing but aching arms and a crick in the back. And he would have been starting for the woods with Miriam about now!

He was staring unseeingly at his line as it began its swing toward shore. Twenty feet or so below the point where the line met the water, a wave appeared — a V-shaped wave, moving rapidly. Something was making that wave. There was a splash, a mighty swirl that left a whirlpool in the water, then the line swung on quietly toward shore. Ye gods! What was that? It was frightening! Why, it was about where his fly must have been. A rise! David's knees sagged so suddenly that he nearly shipped water down the tops of his waders.

Gee, gosh! What had dad said about a salmon missing a fly? He remembered! "Wait one full minute, then cast again in the same place." David dropped his eyes to his wrist watch. Golly! Was a minute that long? Ten seconds more! Five seconds! Well, here goes!

He cast well above the place, so that the fly would float over it. Now the fly was about where it had happened. Past it! Way past it! Nothing!

It must have been a salmon. Then what was wrong? Just his darned luck! Nothing ever went right for him! Better try again. He did. The fly reached the fatal spot. It passed it. Darn! The rod was all but jerked from David's hands. Oh, where was dad? He hadn't known! He hadn't dreamed it would be like that! The savage blow of the strike all but paralyzed him.

Out of the mysterious, hurrying river rose a monster, huge beyond belief, vicious-looking, majestic, terrifying. It curved into the air and crashed into the river with a heart-shaking splash. Its sides were gleaming silver. Its head and back and great spadelike tail were black. There was one tiny spot of bril-

270

liant color at its jaw. It was the bright scarlet and orange of David's Thunder and Lightning.

What should he do? For a moment he thought of dropping the rod and getting out of there. The thing was too huge, too implacable looking. The rod curved. The reel began a steady "ze-e-e." Mechanically he sank the butt into his stomach and slid his hand up the rod. "Ze-e-e, ze-e-e-e, ze-e-e-e-e!" A hundred yards down the river the great fish curved into the air again. That was good! He wasn't so frightening, far off like that. "Ze-e-e-e, ze-e-e-e-e!" The salmon leaped again. Gee, he was a mile away! David looked down at his reel. He was appalled at what he saw. The fat spool of green silk backing was down to a slender spindle. What had dad said? "Follow your fish if he takes too much line!" David waded to shore and started downriver, stumbling among rocks and driftwood, trying to keep the rod well up against the remorseless pull of the fish, and reeling, reeling, reeling! He had recovered a good deal of the line when the steady pull ceased. The rod straightened. Gone! Well, that was that. He couldn't have stood much more anyway.

Swoosh! Ker-swash! Great grief! The salmon had hurtled into the air not more than fifty feet below. Lord, he had all that slack! David's tired fingers flew to the reel handle. He ground away in a frenzy until the fingers were stiff with cramp. He simply couldn't reel in any more! He did, however, until the sag of the line became like a bow-string once more and the rod arched again. The line met the water a hundred feet above David, upstream! The fish had passed him while he was reeling in. "Ze-e-e, ze-e-e-e!" Upstream instead of down! David staggered after. How long was this going to last? He couldn't stand much more. The renewed steady pull on the rod had proved that. His left arm, that bore the strain, was quivering with fatigue. His legs were shaking. His back felt as though it had been pounded with a club.

At the exact spot from where he had risen to the fly, the salmon came to rest. David worked up to him, slowly gathering in line. He stopped on the shore just below the fish and wiped the sweat out of his eyes with the sleeve of his free right arm. He supposed the demon was sulking. Dad had told him about that. Well, let him sulk. That suited David.

271

He shifted hands on the rod and eased his aching left arm. With the bow of the rod keeping the line taut, he stood there waiting and looked about him — at the river, its bank, the mountains, the gray sky just above them into which they seemed to thrust their pine-clad tops.

He was standing on the edge of the pool he had fished so often. He thought he knew every flat, every riffle in it, every tree, every rock that formed its setting. It had become too familiar. He had learned to hate it. He found that he was seeing it all for the first time. Stimulated by the most violent excitement he had ever known. David's senses were razor sharp. The smell of the pines had never been so pungent. He filled his nostrils with it. and drew in lungfuls of the good air that bore it to him. The pines stood out more sharply than ever before. He could see each cluster of green needles on their branches. These somber steadfast trees seemed to be watching him — calmly, darkly watching.

And the river! He heard notes in its song altogether new to his ears. Sighs, gurgles, whispers, chuckles, the varied pattern of its steady roar. The water itself was different. The surface of the pool, beside which he stood, seemed like a smoothly sliding, dark-amber mirror concealing fathomless depths. Below this mirror, savage darting lives were being led by huge black-and-silver salmon. It seemed strange that the mere dropping of a tiny arrangement of gaudy feathers on this mirror could bring one of those monsters from the impenetrable mystery of his dim watery haunts to an intimate struggle with the boy who had put it there.

David looked up at the perfect curve of his rod. How steadily, how splendidly it fought for him! What a delicate thing, and yet how staunch! He loved it! He loved it all — sky, river, pines, mountains. He seemed a part of them. He was a weak continuation of his rod. They were joined forever in a world that contained two living creatures — himself and the great fish at the end of his leader, quiet now, for some reason.

What was he doing down there? Was he pausing for new atrocities to enter his diabolical mind? He must be tired or he wouldn't rest this long. It hadn't seemed possible that anything could tire him a little while ago. Maybe he was all in. Maybe he could be handled, after all. Boy, oh, boy!

The line began to move upriver with a faint hiss as it cut through the water. Where do we go from here? Nowhere! Just a jarring smash on the tackle that shook his arm from his wrist to shoulder. Another and another and another! Good Lord! What was he doing? The fish was jigging. David had not been told about that. Panic seized him as jar after jar was telegraphed through line and rod to his arm. Something had to give if that kept up! Instinctively he reduced the pressure on the rod, but the jigging continued.

"Wish he'd quit that jerking," said David, aloud.

His wish was swiftly granted. "Ze-e-e-e, ze-e-e-e!" Out of the water he came! The wave he made as he somersaulted in again washed inches up on David's wading shoes. "Ze-e-e-e, ze-e-e-e-e!" Tired? He's going to the ocean! Got to go after him!

And now, as David discovered when he got to the salmon at last, the real fight began. Not so spectacular, not so vicious, but a wearing, remorseless series of short rushes, long runs and circling swings around a pool with the line hissing as it cut various impromptu figures through the water. No more leaps. That, thought David, was grandstand stuff. This is the real thing.

On and on it went. No let-up. No slightest sign of weakening in the dogged drive of the great fish. "Ze-e-e" from the reel. 'His-s-s" from the rigid line, knifing up or down or across a pool. David could barely stand. Sweat filled his eyes and dripped off his nose. He could no longer close his hands. If the salmon bored away upstream or down, he staggered after, knowing he could not turn his reel handle to take up the slack. His thin arms were numb to the shoulder. "Oh, God!" he said at last to the watching trees and mountains. "I'll never do it!"

If Dad would only come, or Uncle Jim! He couldn't cut the line; he'd die before he did that! Was this going on forever! Not forever; he'll die, all right, before long, or heart failure or busted lungs, or something. But his heart and lungs continued to serve him for another incredible half hour. Then at last he saw the gleam of a great silver side. He saw it again a moment later. It was flat on the water for an instant. That must mean something. It did! The runs began to shorten. The side was showing more and more, despite the still powerful sweeps of the awesome tail. The salmon was no longer swimming now. It was wallowing

273

just before the surface. David's eyes filled with quick, unaccountable tears. He blinked them away. "I believe I've got him!"

From some unsuspected source he drew enough strength to lift on the rod. He could not believe his eyes as the salmon came wallowing and rolling in.

"Thank you, God!" breathed David.

With the rod bowed to a complete arch, the fish came in, a heartbreaking foot at a time, but he still came, until he was thrashing the water to foam and churning up clouds of sand a few feet off the narrow beach where David stood.

Now what? He was supposed to get him by the tail and drag him onto the beach. He laid down his rod. He found he couldn't stoop over. He staggered out beyond the fish and put the side of his foot against it. With a heave of his leg he got it nearer the shore. Another heave! Another! The salmon was now in a shallow mixture of sand and water. David fell on his knees. He got both arms around the fish despite the flailing tail. He must get to his feet! He must — he must! He did it, somehow, and staggered up the little beach. His arms gave way. The salmon thudded to the sand. David fell on his face beside it.

For ten minutes he lay there without movement, his mind a blank. Then thought returned. Was the fish still there? Was he as big as he had seemed? David sat up. He was still there! He was bigger! He was bigger than any fish could possibly be! David looked at the huge still slab of silver. Then he looked at the slender varnished rod lying in the sand. It just couldn't be done! But he had done it! Once more his eyes filled with sudden tears — he didn't know why.

He sat and stared at the magic river over which one could wave a split bamboo wand and lo, a miracle would come to pass. Footsteps crunched on some gravel behind him. It was Miriam. She was not in a pleasant mood.

"It'll be a cold day when I ask you to go anywhere with me again, mister — and don't you forget that! Just because you're from New York, I suppose you think you can treat a person up here like she was dirt!"

David turned his head slowly and looked at her. She proved to be a girl with sort of reddish hair and big eyes. She brought back to him, vaguely, days of uncertainty and longing, broken

274

by slinking, sneaky, throbbing moments that had left him shaking and unhappy.

"Scra-am!" The snarling of the command was an unconscious imitation of certain noble racketeers that people the fabulous world conceived by Hollywood. "Scram! Beat it! Don't you see I'm fishing?"

Ten days later, David's mother was welcoming her menfolk home.

"And, muz, I got eight more beside the whopper." David searched in his coat pocket and brought out a newspaper clipping. "Thought you might want to see this," he said, with elaborate indifference. "It's from a Halifax paper."

She took the clipping and glanced at the headlines.

BOY ANGLER'S AMAZING FEAT
Sixteen-year-old David Caruthers of New York Kills Second Largest Salmon Ever Taken on The Margaree. The Fish, Weighing 44½ Lbs., Was the First Salmon the Youngster Had Ever Hooked.

She looked up from the clipping at David's father. "Yes, there are two of them, now!" David's father slid a consoling arm about her waist.

"I'm afraid you're right, old lady," he said.

Dog

She was the best bird dog he'd ever seen and she
cost only forty dollars. But buying the dog's
undying devotion would take more than money.

by John Taintor Foote

yrtle is dead, poor funny little snipe-nosed Myrtle. I
left her, bored to extinction, at a gun club in Maryland.
Between shooting seasons, life to her was a void. It
consisted of yawns, the languid pursuit of an occasional flea, the indifferent toying with bones and dog biscuits
and a mournful, lackluster gazing at fields and thickets nearby.

During these dreary months she was never chained or confined in any way. Self hunting, which spoils so many gun dogs,
did not affect Myrtle. Occasionally, when the dragging days
became more than she could bear, she would betake herself
listlessly to quail cover, find a covey, point it for a moment, flush
it and watch the birds whir off into the pines. She would then
return, sighing heavily, to a twitching nap somewhere around
the clubhouse.

She must have perished during one of these efforts to break the monotony of existence in a gunless world, because a letter from the club steward tells me that she was caught in a muskrat trap in the big marsh and drowned. The big marsh is perhaps a half mile from the clubhouse.

Drowned! Except for Chesapeakes and a spaniel or two, I never saw a better swimmer. And yet, in preventing a similar tragedy, she became my dog, body and soul. Also I learned to sniff audibly when scientific fellows announce in my presence that animals cannot reason.

And now, I fear me, I shall have to divulge a secret that has been closely kept for many a day. I am about to spread reluctantly on the printed page the one formula for securing the kind of quail dog that fills an owner with unspeakable joy from dawn to dark, year in, year out, come heat or cold, or drought or rain.

It has nothing to do with sending a check to a professional breeder and then waiting, all expectant, for a shipping crate to be delivered at one's door. It has nothing to do with raising endless litters of distemper-ridden puppies. If you want the rarest, the most perfect instrument for sport in all the world, and not the average plodder and flusher of commerce or home industry, stick to my formula. I set it down exactly as it was given to me by a wise man of the South many years ago.

Here it is: "A Georgia cracker will sell anything — his land, his mule, his house, his wife. By God, he'll sell a bird dog — a real one, I mean. Just show him cash money and he'll reach for it."

These words — after I had learned their true significance — accounted, some years ago, for my spending a winter in Atlanta. My string of gun dogs, so my handler told me, had petered out. I was looking for another string, and Atlanta is the clearing house for information about noteworthy setters and pointers located in various counties of south and central Georgia where the most quail and, ipso facto, the most good gun dogs are found. Working out from Atlanta by motorcar, as rumor of dogs that knew their business drifted into town, I had secured four pointers. I had shot over perhaps fifty dogs in selecting them. The four were all fast, wide-going, covey finders. Class dogs are good for about three hours at top speed. I, therefore, had a pair for mornings and a pair for afternoons, but I needed something that would stay in closer and go slower and find singles — an all-day dog — to back up my four whirlwinds.

One evening a voice spoke over the telephone — a voice that I knew well. The voice said: "Listen. The foreman of our bottling plant was down below Macon last week. He got plenty of birds. He's been telling me about a little setter bitch he saw work that sounds like what you're after. He says he can fix it for us to go down and shoot over her next Saturday. What say?"

"How far is it?"

"'Bout a hundred and twenty miles."

"Does your foreman know a good dog when he sees one?"

"Yep!"

"What does he say she's like?"

"He says she's a ball of fire."

"Doing what?"

"Finding singles — coveys too."

"All right, have him fix it."

Thanks to that telephone conversation, my glance rested upon Myrtle for the first time about eight o'clock the following Saturday morning. She came cat-footing from somewhere behind a paintless shack, set in three or four acres of cotton stalks, at her master's whistle.

I took one look at her. Then my eyes swung reproachfully to the bottling-plant foreman who was responsible for, and had accompanied us, on a one-hundred-and-twenty-mile drive to see her.

"Never you mind," said he stoutly. "You want a bird dog, don't you?"

I did want a bird dog. I have ever been contemptuous of him who goes gunning with a silk-coated, bench-show type of setter calculated to drive a sportsman to undreamed-of heights of profanity with one hour's work in the field. But this specimen before me was — well, I felt that I could never bring myself to admitting the ownership of such a dog.

I had been told she was little. She was. She did not weigh much more than twenty pounds. She had a wavy black-white-and-ticked coat that gave her a claim on the setter family. Her muzzle was so pointed that her head suggested the head of a

278

fox — a black fox — except for a pair of drooping bird-dog ears. Her tail was short, clubby and without any flag. She carried it drooping and a bit to one side. Her eyes were the yellow fox eyes that belonged in such a head. Her gait, as she came loping to us, seemed more cat than fox, but it reminded me of both.

Delicacy made me omit the opening of the ritual expected at such a time. "How's she bred?" was never spoken. I inquired without interest about her age.

"Comin' three. Reck'n me an' yoh better stay together, an' yoh friends hunt their dogs."

"All right," I agreed feebly. I was in for it! A-hunting we must go!

And a-hunting we did go. My friend and the bottling-plant man with two of the former's dogs in one direction; my hapless self, with the unspeakable little setter and her lanky owner, in another. She had been named Myrtle, he told me, after his old woman. I had caught a glimpse of the "old woman" through the door of the shack ere we set forth. She was all of sixteen.

We walked in silence up a lane, and so came to fields and promising cover. "Get along, Myrt," said my companion in a conversational tone, and Myrt drifted to our left into some high grass and disappeared. We found her presently, perfectly still, looking without particular interest straight before her. "She's got birds," I heard. And this, indeed, was true, if our finding a covey twenty yards ahead of her proved it. Accustomed to the tense rigidity on point of more orthodox shooting dogs, Myrt's method was disconcerting.

I shall not attempt to describe that day — my first day afield with Myrtle. She found, in her cat-fox fashion, twelve coveys, as I remember. After each covey find, she proceeded to point and promptly retrieve, when killed, every scattered bird of every covey — or so it seemed to me. And the day was hot, and the day was dry. Incidentally her master shot rings around me.

Her final exhibition that evening would have settled my desire to call her mine if she had not already won me completely hours before. We had joined my friend and the bottling-plant foreman. They had found two coveys and a few singles, had killed four birds, and my friend's pair of pointers were the apple of his eye.

"There just weren't birds in the country we worked over,"

my friend explained.

I saw the owner of Myrtle open his mouth to speak, then close it resolutely. We started down the lane to the house, my friend, with his dogs at heel, in the lead; Myrtle, cat-footing behind her master, in the rear.

The dusk had closed in softly about us. It was already too dark for decent shooting. The lane down which we plodded had a high wire fence on either side, with pine woods to the left and a flat, close-cropped field to the right.

Suddenly I heard a whine behind me. I stopped and turned. Myrtle was trying to squeeze through the right-hand fence to get into the field beyond.

"Birds out yonder," said Myrtle's owner.

I called to my friend and explained.

Now his dogs had just passed that way without a sign. Also, the field was almost as bare of cover as a billiard table.

"Out there!" he snorted. "Wait till we get back to Atlanta. Maybe we'll find a covey in the middle of Five Points."

Perhaps I should say here that Five Points is to Atlanta what Trafalgar Square is to London.

Myrtle's owner met the insult by picking her up and dropping her over the fence. She went straight out into the field and stopped. There followed an exhibition of fence climbing against the watch by my friend and the bottling-plant foreman. They managed to scratch down two birds from the covey that roared up in the gloom somewhere out ahead of Myrtle.

Thirty minutes later she was stretched out on the back seat of the car on her way to Atlanta, too tired to wonder where she was going or with whom.

She cost me — steady, gentlemen, don't throw anything; just observe the workings of the formula — forty dollars. The amount was simply spread carelessly before her owner. The result was inevitable.

And so I became the owner of Myrtle. But that was all. I brought her into the house and begged her to accept my favorite overstuffed chair. I petted her fondly. She accepted food and chair without enthusiasm. She barely submitted to the caresses. She was not interested in a mere owner. She wanted a master. She wanted the lanky cracker — that was clear. As to the matter of forty dollars changing hands, she completely ignored the transaction.

Having endured a few days of this, I accepted an invitation to go down with one of the best quail shots in the South to shoot with friends of his near Americus. I wanted birds smacked right and left over Myrtle. I wanted her to see shooting, with the lanky cracker far, far away. This, I felt, might aid her perception of property rights. I loaded her into the car, among a reassuring welter of gun cases, shell boxes and shooting coats, and lest she be distracted while learning that forty dollars is forty dollars, I left the four whirlwinds straining at their chains, yelping prayers and curses after me, as we drove off.

Eventually we reached a plantation house and its broad acres, over which we were to shoot, to be greeted by two tall brothers who owned it all. A mincing, high-tailed pointer, who seemed to be walking on eggs, and a deep-muzzled, well-feathered setter helped to welcome us. They were a fine-looking pair of dogs. I opened the rear door of the car and Myrtle came forth.

Now our hosts were true gentlemen of the South. After a look at Myrtle, they spoke earnestly of the weather and the crops and of how hard it was to get hold of good corn liquor. The crack shot from Atlanta became absorbed in assembling his gun. All in all, the moment passed off well.

In due time we marched out over the fields, four guns in line. We had planned to separate into pairs when we reached wider country. This we never did. I do not like to shoot with more than one other gun. I wanted the crack shot to help me kill birds instantly and stone dead when Myrtle found them; but in a surprisingly short time, the brothers showed little desire to leave us, despite their pair of dogs ranging splendidly through the cover.

Myrtle, as we started, had run whining from one man to another for some moments. At last she stopped to stand and watch the other dogs quartering out ahead. She turned and looked deliberately at, or rather through, each of the gunners, myself included. Then with a last small whimper, she got to work. It became clearer and clearer from then on that the place to kill birds that day was in the vicinity of Myrtle.

That miniature, misbegotten what-not found covey after

281

covey and heaven knows how many singles. Her work was marred, however. When a bird fell, she would find it at once and pick it up. She would stand uncertain for a moment and whimper, then start with the bird in her mouth for the nearest man. Having visited all four of us, she would begin to move in a vague circle, whining and looking about. Once she dashed for a high black stump in a field, to return dejectedly with the bird still in her mouth.

I blew my whistle at such times. She never seemed to hear it. I would go toward her, calling her name, and ordering her to "Bring it here!" She only retreated from me, whimpering as I advanced. Getting to her at last, I would take hold of the bird and persuade her to let go of it. All this took time. It was also, to me, her legal owner, somewhat mortifying.

I shared my lunch with Myrtle. She accepted a sandwich, then withdrew a little from the rest of us, to stand looking off into the distance. Suddenly she was away like a shot. I looked in the direction she was going and saw a Negro field hand working along the bottoms, gun in hand, looking for rabbits. I blew and blew my whistle. She rushed on. When close to the Negro, she stopped, looked at him, and came slowly back to where we sat. I rubbed her behind the ears and along the back. She submitted, gazing off into space.

Later that afternoon a covey scattered in a narrow thicket along the bank of the river. The river was in flood — a wide, tawny plain with hummocks of fast water in the middle and still reaches of backwater at its edges.

Myrtle pointed a single within inches of the water. The bird, when flushed, swung out over the river. The deadly gun from Atlanta cracked. The bird came down in the backwater just at the edge of the current. Myrtle was in the river swimming for the bird the moment it fell. She got to it quickly, but an eddy or the wind had carried it out into the current. As she turned to come back with the bird in her mouth, the force of the river took her, and downstream she went.

There was a bend just there, curving away from our side. We four stood helpless on its outer rim and watched her work slowly shoreward, going downstream ten feet for every foot she gained toward the backwater and safety. I remember yelling

"Drop it, Myrt — drop it!" knowing that she could make a better fight without that wretched bird. She did not obey. She struggled on until she came at last to the backwater with the bird still in her mouth.

We all breathed sighs of relief and watched her swim swiftly toward us when free from the drag of the current. "Good girl! Bring it here!" I called, and got out a cigarette with shaking fingers. I began to bask in exclamations I heard along the bank: "Hot damn! That's the baby!" And "Come on home with the bacon, gal!" At least I was her owner. But trouble swiftly met that small swimmer. There were cat briers growing below her in the flooded ground. One of the longer of these through which she swam fastened in her collar — the new collar I had bought her only the day before. Swim as she might, it held her fast. Her stroke became less smooth. She began to paw the water with her front feet — splashing as she did so.

My shooting coat, filled with shells, came off and in I went. No swimming, I found was required. I was no more than up to my armpits in icy water when I reached Myrtle. For this I was duly thankful.

Myrtle was showing fright and exhaustion by now. She was no longer swimming. She was dog-paddling frantically to keep her head above water. The quail was still in her mouth.

I disengaged the brier from her collar and carried her to shore. Then I sat down to empty my hunting boots. I thought I felt the rasp of a pink tongue on the back of my hand as I did so. I can't be sure, for I was pretty cold.

The day was well along and my bedraggled state demanded the plantation house and a fire. We started toward both, hunting as we went.

I was at the left end of the line. Myrtle stopped on point, out in front and to the right. It was evidently a single, since flushed birds had gone that way. I called, "Go in and kill it!" And stood to watch the shot.

The bird fell at the report of the gun. Myrtle went into some brambles to retrieve. She emerged with the bird in her mouth. "Bring it here!" I heard from the man to whom it rightfully belonged. If Myrtle heard him, she gave no sign. Nor did she give that whimper of uncertainty that I had heard throughout

283

the day, as she had stood with a recovered bird in her mouth. She came to me on a straight line, running eagerly, to lay the dead quail in my extended palm. Her eyes had that look — half pride in work well done, half love and faith and companionship — which is characteristic of a shooting dog as a bird is brought to the master's hand. "Here it is, boss!" that look seemed to say. "It's yours. And I am yours — to slave for you, to adore you, as long as I shall live."

Although my teeth were chattering, I was warmed suddenly from within.

Myrtle rode back to Atlanta that night, curled up in my lap, a weary but contented little dog.